ALSO BY RUTH REICHL

Mmmmm: A Feastiary

Tender at the Bone: Growing Up at the Table

Comfort Me with Apples: More Adventures at the Table

Garlic and Sapphires: The Secret Life of a Critic in Disguise

For You, Mom. Finally.

Delicious!: A Novel

EDITED BY RUTH REICHL

The Gourmet Cookbook

Gourmet Today

My Kitchen Year

My Kitchen Year

136 Recipes That Saved My Life

Ruth Reichl

Photographs by
Mikkel Vang

Random House • New York

Copyright © 2015 by Ruth Reichl

Published in the United States by Random House, an imprint and division of
Penguin Random House LLC, New York.

RANDOM HOUSE and the HOUSE colophon are registered trademarks of Penguin Random House LLC.

LIBRARY OF CONGRESS CATALOGING-IN-PUBLICATION DATA

Reichl, Ruth.
My kitchen year : 136 recipes that saved my life / Ruth Reichl
pages cm
ISBN 978-1-4000-6998-9—ISBN 978-0-679-60522-5 (eBook)
1. Seasonal cooking. I. Title.
TX714.R4438 2015
641.5'64—dc23
2014029197

Printed in the United States of America on acid-free paper

randomhousebooks.com

2 4 6 8 9 7 5 3 1

First Edition

Book design by Susan Turner

Photographs by Mikkel Vang

For Michael and Nick

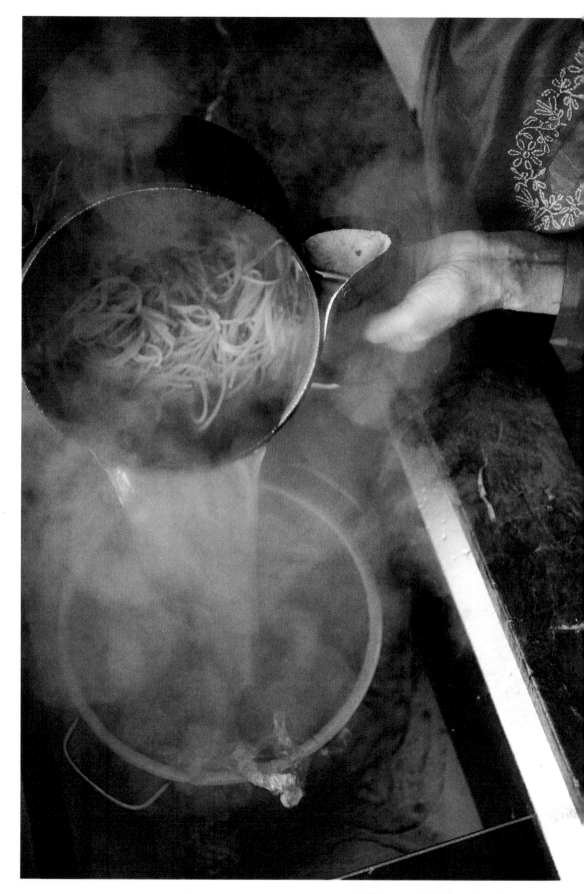

CONTENTS

My Kitchen Year

Mysterious misty morning. Crows
wheeling, cawing. Storm is on the way.
Coffee black. Eggs fried. Toast burnt.
Gourmet's over. What now?

I N THE FALL OF 2009, I'D BEEN THE EDITOR IN CHIEF OF GOURMET FOR ten years. Advertising revenues were falling throughout the magazine industry, and we were no exception. But despite the recession it never crossed my mind that Condé Nast might close the magazine. *Gourmet* was a sixty-nine-year-old institution; many people had lifetime subscriptions. We were constantly hearing from readers who had grown up reading the magazine, learned to cook from it, and continued to stand by the mailbox each month, eager for its arrival.

My response to the challenge of publishing in a recession was to do what the industry calls "expanding the brand"; by 2009 we had two shows on public television and a string of books. I was, in fact, in Seattle promoting our just-published doorstop of a cookbook when I received an ominous call from my boss, Tom Wallace.

"Forget about *Gourmet Today*," he said. "You have to come back to New York." I was in a restaurant, being interviewed by a reporter, and I stepped outside to take the call.

"Is something wrong?" I asked.

"We need you in the office" was all he would say. I took the first plane out and was at 4 Times Square the following morning, standing with my staff, when we learned that *Gourmet* was history.

It took a while for the enormity to sink in: the next day I left for Kansas City. Everyone else was packing up, but I was obliged to go back to promoting the cookbook. When I wasn't doing that, I was working on our television show *Adventures with Ruth,* which was in postproduction.

I had no time to process the events, but as I traveled from one town to the next, people told me, often in tears, how much they were going to miss the magazine. What I thought about most, though, was how much I was going to miss my *Gourmet* family. And how badly I'd let them down. We'd spent ten years together, trying to make a magazine that mattered, but now the staff was scattering across the country. It was over. America's first epicurean magazine had survived for almost seventy years, and it had closed on my watch.

Still, it was not until the book tour ended that I fully grasped how much my life had changed. Home again, I stared at an empty calendar. My husband, son, and family were immensely supportive, and I was surrounded by close friends. Compared to those of many others, my problems were small. I was in good health. I was not about to starve. But I was sixty-one years old, and I wasn't sure I'd ever get another job. I had no idea what to do with the rest of my life and no notion how we'd pay the bills.

And so I did what I always do when I'm confused, lonely, or frightened: I disappeared into the kitchen.

It had been so long since I'd had time to really cook. For years I'd been sticking to familiar foods, rushing home from work to throw quick meals together for my family. Now I began roaming New York, exploring ethnic neighborhoods. On weekends I went upstate to our country house and haunted farmers' markets, coming home laden with unfamiliar ingredients.

Looking back, I see that I was repeating what I'd done when I graduated from college. Back then I was working in a job I hated, and I had no clue about the direction my life should take. Miserable, I began rambling the city, discovering new neighborhoods and collecting recipes from butchers, cheesemongers, and ethnic shopkeepers. I wrote a cookbook trying to explain how much cooking meant to me. I was twenty-two, and *Mmmmm: A Feastiary* is a document of its time, a rollicking period piece that reflects what was happening in 1970, when we were just beginning to discover that there was more to "American food" than hamburgers and hot dogs. I was not a trained chef; I'd never taken a culinary course, and my knife skills were pathetic. But I was an omnivorous eater, a question asker, and a very curious cook.

Fast-forward forty years. In the intervening time I've worked in restaurants, written about food, been a restaurant critic and the food editor of a major newspaper. I've spent time in kitchens all over the world. I've watched food become an important part of popular culture. But two things haven't changed. My knife skills are still pathetic. And I still believe, to the core of my being, that when you pay attention, cooking becomes a kind of meditation.

And so I take my time, admiring the color that's hidden until you peel a peach. I open the oven door, leaning in to savor the fine yeasty scent of bread as it begins its slow rise. Making pie crust, I cut the shortening in by hand, eager to feel it becoming one with the flour. And I never fail to listen for the sizzle of sliced onions as they hit hot butter in a pan.

For me, the shopping is as much a part of cooking as the peeling and the chopping, and I linger in the butcher shop, the farmers' market, and the cheese store. Food people are eager to share their knowledge, and the small exchanges that take place across the counter are precious to me. It's not about the recipes; these daily conversations ground me in the world, anchoring me in time and place.

The physical act of cooking gives me enormous pleasure, but I also like watching what it does for others. Even the angriest person is soothed by the scent of soup simmering on the stove. The aroma of flour, sugar, and butter mingling in the oven is a better tonic than any alcohol. And the best recipe for a good evening is a dish so fragrant that it makes the tongue-tied start to talk. The formula is simple: when you cook for people, they feel cared for.

That hasn't changed. What's different is that forty years ago my interest in food felt like a very solitary passion. Today everybody's interested, and cooks connect in ways we didn't dream of before computers came into our lives. Now, thanks to Twitter I have friends I've never met all around the world. These friendships may be virtual, but to me they are real; I'm no longer alone when I cook.

My kitchen year started in a time of trouble, but it taught me a great deal. When I went back to cooking I rediscovered simple pleasures, and as I began to appreciate the world around me, I learned that the secret to life is finding joy in ordinary things.

A Note on the Recipes

"9 POUND OF FLOUR, 3 POUND OF SUGAR, 3 POUND OF BUTTER, 1 QUART emptins, 1 quart milk, 9 eggs, 1 ounce of spice, 1 gill of rose water, 1 gill of wine."

That, in its entirety, is Amelia Simmons's recipe for Plain Cake. It appears in America's first cookbook, which was published in 1796.

As you can see, it required a fair amount of knowledge—and not a little guesswork—on the part of the cook. ("Emptins" are the dregs—or emptying—from making ale or cider, and they served as leavening for the cake.)

Recipe writing is a direct reflection of culture, which means that it changes along with the times. One hundred years after Amelia Simmons, Fannie Merritt Farmer introduced the notion of "scientific cooking" in her *Boston Cooking-School Cook Book*. Her radical idea was to standardize measurements, then begin each recipe with a list of ingredients followed by a strict step-by-step series of instructions. In 1961, Julia Child took that notion even further, guiding her readers through a carefully choreographed map of each recipe—with no deviations allowed.

I've never been completely comfortable with that. To me recipes are conversations, not lectures; they are a beginning, not an end. I hope you'll add a bit more of this, a little less of that, perhaps introduce new spices or different herbs. What I really want is for my recipes to become your own. I love each of the dishes in this book, but if I were at your house I'd expect every one to taste a bit different than they would when you're at mine.

And so I've tried to write these recipes in a relaxed tone, as if we were standing in the kitchen, cooking together. Rather than a standard list of ingredients, you'll find a shopping list of items you'll likely have to buy—and staples that you probably have on hand. Which means you'll want to know what I consider staples. If you were in my kitchen right now, this is what you'd find:

Refrigerator Staples

anchovies

bacon

butter (*salted and unsalted*)

capers

cream

eggs

lemons

mayonnaise

milk

Parmesan cheese

sour cream

Pantry Staples

baking powder

baking soda

brown sugar

chocolate (*good quality*)

cornstarch

flour (*all-purpose*)

oils: olive, grapeseed, peanut

pasta (*dry*)

pepper

rice (*both long grain and basmati*)

salts—a few different sorts

soy sauce

spices (*with some exceptions, noted in recipes*)

sugar

tomatoes (*canned*)

vanilla

vinegars: apple cider, balsamic, red wine, rice, sherry, white

Worcestershire sauce

Vegetable Staples

garlic

ginger

onions

parsley

potatoes (*both russet and waxy*)

shallots

Unusual Staples

Asian fish sauce

black beans (*fermented*)

bottarga

cream sherry

kimchi

miso (*brown*)

rice wine (*Chinese*)

Sriracha

Freezer Staples

bread crumbs and croutons (*homemade—see page 17*)

extra butter (*you never know when you'll need it*)

chicken stock (*homemade—see page 301*)

At times I've moved staples to the shopping list, but there's always a reason: if you need only a splash of cream it's a staple, but if a recipe requires an entire quart, you'll want to remember to buy extra. All-purpose flour is a staple; most cooks keep it in the pantry. Pastry flour is less common. And what I call "Unusual Staples" will always be on the shopping list; they may be staples in my house, but that does not necessarily mean that they are in yours.

Most of all, though, I hope these recipes will give you as much pleasure as they have given me. And if you want to continue the conversation—just send me a tweet.

Another
side of

ords and M

BALLAD IN PLAIN D
BLACK CROW BLUES
CHIMES OF FREEDOM
I DON'T BELIEVE YOU
IT AIN'T ME BABE
MOTORPSYCHO NIGHTMARE
MY BACK PAGES
SPANISH HARLEM INCIDENT
TO RAMONA
ALL I REALLY WANT TO DO

Price $1.95 IN U.S.A.

mph

Printed in U.S.A.

M. WITMARK & SONS • NEW YORK, N. Y.

FALL

Coffee. Toast. Eggs. Purring cats.
Air sparkling, pulling me outside.
Wish I could spend the day
wandering the city.

Be careful what you wish for: two weeks from the late September day I tweeted the wish on the previous page, my wandering days arrived.

But on this day, oblivious to the clouds gathering over *Gourmet,* I happily made an opulent little breakfast for my family and blithely set off for work. The meal was its own omen, a recipe I would repeat many times in the year to come, because this is the world's most comforting dish.

Potatoes and eggs have had a very long love affair, but their romance has never been more exciting than here, where they embrace with astonishing fervor. When you want to be really, really good to yourself, take the time to make this soft egg, gently cooked on a pillow of butter-rich potatoes. Then eat it very slowly, with a spoon. Each bite reminds you why you're glad to be alive.

SHIRRED EGGS WITH POTATO PUREE

SHOPPING LIST
4–5 young Yukon
   Gold potatoes
   (about 1 pound)
¾ cup cream

STAPLES
salt
pepper
4 tablespoons butter
4 eggs

Serves 4

Peel the potatoes and cut them into half-inch slices. Put them in a pot, cover them with an inch of cold water, and add a teaspoon of sea salt. Bring the water to a boil, reduce it to a mere burble, and cook for 20 minutes, until the flesh offers no resistance when you pierce it with a fork.

Drain the potatoes and put them through a ricer. Or mash them really well with a potato masher. In a pinch, use a fork. Season with a light shower of freshly ground pepper.

Melt the butter and stir in half a cup of the cream. Now comes the fun part. Whisk the cream mixture into the potatoes and watch them turn into a smooth, seductive puree. Season to taste, doing your best to keep from simply gobbling everything up.

Heat an oven to 375 degrees and put a kettle of water on to boil.

Butter 4 little ramekins and put about an inch of the potato puree into each one. Now gently crack an egg on top of each, being careful not to break the yolks. Set the ramekins in a deep baking dish, pour boiling water around them (be careful not to splash either yourself or the contents of the ramekins), and set the dish in the oven for about 8 minutes, until the whites of the eggs have just begun to set.

Spoon a tablespoon of heavy cream over the egg in each ramekin and bake for another 5 minutes or so, until the egg whites are set but the yolks are still runny. Garnish with flakes of salt, bits of chopped chive, or, if you're inclined to true indulgence, crisp crumbles of bacon.

Thank you all SO much for this outpouring of support. It means a lot. Sorry not to be posting now, but I'm packing. We're all stunned, sad.

THE *GOURMET* CONFERENCE ROOM, A COLD, GLASS-ENCLOSED SPACE, WAS BARELY large enough to hold the entire staff, and we stood, packed shoulder to shoulder, as Si Newhouse, the owner of Condé Nast, told us that the magazine was closing. Had in fact already closed.

"What about the December issue?" I asked. It was already at the printer.

"The November issue will be our last." Si didn't look at me as he said it, and I caught the eye of Richard Ferretti, our creative director, who seemed as stunned as I was. The cookie issue, the one that had five covers, one on top of the other, was never going to appear?

Si said something bland about Human Resources, and then he and his entourage left. Nobody moved. We were still too shocked to comprehend what was happening. I blinked, trying not to cry.

Boxes had appeared, as if by magic, and one by one people straggled out of the conference room, picked them up, and went off to start packing their possessions. Many had spent their entire working lives at *Gourmet*. At last only executive editor Doc Willoughby and I were left, and I finally allowed the tears to fall. He put his arms around me, and we stood for a long while, trying to comfort each other.

I went back into my huge office overlooking Times Square. Every phone was ringing. Reporters wanted to talk to me, and I could hear my secretary, Robin, telling them to call the corporate offices. She is the friendliest person on earth, but her voice was cold, clipped. She had been at Condé Nast for almost thirty years.

When the noise level in the hall rose perceptibly, I went out to see what was going on. James Rodewald, our drinks editor, was standing in the conference room opening the hundreds of bottles of wine he had collected. "Drink up," he kept saying, "no point in leaving it here."

By dusk we were all drunk, exhausted, and feeling very fragile. Not one of us was ready to go home. We were beginning to understand how unlikely it was that we'd all be together again in one place. Impulsively I said, "Come to my house!" and we trooped off, carrying bottles of wine and whatever we could salvage from the test kitchen.

It was curiously comforting, spending the night together. The cooks cleaned out their kitchens, each contributing something to the feast. Am I remembering this correctly? I think Gina Marie Miraglia Eriquez, the star baker of the food editors, brought one of her spectacular birthday cakes, which sat incongruously in the middle of the table. Paul Grimes, our ace food stylist, brought the hors d'oeuvres he'd been working on for the May issue, and food editor Ian Knauer packed up some of his brilliant bacon-and-prune-laced meatloaf. Food editor Maggie Ruggiero found some shrimp and scallion dumplings in her freezer and brought those along. My own offering was a few little pots of chicken liver pâté. I always make extra so I'll have some in the freezer should an emergency arise.

It had arisen.

CHICKEN LIVER PÂTÉ

SHOPPING LIST
1 pound chicken
  livers
1 apple (grated)
3 tablespoons calvados
  or cognac

STAPLES
8–12 tablespoons
  (1–1½ sticks)
  unsalted butter
2 shallots (minced)
salt and pepper
cream

Serves 8 to 10

The most important part of this recipe is the shopping. If you begin with a pound of pretty livers from free-range chickens, the rest is easy. Start with the bedraggled bits you often find in supermarkets, however, and you're likely to have trouble. So beg your butcher for the best, take your livers home and cut off the gnarly parts (they're bitter), dry the livers well, and sprinkle them with salt and pepper.

Melt a tablespoon of butter in a large pan, and cook the minced shallots over medium heat until they soften. Toss them into a food processor to wait while you melt a bit more butter and briefly sauté the apple. (Any apple will do, but I prefer a firm, tart variety like Granny Smith.) Add the apple to the food processor and melt a couple more tablespoons butter in the same pan. Turn the heat up

high and quickly sauté the livers, shaking the pan, until the outsides have just begun to go from brown to gray (they should still glow pink within).

Remove the pan from the heat, pour the calvados or cognac into it, return to the heat, light the pan with a match, and enjoy the whoosh. When the flames have died and the alcohol has burned off, add the contents of the pan to the food processor and blend until very smooth.

Cut ¾ of a stick (6 tablespoons) of cold butter into chunks and slowly add them to the livers, as you continue to blend. If you have some heavy cream, add a teaspoon or so, although it's not necessary.

Taste for seasoning and put into ramekins, custard cups, or small bowls. Cover tightly with plastic wrap, pressing it onto the surface of the mousse. Allow the pâté to mellow in the refrigerator for at least 2 hours before serving.

This freezes very well.

At Newark airport. Stop to buy a sandwich and the woman behind the counter says, "I'm so sorry about Gourmet; this one's on me."

STILL SLIGHTLY HUNGOVER FROM THE PARTY THE NIGHT BEFORE, I THREW SOME clothes into a suitcase and dashed to the airport. Kansas City was the last place I wanted to be, but the chef at Starker's Restaurant had called, begging me not to cancel the first stop on the book tour. "I've had farmers raising special chickens for this dinner for months," he pleaded. "We have more than a hundred people coming to see you. Please don't let us down."

My husband, Michael, thought I was crazy. "What do you care if the book sells or not? It belongs to Condé Nast," he said. "You need to take a few days off."

"The chef sounded so desperate," I said. "I just couldn't tell him no."

Michael shook his head as he carried my suitcases to the door. His parting words were "Promise me you'll eat something at the airport."

But by the time I got there I had lost my appetite. This trip was a mistake. I felt hollow, miserable, and utterly alone. I was staring blindly at the sandwiches when I realized the woman behind the counter was trying to get my attention. "I loved that magazine," she said, offering a sympathetic smile. "I could hardly wait for it to arrive each month. Please take anything you like."

She was so kind, and her generosity so unexpected, that my mood instantly lifted. I looked through the refrigerated case, pulled out a steak sandwich, and ate it with as much pleasure as if it had been a Peter Luger porterhouse.

I know the gift was a tribute to the magazine, not to me, but it was a lovely gesture at a terrible time. To this day a steak sandwich can turn me right around. One bite always reminds me of the power of random acts of kindness.

STEAK SANDWICH

SHOPPING LIST
1 pound skirt steak
4 crusty rolls

STAPLES
salt
vegetable oil
condiments

Serves 4

If you love steak sandwiches, you need to make friends with skirt steak. It's a fantastically flavorful cut that doesn't cost much. It does, however, demand a bit of coddling.

The skirt is a bundle of abdominal muscles that have worked very hard, lending them great flavor and a tendency to be tough. Long and thin (a friend calls it "steak by the yard"), skirt steak has many aliases. In Texas it's called "beef for fajitas," and in the Jewish restaurants of New York's Lower East Side it goes by "Romanian tenderloin." But in my house it's sandwich steak because the skinny slices can stand up to salsa, chimichurri, pesto—or simply mustard and a bit of butter.

If you buy your meat from an artisanal butcher, ask for the "outside" skirt, which is fattier and juicier than the inside cut. (If you're buying meat from industrially raised animals, this is a pointless exercise; the Japanese import 90 percent of American outside skirt steak.)

Rub the meat all over with salt—¾ of a teaspoon per pound of meat—and let it sit in this dry brine for 4 or 5 hours before cooking. This will draw out the liquid and concentrate the flavor. Just before cooking, blot the meat very well with paper towels to remove all the surface moisture, and brush it with a bit of vegetable oil. (I prefer a neutral oil like grapeseed, but it's your call.)

Skirt steaks prefer high heat (cooked low and slow, the meat turns chewy), so get a grill or grill pan very hot. The steak will cook quickly; 2 minutes a side should give you beautifully rare meat.

Rest the steak for 10 minutes. Now comes the most important part: the slicing. If you cut with the grain, each slice will be a single tough muscle. If you cut against the grain, into very thin slices, you'll end up with tender meat. (This means that when you're cutting you want the grain to run up and down in vertical stripes, not horizontal ones.)

Now cut a crusty roll in half, butter one side, spread mustard on the other, and heap it with steak slices. You can add any condiments you like, but this meat is so tasty it really deserves the spotlight to itself.

Leaves turning. Early fall farmers' market. I'll buy apples, pork, kale, squash, and spend the weekend dancing in the kitchen. Can't wait.

On tour I'd been forced to smile at strangers and pretend everything was fine while I made pleasant small talk. I was longing to go up to our country house and spend time with Michael. I looked forward to just being myself for a bit. The magazine had been closed for ten days, but this was my first morning at home.

Michael rolled over in bed. "Are you making breakfast?" he asked hopefully.

I squeezed fresh orange juice. I ground coffee beans. I fried bacon, enjoying the aroma that went hissing into the air. I scrambled eggs with slow concentration, taking my time so the curds were small and as tender as custard. We ate together, discussing the news, and I thought how pleasant it could be, not working.

But that mood didn't last. Dishes done, I prowled around the house, edgy and uncomfortable, unable to come to rest. Even the cats, Halley and Stella, watched me warily, as if I had suddenly turned into someone dangerous. Disgusted with myself, I picked up my car keys and headed to the farmers' market.

Halfway across the parking lot I could see smoke spiraling upward; the spicy aroma of sizzling meat drew me to a grill where a young farmer was cooking sausage. He raises pigs whose flesh has a clean, almost nutty flavor, and when he spotted me he smiled broadly. "I've been hoping to see you." He leaned into his cooler, coming up with a huge hunk of pork. "I brought that pork shoulder you're always asking for."

The adjacent stand was heaped with just-picked apples and jugs of fresh cider, and I began imagining that sweet meat melted into onions and apples. Farther on I found kale, the leaves dark and inviting. The garlic man had a huge variety, and a sign on the potatoes read JUST DUG. A New England farmers' market on a warm autumn morning is a captivating place, and as I moved from one abundant stall to the next, I allowed it to seduce me. Before long I was cooking in my head, thinking on my feet, deep into the food. At one stand I found real buttermilk, thick and tangy, and I snatched that up. I love what it does to potatoes. A meal began to come together.

I had bought more than I could comfortably carry, which meant it was time to go. But just as I was leaving, the last lonely nectarines, rosy but hard as rocks, called out to me. I couldn't resist; tucked into pastry and baked in a hot oven, they'd make a fine farewell to summer.

CIDER-BRAISED PORK SHOULDER

SHOPPING LIST
8- to 9-pound bone-
 in pork shoulder
1½ cups apple cider

STAPLES
3 cloves garlic
salt
pepper
6 large onions
vegetable oil

Serves 8

I love pork shoulder because it's one of those cheap, fatty, flavorful cuts that reward the patient cook. This particular dish, which is just about the easiest way I know to feed a crowd, is mostly cooked the day before it's served. It does, however, require a covered pot big enough to hold a hefty joint of meat.

Ask your butcher (or your farmer) for a bone-in fresh pork shoulder. Score the skin into a crosshatch pattern, cutting down through the fat to the meat. Then take a thin-bladed knife and pierce little slits all over the pork. Cut the garlic into slivers and poke them into the slits. Dry the meat well, then shower it liberally with salt and freshly ground pepper.

Cut the onions by halving them lengthwise and then ribboning them into long slices. Set them aside while you heat a couple of tablespoons of grapeseed or canola oil in a heavy pot and brown the pork on all sides. It's not easy to turn a piece of meat this heavy, so use your most substantial fork, or two.

When the meat is browned on all sides, remove it to a platter and add the onions to the pot. Cook, stirring occasionally, until they're fragrant, golden, and caramelized. Stir in 1½ teaspoons of salt and the apple cider, return the pork to the pot, cover it securely, and put it into a 325-degree oven. You can forget it for the next 3 hours.

When the time's up, remove the pot from the oven, uncover it, and allow it to cool. Put the cover back on and set the pot in the refrigerator overnight.

Two or three hours before you plan to serve dinner, take the pot out of the refrigerator and lift off and discard the solidified fat that's risen to the top. Allow the meat to come back to room temperature, then reheat it in a 325-degree oven for another hour. By now it should be extremely tender. Lift the pork onto a platter and measure the onion-cider mixture that's left in the pot. If it is more than a quart, bring it to a boil and let it cook furiously until it's reduced to one quart (4 cups). Taste and add as much salt and pepper as you think it needs.

This is great with mashed potatoes and warm applesauce on the side.

(A note on the liquid measurement: both the pork and the onions release a surprising amount of liquid.)

BUTTERMILK POTATOES WITH BROWN BUTTER

Real buttermilk is thick and has a bit of bite; it's made from what's left after butter's been churned. It's wonderful stuff, delicious on its own and great for baking. It's also excellent in mashed potatoes when you don't want them to be rich with butter or swimming with cream.

Peel the potatoes, slice them fairly thin, and put them into a large pot with the buttermilk, 4 cups of water, and salt and pepper. Simmer, covered, for about half an hour, until the potatoes are soft and slumping in on themselves. Remove the lid—the buttermilk will look curdled, but that's natural. Cook for another 5 to 10 minutes, reducing the liquid while stirring and mashing, until the potatoes have cooked into a thick wonderful mush.

These are particularly good with brown butter stirred in just before serving. Butter becomes brown, with an elusive flavor of nuts, if you melt it slowly, stirring frequently, in a small light-colored saucepan (so you can see the color of the butter change), watching carefully until it turns a light golden brown; this usually takes about 5 minutes. (The butter will continue to brown a bit after you take it off the heat.)

SPICY TUSCAN KALE

SHOPPING LIST
3 large bunches
   lacinato kale
   (about 3 pounds)

STAPLES
salt
2 large onions
olive oil
4 anchovy fillets
chile flakes
pepper
4 garlic cloves
   (smashed)
¼ pound Parmesan
   cheese (grated)
½ cup bread crumbs
   (see recipe below)

Serves 8

Tuscan kale goes by a lot of different names: lacinato kale, dinosaur kale, flat black cabbage. Wash the bunches and then strip the leaves off the ribs. (I find this easiest to do with my fingers, in one long, smooth stripping motion.) Tear the leaves into large pieces and cook them in a pot of boiling salted water for a minute or so. The kale should stay a vibrant green. Drain it and run it under cold water until it's cool enough to comfortably hold in your hands, then squeeze out as much water as you can and set the kale aside.

Chop the onions into a casual dice; no need to be fussy about this step.

Heat a healthy splash of olive oil in a large skillet. Throw in the anchovies and worry them with a wooden spoon until they've completely disintegrated. Add the onions, a few pinches of chile flakes, a few grinds of pepper, and cook, stirring occasionally, for about 10 minutes, until everything is soft and fragrant. Toss in the kale, along with the garlic, and cook for another 10 minutes or so, until it's all come together in a lovely green mass. Taste for salt, add a bit more olive oil if you like, and stir in the Parmesan cheese and the crisp bread crumbs for texture.

HOMEMADE BREAD CRUMBS

SHOPPING LIST
one loaf stale French,
   sourdough, or Italian
   bread

STAPLES
olive oil
salt

Cut bread into cubes and grind it into crumbs in a blender or food processor. (A blender is better; it gives you a more uniform texture.) If your bread is not stale enough to crumb, you can dry the cubes in a 200-degree oven for about 15 minutes before grinding.

Spread the crumbs on a baking sheet and toast in a 350-degree oven for about 20 minutes until they are crisp and golden. Drizzle with olive oil (about ¼ cup for every 2 cups of crumbs), season with salt, and allow to cool completely before putting into containers.

These will keep in the freezer almost indefinitely. Just stick the crumbs in the microwave for a few seconds to take the chill off before using.

NECTARINE GALETTE

(This recipe will work with any unripe stone fruit.)

SHOPPING LIST
4–5 unripe nectarines
  (about 1 pound)

STAPLES
1⅓ cups flour
1 tablespoon plus
  ½ cup sugar
salt
6 tablespoons
  unsalted butter
1 egg
1 lemon
cream

Begin by making this hardy crust. Put the flour, a tablespoon of sugar, and a bit of salt into a food processor. Give it a whirl, then add the butter, cut into little pieces, and whirl again, gently, until the butter is ragged. Throw the lightly beaten egg into the flour and whirl again, just until the dough starts to come together. Empty the dough onto a flour-dusted counter and knead it gently into a thick disk. Wrap it in plastic and chill it for at least an hour (up to a couple of days).

Roll out the dough into an approximately 12-inch round, transfer to a rimmed baking sheet, and put it back in the refrigerator for an hour or so.

Meanwhile, slice the nectarines until you have 3 cups. Toss in half a cup of sugar, squeeze in the juice of half a lemon, and give it a stir.

Remove the dough from the refrigerator and mound the fruit into the middle of the pastry circle, leaving 2 inches all around. Spoon the juice from the fruit over the nectarines and fold the crust around the fruit, pleating as you go and leaving most of the nectarines exposed. Brush the galette with cream and bake at 375 degrees for about 40 minutes. Cool for 10 minutes, then transfer to a wire rack. If you don't have a rimmed baking sheet, be sure to line the bottom of the oven with foil; the juice often bubbles over.

Heading off to launch party for Adventures with Ruth. Strange feeling. The last Gourmet party ever.

THE WEEKEND ENDED AND I WENT BACK ON THE ROAD FOR THE COOKBOOK. THE schedule was grueling; most mornings when my 5 A.M. wake-up call came, I had to ask the desk clerk what city I was in. It didn't matter much; I saw little more than airports, hotel rooms, and bookstores. But I was grateful; I was too busy to feel very much.

I returned to New York to do the final voice-overs for *Adventures with Ruth,* the public television show we'd spent the last six months creating for *Gourmet.* I'd loved shooting the ten episodes, loved traveling to exotic places (Laos, Morocco, Brazil!) to take cooking classes along with fascinating people like Fran McDormand, Jeffrey Wright, Lorraine Bracco, and Dianne Wiest, and in the darkness of the studio it was easy to imagine that nothing had changed. Watching myself on the screen, I even managed to overlook the fact that the corresponding articles we'd planned to run in the magazine would never see the light of day.

The last show we worked on was the China episode, and as I redubbed the material, I remembered Yangshuo, one of the strangest places I've seen. An achingly beautiful natural setting bumps up against frantic neon honky-tonk, so that in a single mile you travel from the sixteenth century to the future. I'd been so happy in that curious little town, and I went home and attempted to recapture the feeling by making the dumplings I learned while I was there.

You have to concentrate when you make these dumplings, because it takes a while to master the gesture of creating the thin egg wrapping and then rolling it around the filling. I think that's why I find the process so soothing. I had to be completely in the moment while I cooked, and it was so absorbing that by the time the dumplings were done I was in a better mood.

But then it was time to get dressed and go off to the gala launch party. Approaching the Time Warner Center, I saw the limousines, red carpet, and throngs of celebrity guests. To please the show's sponsors, no expense had been spared, and I looked at all that luxury and tried to fix it in my brain. This was, I realized, my farewell to the *Gourmet* universe. I'd enjoyed my sojourn in the lavish land of Condé Nast, but I'd only been a visitor. It was time to leave.

"Let's go down to Chinatown," I said when I could take it no longer. The *Gourmet* troops gathered and we decamped to a funky little restaurant with a karaoke room, where we feasted on gingered crab, pork ribs, noodles, and fried rice as we drank endless bottles of cheap wine. As I did a very bad rendition of "Proud Mary," it occurred to me that we were having a lot more fun than the people uptown at that expensively stuffy party. I was leaving again, going to Massachusetts to continue promoting the book, but this memory would help.

GLUTEN-FREE EGG-WRAPPED DUMPLINGS FROM YANGSHUO

SHOPPING LIST
¼ pound ground
  chicken
Chinese chile sauce
oyster sauce
sesame oil

STAPLES
1 clove garlic
  (minced)
fresh ginger
soy sauce
3 large eggs
vegetable oil
rice or balsamic
  vinegar

Makes 1 dozen dumplings

Mix the ground chicken with the garlic, a bit of grated ginger, a teaspoon of chile sauce, and a teaspoon of oyster sauce. Add a splash of soy sauce and form into a dozen little rounds.

Beat eggs well with a fork. Pour a tablespoon of egg into a very hot, oil-slicked wok until it begins to set; it won't take more than about 8 seconds. Immediately put one of the chicken balls into the middle of the egg round and fold it over to make a half-moon. Push the dumpling up the side of the wok, turn it over, and cook it for a minute. Remove it to a plate. Repeat this—it gets easier—until you have a dozen little egg-wrapped dumplings.

Put them all back into the wok, add a half cup of water, cover, and steam for about 3 minutes, turning halfway through. Serve immediately, with a dipping sauce made of soy sauce, a bit of julienned ginger, a small splash of rice or balsamic vinegar, and another splash of toasted sesame oil.

Dreaming of the pungent, crowded
Golden Mall in Flushing. Woke up longing
for chile noodles and fat dumplings.
Alas, we ate them all.

———

THE BOOK TOUR, PLANNED MANY MONTHS IN ADVANCE, HAD INCLUDED A BREAK FOR
me to return to New York to close the December issue. There was, of course, no
December issue, but Condé Nast had other plans; it was time, they said, that I
cleared out my office.

The rest of the staff was long gone, and I wandered through all those deserted
rooms with a feeling of despair. The empty desks were littered with handleless
mugs and broken paperweights. Unwatered plants withered in their pots on dusty
windowsills. In the halls, huge recycling bins, overflowing with old files and
photographs, created a crazy obstacle course. But the worst was the test kitchen: it
had been such a lively place, filled with music, laughter, and endless argument. One
of the sinks was dripping loudly in the abandoned room, and I found the sound so
forlorn that I turned and fled back to the one place that remained unchanged.

I was staring at the clutter in my office—where to begin with all those books
and photographs?—when four friends swept through the door. Nancy Silverton's
a famous chef, Laurie Ochoa is an editor I've worked with most of my life, and
Margy Rochlin's a wonderful writer; they'd all flown in from California to surprise
me. Robin Green, a television writer, was with them, too. "You shouldn't be here
alone," they said. "In fact, you shouldn't be here at all."

"But I'm supposed to pack my things," I protested. Waving my objections aside, they bundled me into my coat and towed me off to the subway. "We'll come back later and help you pack."

We rode the 7 all the way to the end of the line. In Flushing they led me in and out of Asian restaurants—Chinese, Taiwanese, Korean—where we indulged in great floppy chive turnovers, bowls of searingly spicy tofu, and deliciously juicy dumplings. On one corner we watched a woman deftly slice the burnished skin off roasted ducks, tucking the crisp morsels into small, snowy buns. On another we stood transfixed as a chef converted a solid lump of dough into hundreds of gossamer strands, his hands agile as a magician's. And in a small Korean restaurant we ate rice sticks that were chewy, spicy, and utterly unfamiliar.

"I bought you something." Laurie emerged from a small shop and handed me a package. Inside were the rice sticks, looking like nothing so much as pliant sticks of chalk. "You liked them so much, I bet you could make up a really great recipe."

SPICY KOREAN RICE STICKS WITH SHRIMP AND VEGETABLES

SHOPPING LIST

300 grams Korean
   rice sticks (ddeok)
2 tablespoons Korean
   red pepper paste
   (gochujang)
1 pound asparagus
   (or cabbage or
   broccoli, sliced)
½ pound peeled
   shrimp
3 scallions (sliced)

STAPLES

vegetable oil
2 tablespoons brown
   sugar
1 teaspoon cayenne
   pepper
3 cloves garlic
   (smashed)
soy sauce
vinegar
1 onion
   (sliced thin)

Serves 2

Korean rice sticks (ddeok) were a completely new ingredient to me, and I loved experimenting with them. Left to their own devices they are innocuous and rather bland. But they play very well with other ingredients. This recipe offers you the crunch of rice sticks, the joy of crisp vegetables, and the chile-garlic heat that characterizes Korean cooking.

Rice sticks usually come in 300-gram packages (about half a pound), and I've found that they're best fresh. If the ones you find are frozen, let them sit on the counter to thaw. Do not buy the kind labeled "unfrozen"; they have an odd, almost dehydrated texture and won't work for this recipe.

Koreans usually eat rice sticks boiled or cooked right in with the vegetables, but to me they taste best pan-roasted, which gives them a delightfully crunchy exterior. Heat a lightly oiled cast iron skillet over medium high heat for a few minutes and roast the rice sticks just until they begin to brown. Remove them from the heat, and if you want them in smaller pieces, cut them up.

Make a sauce by mixing the gochujang (Korean red pepper paste), with the brown sugar, cayenne, garlic, a splash of soy sauce, and another splash of balsamic, sherry, or rice vinegar.

Heat a wok, add a bit of neutral oil, and toss in the onion until it just begins to send its perfume into the air. Add an equal amount of the cabbage, broccoli, or asparagus, and the shrimp, tossing until the shrimp begin to turn rosy. Add the sauce and the rice sticks, and if it looks as if it needs it, a bit of water. At the very end, add the scallions, toss well, and serve.

The joy of texture: yamaimo.
Pure white bite of crispness. Amazing
change. The sticky pleasure of goo.
Why do Americans hate it?

A DISASTER IS A FINE EXCUSE FOR A PAJAMA PARTY, AND WE STAYED UP HALF THE night talking. We finally fell asleep, waking to a day so bright and crisp it was impossible to think of packing.

"Let's go to New Jersey," said Nancy. "You're always saying you want to visit the big Mitsuwa supermarket." We've done a fair amount of traveling together, and we share an almost insatiable appetite for food markets.

"I really should be packing . . . ," I began, but they were having none of it. "Enjoy your leisure while you have it," Margy insisted.

When I replied "I might be at leisure for the rest of my life," she rolled her eyes in eloquent exasperation. Later it hit me that her faith in me might have been the greatest gift of all.

The supermarket was all I could have hoped for, a vast emporium stocked with every possible Asian ingredient. I hovered over the fresh wasabi roots, wondering if I should indulge (they're very expensive). In the end I bought two of the long, pale green roots, which look like nothing so much as elongated pinecones. They have a sneakily elegant heat, quite unlike the harsh powdered horseradish you're served in most sushi bars. I bought sheets of crisp blue-black seaweed, jars of plum paste, and leaves of shiso. But my favorite find was a length of yamaimo, the hairy beige tuber the Japanese call "mountain potato."

"You really like that stuff?" Margy looked at the strange vegetable and shuddered visibly. Although Margy hangs around with food people, she has no appetite for the exotic. But I was remembering my very first taste, when a sushi chef had handed me a crisp sheet of seaweed folded around a shiso leaf, a bit of plum paste, umeboshi, and some little white sticks that I thought were daikon. But while yamaimo begins with a crunch, it quickly dissolves into a creamy paste and then while you're chewing becomes stickier and stickier until it devolves into something approaching a liquid. This transformation never fails to entertain and delight me.

At home I put on rubber gloves and peeled off the brown outside; yamaimo is mildly irritating to the skin, causing a slight (and fleeting) prickle. Then I cut the pure white tuber into little sticks and drizzled them with soy sauce. I took a bite, enchanted by this small circus of the mouth. Life is full of surprises.

Friends who came for dinner said they'd bring steak. They forgot. We made fresh pasta. A robust sausage sauce. More fun, really.

————

THE NEXT DAY WE FINALLY WENT BACK TO TIMES SQUARE AND PACKED UP MY office. It was miserable work, and I was glad to have company. Being in the office had brought all my feelings of grief and failure simmering to the surface. On top of that, I was scheduled to tape a radio interview late in the day, and I was dreading it. It was supposed to be about *Gourmet*'s cookbook, but I knew that once again I'd be getting questions about the demise of the magazine.

"You'll be fine," Margy assured me as we left my office, empty now but for the taped-up cartons. I'd never see this room again. I went over to the huge window, gazing down at Times Square; the neon signs winked and glowed. Everything was moving. Robin came over to where I was standing. "Time to go." She took my hand. "Let's meet back at your house when your interview's over. We'll cook dinner. Something simple. I'll bring steak."

The interview was even worse than I'd expected, and I left the station shattered. I went home, cooking frantically, hoping to forget what a fool I'd made of myself. I baked a pie. I washed lettuce for salad, trying very hard not to fret. I was starting to peel potatoes when Laurie, Robin, Nancy, and Margy walked in. Their hands were empty. "Where's the steak?" I asked.

They looked at one another, aghast. Somehow this little drama made me feel better; I wasn't the only incompetent one! I put the potato peeler down, opened the freezer, and peered inside. When I saw the sausage I smiled. "No problem," I said. "We'll make pasta."

We could have used dried pasta; if I'm honest I'll admit that I prefer it. But rolling pasta is a great group project, so I got out flour, eggs, and the pasta machine; Robin opened a bottle of wine; and for the next few hours we rolled pasta and stirred the sauce. Then we stirred the sauce some more. Drank some more wine. This sauce is easy, but it isn't fast.

Later, as I washed the dishes, I thought how much fun this communal meal had been. So much fun, in fact, that I'd forgotten to listen to the radio show. How bad was it? I'll never know.

EASY "BOLOGNESE"

SHOPPING LIST
1 pound spicy pork
  sausage
1 can San Marzano
  whole tomatoes

STAPLES
olive oil
1 onion
  (coarsely diced)
salt
pepper
crushed red pepper
2 cloves garlic
  (smashed)
1 pound spaghetti
  (dry, or see recipe on
  page 30)
butter
Parmesan cheese

Serves 4

This dish demands good, spicy Italian sausage. When I can, I buy mine from a farmer who raises his own pigs. Otherwise, I go to an Italian butcher. I try always to keep some in the freezer.

It also requires patience. The secret is to cook the sauce for a long time, so that it caramelizes into something that's more than the sum of its parts.

Pour a bit of olive oil into a skillet and sauté the onion until the fragrance is irresistible and the onion translucent. Add salt and pepper and red pepper and garlic. If you have some carrots, dice them and add them to the pot. A bit of shredded basil always adds a lovely fragrance.

Squeeze the sausage out of its casing into the pan and fork it around until it loses its raw color. Open the can of tomatoes (this is the moment to use the best imported ones you can find) and crush them into the pan, tearing them with your fingers. (I love the feeling of the tomatoes squishing through my hands.) Set aside the remaining liquid from the can. Cook, at fairly high heat, until the liquid has evaporated, stirring every once in a while. Slowly add the rest of the liquid from the can, a bit at a time; the secret to this sauce is allowing the liquid to evaporate each time before adding more. When the liquid is gone, turn the heat down, add a bit of water, and cook for at least two more hours, watching the pot and adding more water as needed. This is best when it's become quite dry and the tomatoes are beginning to caramelize against the bottom of the pan.

Cook a pound of spaghetti, drain it in a colander, toss it into a bowl, and add enough butter so that you can smell it melting as you toss it about. Add the sauce, and pass just-grated Parmesan cheese.

FRESH PASTA

STAPLES
2½ cups
  all-purpose flour
salt
4 large eggs

Pour the flour onto a marble surface or a large wooden table or cutting board. Add a pinch of salt and stir it about with your fingers. Now mound the flour back up, make a dent in the center, and crack the eggs into it.

Making pasta always reminds me of playing in the sandbox as a kid. It's tactile, messy fun. Stir the eggs with a fork, gradually whisking the flour from the inner rim into the eggs. As the eggs become one with the flour, use your other hand to push the flour walls toward the center. If it looks like a big shaggy mess, you're doing it right.

When you've incorporated as much flour as you can—the amount will vary with the weather—start kneading the dough, using both hands. The dough will be sticky; add more flour as you go. When it's come together in a way that feels right, pick up the ball of dough and clean your work surface, scraping well, so you don't get dry bits into your final dough. Dust the surface with a bit more flour and knead the dough for another 5 minutes or so. It should be smooth, elastic, and just a little bit sticky. If it sticks to the board, throw on another dusting of flour.

Wrap the dough in plastic wrap and leave it to rest for half an hour.

Cut the dough into 12 portions, then flatten each ball with a rolling pin and run it through the widest setting on your pasta machine 4 or 5 times. Gradually run each section of dough through the settings, dialing down to a narrower one each time. (If the dough becomes awkwardly long, cut it in half.)

For fettuccine I generally like the second-to-last setting, but for lasagna or ravioli—all stuffed pastas—nothing beats the last setting, which will stretch your dough until it is as delicate as flower petals.

When the dough has gone through the final stage, drape it over the back of a chair to dry for 15 minutes or so, then cut it into 10-inch lengths and run it through the cutters of the pasta machine to make your desired variety. Drape the resulting pasta over a chair, or hang on hangers. Or dust the strands lightly with semolina and set them on kitchen towels. Do not wait too long before cooking or the pasta will dry out.

Boil the noodles in copious amounts of well-salted water; for al dente fresh fettuccine, linguine, or tagliatelle, cook only 2 minutes or so after the water has returned to a boil.

Fall. Orange leaves go swirling past the window. Butternut soup. Smooth. Hot. Savory. Winter's coming. Too soon.

PHILADELPHIA, ST. LOUIS, MIAMI, SAN FRANCISCO . . . THE CITIES ON WHAT WAS starting to seem like a never-ending book tour became a blur, the airports indistinguishable. I began to feel like a robot, and in the second week of November, when I went home for the weekend, I headed off to the farmers' market, eager to cook.

But the changing color palette told me that I'd missed the best of fall. On my last visit there had still been tomatoes, peppers, and eggplants, but now the dominant hues were orange, brown, and the dark green of the kales. It was dispiriting. I bought a pumpkin, some apples, and then, at the last minute, a giant butternut squash.

With its awkward shape and plain brown wrapping, butternut squash is an un-assuming vegetable. I began to strip away the tough beige skin, revealing the bright neon flesh, and in a few minutes that great dull blob of a vegetable was a vibrant pile of color; it was like watching the sun come out. By the time I'd cut it into chunks and started the slow caramelization of the onions, I was entirely relaxed.

But butternut squash is more than merely colorful. It cooks down into a wonderfully textured soup: soft, thick, almost creamy. Requiring nothing more than water, it makes the most luxurious vegan dish I know.

BUTTERNUT SQUASH SOUP

Begin by coarsely chopping the onion, celery, and carrots; you don't have to be fussy about this step since you're going to end up pureeing everything. Slick the bottom of a casserole or Dutch oven with olive oil, add the vegetables, and let them tumble into tenderness, which should take about 10 minutes.

Peel the butternut squash and cut it into ¾-inch (or so) cubes. Peel the potatoes (Yukon Golds are good) and cut into chunks of the same size. Stir them into the vegetables in the casserole, add a couple of teaspoons of sea salt and 2½ cups of boiling water, cover, and simmer until everything is very soft. This will take about half an hour.

Very carefully puree the soup in a blender, in small batches, making sure the top of the blender is secure (hot soup can be painful).

Taste for seasoning and serve drizzled with a few drops of olive oil and/or good balsamic vinegar. A crisp dice of apples on top makes this look lovely and adds a very pleasing note of sweetness and texture. Diced pickled walnuts also make a wonderful topping.

What's best about Thanksgiving?
The house filled with people, meals that
never end, everyone in the kitchen.
Off to make turkey stock.

WEEKDAYS I WAS STILL SPENDING TIME IN AIRPORTS, STILL TRAVELING, STILL promoting the cookbook. Audiences continued to hurl questions at me about *Gourmet*'s end. Why hadn't I known? Had we been too ambitious? Shouldn't I have been able to save the magazine? I was asking myself the same questions, but the book was selling well. People lined up to buy multiple copies, thinking this was their last chance to connect with the magazine they'd loved.

By the time I went home for Thanksgiving the magazine had been closed for six weeks, and I was tired of being on the road, tired of smiling all the time, tired of trying to be upbeat. I had no idea how I really felt, and it was a relief to throw myself into preparations for the holiday. I felt a bit like Scarlett O'Hara: tomorrow was another day, but at the moment I had people to feed.

I began by making turkey stock. I always do: as far as I'm concerned the turkey can be dry, the stuffing too wet, the mashed potatoes filled with lumps, but so long as the gravy holds out, none of that matters. And the better the stock, the better the gravy. I rolled up my sleeves and went into the kitchen.

TURKEY STOCK

SHOPPING LIST
6- to 7-pound turkey
  or turkey parts
2 carrots
2 celery stalks

STAPLES
1 or 2 onions
parsley
bay leaves
whole peppercorns
salt

Buy a small turkey and wash it well. Plunk it into a large stockpot and add enough water to just cover it. Turn up the heat and bring almost to a boil. Skim off the foam that rises to the top, and keep skimming for about 7 minutes, until the foam stops coming. Add the onion (or 2), the carrots—washed and cut in half—the celery, some parsley, a bay leaf, and a handful of peppercorns. Add 2 teaspoons of salt. Partially cover the pot and cook very slowly, so that a bubble rises lazily to the surface every minute or so, for about 4 hours. Strain the broth, discard the solids, let the broth cool to room temperature, then chill overnight. (You can use the turkey itself to make turkey salad or turkey croquettes, but the truth is that what remains is an utterly exhausted bird with very little flavor left.)

Remove the fat from the top of the broth. You now have the makings of gorgeous gravy. You can refrigerate the stock (for up to 5 days) or freeze it (for a few months). All is well.

TURKEY GRAVY

On the big day, when you remove your turkey from the oven, tilt it over the pan to let the juices run out. Then set it on a board to rest. Put a large strainer over a bowl and pour through it all the juices that have gathered in the bottom of the roasting pan. Then put the juices into a narrow vessel (I use a small glass vase), and wait awhile until the fat rises to the top. When it's settled down, skim off the fat.

Meanwhile, gently heat 8 cups of your turkey stock.

Set the turkey roasting pan astride two burners on the stove, pour in a cup of stock, bring to a boil, and stir the bottom of the pan for a couple of minutes until you've scraped up all the delicious drippings. Strain this into the warm turkey stock.

Melt 8 tablespoons (1 stick) of butter in a wide-bottomed pot, whisk in a generous half cup of flour over medium heat, and whisk constantly for about 5 minutes. Slowly whisk in the hot stock and bring to a boil. Lower the heat and simmer for about 10 minutes, giving it a little turn with the whisk every minute or so.

Pour in any juices that accumulate on the platter as the turkey is carved. Taste for seasoning. If you want a dark brown gravy, add a tablespoon of soy sauce (you won't taste it). I like to add a bit of Madeira or sherry at this point, or a little cider vinegar, but this gravy is so delicious you don't really need it.

Black birds swooping onto orange trees; beautiful ballet of the air. Ashmead's Kernels whisper from their skins. Apple crisp!

REVELING IN MY COOKING VACATION, I WANDERED THROUGH THE FARMERS' MARKET tasting apples, trying to decide what to do with each variety. One of the great joys of fall is the explosion of apples, each with its own unique character, and I took my time, tasting carefully.

At one stand I found Ashmead's Kernel, an ancient English russet apple with a thick skin that's more brown than gold. I took a bite, and the flesh was crisp, snappy, exploding with flavor. I swallowed, and was left with the faint lingering scent of orange blossoms.

Another stand proudly displayed Esopus Spitzenburgs. Such a wonderful name! It's a handsome, old-fashioned apple, with great integrity and fine flavor. Knobbed Russets, on the other hand, are extremely ugly. They taste good, but their biggest asset is the way they hold their shape beneath the hottest assault. I bought all three, thinking that I was going to have a crisp with serious character. (If all you can find are insipid apples, you'll probably want to look for a recipe that offers them a bit more help.)

APPLE CRISP

SHOPPING LIST
5 heirloom apples

STAPLES
1 lemon
⅔ cup flour
⅔ cup brown sugar
salt
cinnamon
6 tablespoons
  unsalted butter

Peel a few different kinds of apples, enjoying the way they shrug reluctantly out of their skins. Core, slice, and layer the apples into a buttered pie plate or baking dish and toss them with the juice of the lemon.

Mix the flour with the brown sugar, and add a dash of salt and a grating of fresh cinnamon. Using two knives—or just your fingers—cut in the butter, then pat the mixture over the top of the fruit. The cooking time is forgiving; you can put your crisp into a 375-degree oven and pretty much forget it for 45 minutes to an hour. The juices should be bubbling a bit at the edges; the top should be crisp, golden, and fragrant. Served warm, with a pitcher of cream, it makes you grateful for fall.

Mountains of marinated eggplant, meatballs, spiced nuts, pound cake ... people who show up early for Thanksgiving will not go hungry!

OUR THANKSGIVINGS ARE WEEKLONG AFFAIRS, WITH SOME PEOPLE SHOWING UP Monday or Tuesday and others staying through the weekend. By Wednesday night every room is filled and people are camping on the sofas. The eating never stops.

When I'm expecting a lot of guests I always bake a simple pound cake. It's the little black dress of the pastry world; at night you can dress it up with ice cream, fruit, or sauce, while in the morning, toasted pound cake is a promising way to start the day. It's also a good keeper, so guests can help themselves whenever hunger hits.

PERFECT POUND CAKE

SHOPPING LIST

2 cups cake flour

STAPLES

1 cup (2 sticks)
  unsalted butter

1 cup sugar

4 large eggs

1 teaspoon vanilla

1 teaspoon baking
  powder

salt

There are a few tricks to making perfect pound cake. For starters, you want to have all your ingredients at room temperature; cold ingredients do not blend evenly. You also want to use good unsalted butter with a high butterfat content. I prefer cultured butter (like Echiré or Plugrá), which imparts a delicate complexity of flavor.

Preheat your oven to 350 degrees. Butter a 9x5 loaf pan.

Beat the butter at high speed in a stand mixer until it's fluffy and starting to turn white; it is not possible to overdo this step, which should take at least 5 minutes. Slowly add the sugar, a bit at a time, and keep beating, scraping down the bowl with a rubber spatula whenever it seems necessary. Add 1 large egg and beat for a couple of minutes. Your eggs are your major leavening, so you want to take your time here, incorporating as much air as possible. Add another egg, beat it in, and then another and another, until 4 eggs have become one with the butter. Add the vanilla and mix again.

In a separate bowl whisk together the cake flour, the baking powder, and a pinch of salt. Remove the bowl from the mixer and gently fold in the flour by hand. Stop as soon as the flour is incorporated into the butter and egg mixture; at this point you don't want to overmix.

Turn the mixture into the buttered loaf pan and smooth the top.

Bake for about an hour, until a toothpick comes out clean.

Let it rest on a rack for 10 minutes before turning out of the pan. Allow the cake to cool completely on the rack before serving.

Nick's home. Eating anchovy bread, drinking Kermit's plummy Rhône. Making short ribs. Mashing potatoes. Washing salad. Love my family.

"THE TRAFFIC WAS TERRIBLE. WE'RE STARVING. GOT ANYTHING TO EAT?" TWO DAYS before Thanksgiving, Nick walked in with a group of college friends. The sight of my son always makes me happy. I pointed at the loaf of anchovy bread I'd just pulled from the oven.

ANCHOVY BREAD

SHOPPING LIST
2 teaspoons dry yeast
1 cup pastry flour
1 cup semolina flour
1 tablespoon chopped
  fresh oregano

STAPLES
1 teaspoon sugar
⅓ cup plus
  2 tablespoons good
  olive oil
salt
6 anchovy fillets
1 tablespoon paprika
pepper

I think of this pretty, spicy, salty bread, which comes from Italy's Basilicata region, as an elegant inside-out pizza. It's a simple yeast dough rolled around a pungent mix of paprika, oregano, and anchovies that leaves little pinwheels of color racing through the dough. Nothing tastes better with a glass of robust red wine.

Put ¾ cup of warm water into a bowl, sprinkle on the sugar and the yeast, and watch the yeast begin to foam. (If it doesn't, it's dead, or your water was too hot: start again.) Stir in 2 tablespoons of olive oil.

In another bowl mix the pastry flour with the semolina flour and a teaspoon of salt. Stir in the yeast mixture until it comes together in a ball, knead it for a minute or so on a floured surface until it's as soft and smooth as a baby's bottom

(a cliché, I know, but apt), plop it into a well-oiled bowl, cover it, and leave it alone for an hour and a half or so. It should puff itself up to twice its original size.

Meanwhile, mince the anchovies and drop them into a small bowl with the fresh oregano, the paprika, a teaspoon of salt, a grinding of pepper, and the rest of the olive oil.

Roll the dough out into a large round (about 15 inches). Spread most of the seasoned oil almost to the edge of the dough, leaving a small rim. Roll the dough up into a thin jelly roll and pinch the edges closed. This is a fun and messy process, and if you lose some of the oil, don't fret. Curl your long, thin roll into a spiral and set this into an oiled pie plate or baking pan. Brush the top with the remaining oil, sprinkle with a teaspoon of sea salt, cover with plastic wrap, and allow to rise another hour.

Preheat your oven to 375 degrees and bake for about 35 minutes until you have a loaf that's crusty and golden. Put it on a rack and allow it to cool completely before cutting into very thin slices, each one a layer of color. (One warning: this is not a good keeper. Plan on eating it the day it's baked. On the other hand, any leftovers make wonderful toast, spread with a bit of butter. You can even make the bread ahead, freeze it, and then toast it.)

High-heat turkey method really works.
Caveat: make sure your oven is clean,
clean, clean or you will have billows of smoke.

AFTER TWENTY YEARS AS A NEWSPAPER FOOD EDITOR AND TEN AS EDITOR OF AN epicurean magazine, I doubt there's a turkey recipe I haven't tried. (Most embarrassing example? The year I tried to persuade the readers of the *Los Angeles Times* that the best way to roast turkey is by putting the stuffing beneath the skin. No sane person would do it twice.)

In the end I've come to the conclusion that this high-heat method is a boon to everyone who understands that it's absurd to agonize over a turkey. No brining, no stuffing, no basting: it really is this easy. Best of all, it leaves you plenty of time to think about the more important parts of the meal, like the dressing, potatoes, and pie.

HIGH-HEAT TURKEY

Serves 8 to 10

Preheat your extremely clean oven to 450 degrees.

Rinse and dry a 16-pound turkey and bring it to room temperature. Put it on a rack in a roasting pan, add a cup of water, put it into the oven, and forget about it for an hour. Rotate the pan, make sure there's still about a cup of water in the bottom (if not, add more), and cook for another hour and a quarter to an hour and a half, until a thermometer in the thigh registers 170 degrees. Remove the pan from the oven and allow the turkey to rest for half an hour before carving. That's all there is to it. Really.

Up early. Clouds lying in the valley.
Wild turkey parade. Cutting
butter into flour. Urgent desire
for cranberry crostata.

SURROUNDED BY SLEEPING PEOPLE, I CREPT OUT OF BED, FED THE CATS, MADE A POT OF coffee, and began to bake, still in my bathrobe. I love those solitary early-morning hours, and on this particular one, with a houseful of people I love and wild turkeys strutting their ridiculous way across the lawn, I had the first sense of deep peace since learning that the magazine was about to fold. I knew the feeling wouldn't last, but in that moment, in my kitchen, I was firmly anchored in the present.

CRANBERRY PECAN CROSTATA

SHOPPING LIST
½ cup pecans
1 12-ounce package
  cranberries
1 orange
4 ounces apricot
  preserves

STAPLES
12 tablespoons
  (1½ sticks) unsalted
  butter
1 cup sugar
1 egg
salt
1 teaspoon vanilla
2 cups flour
1 lemon

The nice thing about this particular tart is that the crust is essentially cookie dough, which means that this tart is as good on day two as on day one. You can make it ahead of time—or really enjoy the leftovers.

Gently toast the pecans in a small skillet until they're fragrant, allow them to cool, then grind them fairly fine.

Beat the butter with ½ cup of the sugar until very light. Add the egg, the ground pecans, a pinch of salt, the vanilla, and the flour. Grate in the zest of the lemon and mix well.

Form into two disks, wrap in waxed paper, and chill for 30 minutes (or more).

Meanwhile, cook the raw cranberries with the juice of the orange, the apricot preserves, and the other ½ cup of sugar, stirring, for about 5 minutes. Set aside to cool.

Roll out one disk of dough into a 12-inch circle. Don't worry too much about this step; the dough will tear, but you can just press it into a 9-inch springform pan, bringing the sides up about ½ inch. Spread the cranberry filling onto the crust.

Roll out the remaining disk on a sheet of waxed paper, put it on a sheet pan, and cut it into 8 to 10 strips. Put the pan into the refrigerator for 5 or 10 minutes, which will make the next step easier.

Form a lattice over the cranberries. Don't worry if the strips are so soft they break; you can patch them together, and when the crostata emerges from the oven it will still be gorgeous.

Bake in a preheated 375-degree oven for about 45 minutes, until golden.

Set on a rack to cool for half an hour, then remove the sides of the springform pan. Cool completely, on the rack, before serving.

Pies just went in. On to chili for hungry early arrivals. We're nine now, will be twenty-five before day's end.

MOST PIES TASTE BEST THE DAY THEY'RE BAKED, SO WHY WOULD YOU SERVE day-old pie on the most important holiday of the year? I get up early so the traditional pumpkin pie is out of the oven in time for the turkey to go in.

I'd offer a recipe, but I rely on the one on the back of the can. I do, however, spruce it up a bit by straining the pumpkin a couple of times to give the pie a smoother, creamier texture. Then I spread the strained puree onto a nonstick surface (like a Silpat) and roast it in a hot (400-degree) oven for a few minutes. Then I let it cool before adding the eggs and milk.

Once the pies are in the oven, I really get cooking. We don't eat Thanksgiving dinner until dark, which means that the day turns into an endless meal. Breakfast is no problem; as people wake up I cook them eggs, bacon, pancakes—whatever they want. For those who arrive around lunchtime, there's cheese, sliced salami, dried fruit, and olives. And there's always a big pot of chili bubbling on the stove, so people can help themselves.

I've got two chili secrets. The first is ground bison, which cooks up cleaner than ground beef and doesn't throw off much fat. More important, I make my own chili powder so I don't have to rely on the tired commercial kind.

The classic ingredients for chili powder are a variety of ground chiles mixed with cumin, oregano, and garlic powder. I put fresh garlic, oregano, and freshly toasted cumin right into the meat mixture, then add a blend of chiles that I've toasted and ground myself. Then, as the chili cooks, I stir the sultry smokiness of chipotles in adobo right into the meat.

BASIC CHILI RECIPE

SHOPPING LIST
1 tablespoon chopped
  fresh oregano
1 pound ground bison
1 small can chipotle
  peppers in adobo
  sauce
1 bottle robust dark
  beer
1 can black beans

STAPLES
3 medium onions
olive oil
6 cloves garlic
  (smashed)
salt, pepper
cumin
chili powder (see
  recipe, page 46)
1 large can chopped
  tomatoes
1 cup chicken stock
  (see recipe, page 301)

OPTIONAL
1 ounce dark
  chocolate
fish sauce
balsamic vinegar
cream sherry
soy sauce
cilantro
scallions
sour cream
grated cheddar

Serves 4 to 6

Dice the onions and sauté them in olive oil until they're soft. Add the garlic and let it soften, too. Add the oregano, some salt and pepper, a bit of cumin, and 2 teaspoons of your homemade chili powder—more if you like really hot food.

Add the ground bison and cook, stirring, until it loses its redness. Puree 3 or 4 of the chipotle peppers and stir that in along with the tomatoes and another teaspoon of your chili powder. Add the chicken stock (preferably homemade) and a cup of the beer and let it all simmer at a slow burble for a couple of hours.

Before serving, stir in a cup or so of cooked black beans. Now you get to play with the flavors. Is it hot enough? Do you want more chili powder? Sometimes I'll melt an ounce or so of really good chocolate and stir that in to give it depth. Other times I'll add a spoonful of fish sauce, or a splash of excellent balsamic vinegar. Sometimes soy sauce to spark it up, other times cream sherry to mellow it down. It all depends on my mood. The point is, when you've made your own chili powder, everything else is just window dressing.

You can serve this with cilantro, scallions, sour cream, and grated cheddar. Or not. It's that good.

HOMEMADE CHILI POWDER

SHOPPING LIST
dried ancho,
  New Mexico, and
  habanero chiles

STAPLES
1 teaspoon cumin

I like to use anchos for their winey richness, habanero for their fruity heat, and New Mexicos for their earthy sturdiness.

Wearing rubber or latex gloves to protect your hands, sponge off 2 ancho, 3 New Mexico, and 3 habanero chiles (they're almost always dusty). Cut them in half and remove the tips, where the majority of seeds congregate in dried peppers. Discard the seeds.

Put the chiles into a heavy-bottomed pan (I use cast iron) and toast them over medium-high heat for about 4 minutes, turning from time to time with tongs, until they have darkened slightly. Allow them to cool and then grind the chiles to a powder in a spice grinder or coffee mill. Stir in a teaspoon of toasted ground cumin.

Mr. Trillin gets the award for best house present: arrived for Thanksgiving with spiced matzo and frozen Chinese dumplings.

FOR THE PAST FEW YEARS, CALVIN TRILLIN, THE LONGTIME *NEW YORKER* WRITER (and author of classic books such as *Alice, Let's Eat*), has been coming up to the country for Thanksgiving, arriving Thursday morning with spiced matzo from Blue Ribbon Bakery (it always vanishes in a few minutes) and giant bags of frozen dumplings from Chinatown. This has become such a tradition that I've learned to make my own dumplings, just in case he gets a better offer one of these years.

The truth is that dumplings provide a great diversion for bored guests, who can sit in your kitchen and help pleat them. Cook them at once, or toss them into the freezer to eat when the turkey's gone.

CHINESE DUMPLINGS

Chop the scallions (both white and green parts) and mix them with the ground pork. Grate in a generous bit of ginger. If you found dried shiitake mushrooms, reconstitute a couple, chop them, and add them, too; they add a very appealing flavor note. Chopped water chestnuts are also a lovely addition, giving terrific crunch—but only if you can find fresh ones; the canned kind have a nasty metallic taste and a slightly mealy texture.

In another bowl mix the soy sauce with the rice wine (or dry sherry) and the sesame oil. Add the sugar, a good grind of black pepper, and the white of the egg. Stir this gently into the pork mixture until it's completely incorporated, and allow it to rest for at least half an hour (or overnight in the refrigerator).

When you're ready to assemble your dumplings, mix the corn-starch into a half cup of water in a small bowl. Set it next to a pile of round wonton wrappers. I find commercial wonton wrappers rather thick, so I like to roll each one out a bit with a rolling pin to make it thinner (this also allows you to make fatter dumplings).

pepper
1 egg, separated
1 tablespoon
  cornstarch

*Makes 40 to 50
dumplings, depending
on how generous you
are with the filling*

Put a heaping teaspoon of filling onto the wonton wrapper, brush the top edge lightly with the cornstarch mixture, fold the wrapper over into a crescent, and press and pinch the edges firmly together, trying to press all the air out of each dumpling. Set each one on a baking sheet as it's finished, making sure it's not touching another dumpling. Cover with plastic wrap as you work.

Freeze the dumplings, in a single layer, on their baking sheet. When they're frozen, put them into plastic bags (they'll keep in the freezer for 6 weeks).

To cook, bring a big pot of water to a boil. Throw as many dumplings as you'd like into the pot, bring the water back to the boil, and cook for 7 minutes. (If you're cooking unfrozen dumplings, it will take about 5 minutes.) They'll rise to the top when they're ready.

Serve with a dipping sauce you've made by combining good soy sauce with a bit of grated ginger and a splash of vinegar.

Sunshine! Balmy weather. Bacon, eggs, coffee. Juice. Pumpkin pancakes. Turkey hash. And now the guests begin to depart.

I HATE IT WHEN EVERYBODY LEAVES. ON SUNDAY MORNING, AS THE GUESTS began packing up, I tried to delay their departure by cooking an enormous breakfast feast.

The night before, I'd boiled four large Yukon Gold potatoes and put them in the refrigerator. In the morning I made fresh orange juice and put water on for coffee. But when I reached into the refrigerator for the cold potatoes, I encountered that annoying little bit of pureed pumpkin left over from the pumpkin pie, and I decided to turn that into pancakes. For a few wonderful minutes I forgot that the holiday was almost over.

TURKEY HASH WITH FRIED EGGS

SHOPPING LIST
4 large Yukon Gold
 potatoes
1 cooked turkey
 thigh

STAPLES
1 large onion (about
 2 cups diced)
butter
chile flakes
salt
pepper
3 or 4 eggs

Serves 3 to 4

In our house the dark turkey meat always goes begging. This hash is the perfect way to use it up. It will be easier if you remember to boil the potatoes the night before and leave them in the refrigerator to chill; cold potatoes grate more gracefully.

Grate the cold boiled potatoes (Yukon or white—not russets) on the coarsest holes of a box grater.

Dice the turkey.

Cook the onion in as much unsalted butter as you feel comfortable with (anywhere from 6 tablespoons to a stick) until it's just fragrant and translucent. (If you want this dish to be spicy, add chile flakes to the mix.) Add the grated potatoes and a big handful of diced cooked turkey, salt and pepper generously, and cook for about 20 minutes, turning now and then, until it turns into a golden brown hash.

Divide into 3 or 4 portions and top each with a crisp-edged fried egg.

PUMPKIN PANCAKES

SHOPPING LIST
¾ cup pumpkin
  puree

STAPLES
1¼ cups flour
3 tablespoons brown
  sugar
2 teaspoons baking
  powder
cinnamon
ground ginger
nutmeg
ground cloves
salt
4 eggs
8 tablespoons
  (1 stick) butter
1¼ cups milk
vanilla

Serves 4 to 6

In a fairly large bowl, whisk together the flour, brown sugar, and baking powder. Stir in a small amount (about ¼ teaspoon) of each of the following spices: cinnamon, ginger, and nutmeg. Add a pinch of cloves and a bit of salt.

Separate the eggs, putting the yolks into a small bowl and the whites into a larger one. Beat the whites with clean beaters until they're just beginning to hold stiff peaks, and set aside.

Melt the butter (this recipe will also work with a mere 4 tablespoons of butter—but it won't be quite as good), and stir it into the egg yolks, along with the pumpkin puree, the milk, and just a dash of vanilla. Stir the blended liquids carefully into the flour mixture.

Fold the whites into the flour and pumpkin mixture.

Heat a griddle, slick it with oil or butter, and cook the pancakes at the size that you like best. I tend to like these better when they're on the small side. Serve with maple syrup.

Still dark. City glitters. Awake, alone.
Comfort of congee laced with ginger:
scatter of scallion, splash of soy,
crunch of nut.

———

THANKSGIVING OVER, I WENT BACK TO PROMOTING THE COOKBOOK. HAD I been trying to conjure up the most poignant way to launch the post-holiday season, I could never have come up with anything to equal this particular day.

I climbed out of bed at four A.M., made a cup of coffee, and left the house, bound for the early shuttle to Washington, D.C. The next stop on the book tour was a mammoth big-box store.

My mission was to stand hopefully beside a towering pile of cookbooks while customers with heavily laden carts sped past in pursuit of bargain appliances. At first it was embarrassing, and I felt awkward and out of place. But as the day progressed, an entire constellation of cooks stopped to share recipes and memories. A curator from the Smithsonian told me stories of Julia Child, a Vietnamese man brought me a bowl of pho, and a little girl shyly offered a brownie. "I made it from your recipe."

As the day ended, a regal older woman asked me to sign books for her five grandchildren. "I was hoping to give them each a subscription to the magazine when they turned twelve," she sighed. "Now this will have to do." I left in a melancholy mood. Flights were delayed. By the time I got home,

Michael was already in bed. But the cats came running to greet me, twining around my ankles as I made a bowl of congee. Then they followed me into the dark living room and sat beside me as I spooned up the restorative soup.

CONGEE

SHOPPING LIST
scallions
peanuts

STAPLES
1 cup rice
chicken stock
 (see recipe,
 page 301)
ginger
soy sauce

Serves 4

Nothing is easier to make than the classic Chinese breakfast. It's basically rice slowly cooked with lots of liquid. I like to use arborio rice, although it's not traditional; any kind of rice you have on hand will do. The ratio is about 1 cup of rice to 8 cups of liquid; I think it tastes best with chicken stock, although you can certainly use plain water.

Put the rice and liquid in a pot, bring it to a boil, reduce the heat to low, partially cover the pot, and let it simmer for an hour. Stir it once in a while. The result is a thick, creamy porridge, a canvas for flavor. What you choose for garnish is completely up to you, but to me a julienne of ginger is essential, as is a little shot of really good soy sauce. Peanuts and scallions are nice, and shredded chicken or shiitakes are lovely, too. It is the ultimate tonic: basic, fragrant, satisfying.

A confession: in a pinch I've used leftover cooked rice, simply cooking it with lots of water and stirring until it collapses into the correct consistency.

Long walk in snowy rain. Wet feet,
cold hands. Lupa: the comfort
of a counter. Good company.
Contained fire: pollo alla diavola.

I WAS HOARSE. I'D SPENT ALL MORNING ON THE RADIO, DOING SOMETHING CALLED "the radio satellite tour."

This is how it works: A company sets up a "drive-time schedule" that begins around seven on the East Coast and moves west as the country wakes up. You sit at home, in your bathrobe, holding the phone to your ear while a disembodied voice says, "Next you'll be talking to Joe in Waco, Texas." Then Joe's producer comes on, saying, "Joe will be with you in forty-five seconds." Most of the time Joe doesn't know anything about the book you're promoting, so it's your job to "control the interview" and make sure you hit all the important selling points.

They had set up a robust schedule. I spoke with a different station every ten minutes or so, seesawing from the stately cadences of National Public Radio to the rah-rah pace of small-town all-talk stations and the manic speed of shock jocks. By noon, people all over the country had arrived at work. Drive time was over. I could hang up.

I was talked out, incapable of uttering another syllable. It was one of the cold, damp days of early December, the air filled with the promise of snow, and I walked until my feet were wet and my hands chilled and I was standing in front of Lupa, one of my favorite restaurants. I went inside, took a seat at the counter, and treated myself to a deviled chicken so stunningly spicy it jolted me back into the world. When I'd reduced the bird to a pile of bones, I went home and entertained myself by trying to work out the recipe. It proved to be an excellent diversion; it was a couple of days before I was satisfied, and I set off the smoke alarm half a dozen times. It was worth it.

MY VERSION OF POLLO ALLA DIAVOLA

Start by making chile oil. Chop the jalapeño and serrano chiles and put them in a small saucepan with ¾ cup of olive oil. Add a couple of tablespoons of hot paprika. Grind a fair amount of black pepper into the pot and steep over medium heat for about 15 minutes. Let the oil sit overnight (or all day). Or, if you're in a hurry, you can simply buy a bottle of chile oil.

Put a strainer over a large bowl and pour the chile oil through. Slice the lemons and add them to the bowl. Season with 1 teaspoon salt. Put the oil and lemon into a large ziplock bag, add the chicken, and squish it all around so the lemons are evenly distributed. Put it in the refrigerator and let it sit for at least 4 hours (up to a day).

Heat a cast iron skillet until it's quite hot (about 5 minutes). Preheat your oven to 500 degrees. Meanwhile remove the chicken from the chile oil and pat it dry. Sprinkle it with salt and shower it with freshly ground pepper; you need a lot. Slick the bottom of the pan with olive oil and put the chicken, skin side down, in the hot skillet. Cook until the skin is crisp and golden, which should take 8 to 10 minutes. Turn the chicken over so it's skin side up.

Put the skillet in the oven and roast about 20 minutes, or until a thermometer registers 170 degrees in the thickest part of the thigh.

Sprinkle the chicken with lemon juice, grind more pepper over it, and allow it to rest 10 minutes before serving.

Chilly gray morning. Empty day looms.
I will make ma po tofu sparked
with the strange prickly heat
of Szechuan peppercorns.

———————

GOURMET TODAY HIT THE BESTSELLER LIST. IT HAD BEEN NINE WEEKS SINCE THE magazine closed. My job was done.

On the first day of my new life I woke, alone, to frosted windows in New York City. Michael was out of town, and for a moment I thought gratefully that I had no responsibilities, nowhere to go. Then the empty day rose before me, and I realized that that was literally true. I had nowhere to go. What would I do with myself? I went into the kitchen and opened the refrigerator door.

This classic Szechuan dish struck me as a perfect way to start fresh. Blistered with chiles, it's warrior food; the sharp red intensity of the peppercorns battles the smooth white blandness of the bean curd. I will happily eat this at any time of the day, but on this anxious morning I found it especially heartening.

MA PO TOFU

SHOPPING LIST
2 tablespoons
  Chinese black bean
  sauce with chile
1 bunch scallions
1 pound soft tofu
2 teaspoons Szechuan
  peppercorns
toasted sesame oil
½ pound fatty
  ground pork

STAPLES
1 cup chicken stock
  (see recipe,
  page 301)
2 tablespoons soy
  sauce
1 knob fresh ginger
2 tablespoons garlic
  (minced or
  smashed)
1 tablespoon
  cornstarch
peanut or grapeseed
  oil

Serves 4

Like most Chinese dishes, this is all about the prep. Once you've got your ingredients lined up and ready, it comes together in a fast flash of joyous heat.

Pour the chicken stock into a measuring cup. Add the Chinese black bean sauce with chile (I use Lan Chi brand) and the soy sauce. Set aside.

Chop 2 tablespoons of the ginger, and mince or smash an equal amount of garlic.

Slice 4 scallions very thin, separating the white and green parts.

Drain the block of tofu and cut it into 1-inch cubes.

Put the cornstarch into a small dish and stir in 2 tablespoons of water to make a completely smooth slurry.

Toast the Szechuan peppercorns for a minute or so in a hot, dry skillet until they are just fragrant. Allow to cool and then grind to a powder.

Set all these little dishes out next to your wok, along with some peanut or grapeseed oil, the bottle of toasted sesame oil, and the ground pork.

Heat the wok until it is very hot, coat the pan with the peanut or grapeseed oil, and toss in the garlic, the white part of the scallions, and the ginger, tossing quickly just until they become fragrant. Add the pork and cook quickly, stirring and breaking up the meat until it goes from pink to gray. Add the chicken stock mixture, stir, and toss in the tofu. Cook for a couple of minutes, until the tofu begins to fall apart. Stir in the cornstarch mixture and allow the sauce to thicken. Add a splash of sesame oil and the scallion greens, toss it all together, and sprinkle on the Szechuan peppercorns. Serve with white rice.

Glorious white winter wonderland.
Sparkling sun. Melting ice.
A perfect day for chocolate cake.

———

I WAS SLEEPING IN A DOORWAY ON A DESOLATE STREET, HUDDLED AGAINST THE cold. The stone steps were an icy pillow against my cheek. A doorman's boot banged against my head, and I woke up falling into freezing snow. Disoriented.

Men apparently worry that they'll end up alone in a hotel room. Women take it one step further: our fear is that we'll end up alone and homeless. But this morning my recurring nightmare felt like more than fear: it felt like a warning. My friends and colleagues were starting to find jobs, recover, put *Gourmet* behind them. For me the bad times were just beginning. I had entered the land of grief.

It hit me like a wave, a physical force that knocked me back against the sheets. Was it worse because I'd staved it off so long? Perhaps. Now the reality hit me, and the line that ran through my head was the old blues refrain, "Sometimes I feel like a motherless child." I'd forgotten that loss can be so painful, that life can feel so bleak. I looked into the future seeing endless empty days, incapable of imagining how my life would ever change.

I tried reminding myself of all the good things. Michael. Nick. My friends. The cats came padding onto the bed, pressing their cold noses against my face and gently kneading my skin with their soft paws. They became more insistent, reminding me that they were hungry, that it was time to get up and think about them.

I reluctantly pulled back the covers, got out of bed, and opened a couple of

cans of cat food. I made a pot of coffee, knowing I needed an antidote to the poison of self-pity. What I needed, I decided, was to bake a chocolate cake.

I emailed a few friends, asking them to tea; I was giving myself a deadline, creating insurance against backing out. I slowly started gathering ingredients.

Why a cake? Because the precision of baking demands total attention. Why *this* cake? Because the sheer size of it makes special demands. But most of all, because it is impossible to hold on to gloom with so much chocolate wafting its exuberant scent into every corner of the house.

THE CAKE THAT CURES EVERYTHING

1⅛ cups
   unsweetened cocoa
   powder (not Dutch
   process)

¾ cup whole milk
1½ teaspoons vanilla
3 cups flour
2 teaspoons baking
   soda
salt
1½ cups (3 sticks)
   unsalted butter,
   softened
1½ cups dark brown
   sugar
1½ cups white sugar
6 eggs

Serves 20 to 25

In times of stress, only excess will do: this is an enormous cake. But it keeps very well. And there is no such thing as too much chocolate cake.

Preheat the oven to 350 degrees.

Butter two large rectangular baking pans (13x9x2) and line them with waxed or parchment paper. Butter the paper and dust the pans with cocoa (you could use flour, but cocoa adds both color and flavor to your cake). Hold the pans over a sink and give them a gentle tap so the excess cocoa floats off.

Measure the cocoa powder into a bowl, and whisk in 1½ cups of boiling water until it is smooth, dark, and so glossy it reminds you of chocolate pudding. Whisk in the milk and vanilla.

In another bowl, whisk the flour with the baking soda and ¾ teaspoon salt.

Put the butter into the bowl of a stand mixer and beat in the sugars until the mixture is light, fluffy, and the color of coffee with cream (it will take about 5 minutes). One at a time, add the eggs, beating for about 20 seconds before adding the next. On low speed, beat in the flour mixture in 3 batches and the cocoa mixture in 2, alternating flour-cocoa-flour-cocoa-flour.

Pour half of the batter into each pan and smooth the tops. Bake in the middle of the oven until a tester comes out clean, 25 to 35 minutes. Let the pans rest on cooling racks for 2 minutes, then turn the cakes onto racks to cool completely before frosting.

Assemble the cake by spreading about a third of the frosting on one of the cooled layers, putting the second layer on top, and swirling the rest of the frosting over the top and sides.

FROSTING

SHOPPING LIST

5 ounces
  unsweetened
  chocolate
1 cup whipped
  cream cheese
2½ cups
  confectioner's sugar

STAPLES

¾ cups (1½ sticks)
  unsalted butter
1 teaspoon vanilla

Chop the chocolate and melt it in a double boiler. Let it cool so that you can comfortably put your finger in it. While it's cooling, mix the butter with the whipped cream cheese. Add the chocolate, the vanilla, and a dash of salt, and mix in the confectioner's sugar until it looks like frosting.

The sexy sweetness of bay scallops. Such a fugitive flavor. So subtle. Raw. Sparked with shards of jalapeño. Showered with lime.

———

CHOCOLATE CAKE IS A FINE CURE, BUT IT DOESN'T LAST. I WOKE UP THE NEXT morning still filled with the same empty feeling. Dread. I looked at my calendar, knowing there was nothing on it. I set off for the bookstore, hoping to distract myself, and ended up at the fishmonger's instead. "The Peconic Bays are in!" trumpeted the sign in the window that lured me inside.

Scallops from the Peconic Bay are tiny and as lovely as pearls. They have a remarkable sweetness that resembles nothing else that lives in the ocean. Their season is extremely fleeting, usually no more than a few weeks. But much as I yearned for them, their astonishingly high price gave me pause. For a woman with no job it was a reckless extravagance.

I bought them anyway. At home I opened the package and put a scallop in my mouth; it was like diving into the sea on a warm summer day. I couldn't bear to cook them, so I simply heaped the pile onto a pretty plate, dusted the scallops with coarse salt (Maldon is particularly good because of its flaky, triangular shape), and added a few flecks of jalapeño pepper and a small, refreshing shower of lime juice. They were so sweet, so straightforward, so refreshing. *Simple pleasures,* I thought, as I tweeted my solitary meal.

I had not been expecting the returning rush of tweets. "Raw?" someone answered. "Do I dare?"

"Yes!" someone else replied, and before long we were having an online debate about uncooked seafood. Engrossed in this virtual conversation, I had the sudden realization that this was very much like being in the *Gourmet* test kitchen.

It was not what I expected when I first signed up for Twitter in the fall of 2008. I hadn't even done it myself; two friends, astonished to discover that I was ignorant of Twitter, went online during a dinner party and signed me up. The next morning I tweeted at them, thinking it was a fine way to stay in touch with old friends. I had no inkling that this would become a way to make new ones, or that before long I would be completely engaged with a passionate group of food people whom I had never met.

Thunder rumbling. Bitter broccoli rabe: sweetened with garlic, softened in olive oil, heaped on crisped bread. Just right.

DECEMBER WORE ON, FEELING AS IF IT WOULD NEVER END. THE WEATHER WAS awful. Michael went into the hospital for shoulder surgery. Everything felt wrong. My mood was sour.

I trudged into freezing rain to buy some broccoli rabe; an acerbic taste, I thought, for a sullen mood. Indeed, as I began to cook, the green scent hovered at the very edge of unpleasantness.

But once I had drained the vegetable and started sautéing it with oil and garlic, the aroma morphed into something entirely different. The fragrance turned pleasant, inviting, and by the time I was piling it onto grilled bread and topping it with softly melting cheese, the broccoli rabe had become an extremely amiable mouthful. How quickly things can go from bitter to sweet. How reassuring.

BROCCOLI RABE BRUSCHETTA

SHOPPING LIST
1 bunch broccoli rabe
Italian bread

STAPLES
olive oil
garlic
salt
pepper
Parmesan cheese

Serves 4 to 6

Throw the broccoli rabe into a pot of salted boiling water and cook it until all the rough edges have disappeared and the color has deepened. (It will take 10 minutes or so, but don't worry about overcooking it; this is not an al dente moment.) Drain well, and cut up the vegetable in a casual fashion.

Heat a generous amount of olive oil, throw in 3 or 4 cloves of chopped garlic, and wait for the scent to perfume the air. Add the broccoli rabe, salt, and pepper, and stir until it glistens. Serve on slices of country bread that have been brushed with olive oil and crisply grilled. Top with grated Parmesan cheese.

Wish I were in Venice. Yearning for the sexy little ribs I ate there with my fingers. Wine-drenched. Garlic-crisped. Slightly sticky. Fine.

WELL, OF COURSE I WISHED I WAS IN VENICE. OR PARIS. OR SHANGHAI. THERE IS NO place more depressing than a hospital waiting room. We frightened relatives huddled like disconsolate sparrows, every eye looking up each time a doctor entered the room. Other people typed, read newspapers, whispered into their phones. I sat there thinking about recipes.

Then Michael's doctor walked in to tell me that the operation had been a failure. He'd been unable to repair some torn muscles. It wasn't life-threatening, but it was a blow. Michael was going to be not only in pain, but also in despair.

I sat there wondering if there was anything I might cook that would make him feel better. These ribs, a simple Venetian classic, figured prominently in my thoughts.

VENETIAN PORK

SHOPPING LIST
2 pounds spareribs
  or baby back ribs
fresh rosemary
1 cup white wine

STAPLES
salt
pepper
olive oil
4 or 5 cloves garlic
  (sliced thin)

Serves 4

Ask your butcher to cut a couple of pounds of spareribs into small pieces—about 2 inches wide—or do it yourself with a cleaver. If you're using baby back ribs, cut them apart. Dry them as well as you can and sprinkle them all over with salt and pepper.

Coat the bottom of a skillet with olive oil and sauté the pork over high heat until it has become crisp, brown, and fragrant. You will probably need to do this in two or three batches.

Put all the pork back in the skillet with the garlic, a bit of chopped rosemary, the white wine, and 1 cup of water. Bring the liquid to a boil, cover the pot tightly, and simmer over low heat for an hour and a quarter, or until the pork is entirely tender.

Just before serving, remove the lid and reduce the sauce to a lovely shiny glaze.

Spicy shrimp. Fiery red heat of Sriracha. Cool jumble of asparagus, garlic, ginger. Onions. Gentle tropical sweetness of coconut rice. Good!

THE HARDEST THING I KNOW IS WATCHING SOMEONE YOU LOVE IN PAIN. I fluttered anxiously around Michael, driving him crazy, wanting to do something and utterly incapable of anything more than pills, pillows, and sympathy. The least I could do was cook his favorite dishes.

SRIRACHA SHRIMP OVER COCONUT RICE

Begin with the best shrimp you can buy. Look at the labels. Shrimp vary enormously in quality. If you can find wild-caught American shrimp, that's what you want. Most farm-raised shrimp are either tasteless or have an unpleasant iodine tang; on top of that, many shrimp farmers are ecologically reckless.

Peel the shrimp, squeeze the juice of the lime over them, and sprinkle them generously with a few tablespoons of Sriracha sauce; allow to marinate for about 15 minutes.

Wash the basmati rice, and keep washing until the water runs clear. Drain the rice, and sauté it in a bit of butter; when it's glossy add the coconut milk mixed with ¾ cup of water (you can vary the proportions if you have less coconut milk on hand). Add a pinch of salt, bring to a boil, cover, turn down the heat, and cook for 20 minutes. Remove from heat, but leave the lid on for 10 more minutes before fluffing and serving.

While the rice is cooking, sauté the onion, the garlic, and a bit of thinly sliced ginger in vegetable oil in a large sauté pan. When the mixture has become impossibly fragrant and the onions are translucent (about 5 minutes), add the asparagus and toss for a couple more minutes. Add the shrimp and their marinade. Toss and sauté over high heat until the shrimp lose their translucence, 2 to 3 minutes.

Pile the shrimp on top of the rice and serve, with extra Sriracha sauce.

Cold. Clear. White world.
Almost Xmas. Eating Linzer torte.
Thinking of my father; he loved it so.

MICHAEL SLOWLY RECOVERED FROM BOTH HIS PAIN AND HIS DEPRESSION, AND NICK came home for winter break. The world rocked into holiday orbit, and I gave myself to the moment. Phones ringing, kids dashing in and out, long games of Scrabble, movies on TV . . . I was back in Scarlett O'Hara mode. I knew that bad times were ahead, but for the moment I was concentrating on Christmas.

LINZER TORTE

SHOPPING LIST
1 cup confectioner's
  sugar
1¾ cups almonds
½ cup raspberry
  preserves (the best
  you can find)
⅓ cup red or black
  currant jam

STAPLES
12 tablespoons
  (1½ sticks) unsalted
  butter, softened
2 eggs
1¾ cups flour
salt
1 teaspoon ground
  cinnamon
1 lemon

Every Christmas my father went uptown to Yorkville to purchase a Linzer torte; it reminded him of his Berlin childhood.

The year I was twelve I surprised him by baking one myself.

Much later I learned that the classic recipe requires considerably more effort than mine, but to this day I prefer this super-easy version. To me it will always be the taste of Christmas.

Cream the butter with the confectioner's sugar. Beat in 1 egg and 1 egg yolk (save the leftover white).

Toast the almonds and grind them very fine. Add the nuts to the butter mixture, along with the flour, a pinch of salt, and the cinnamon. The dough will be very stiff. Form it into a disk, wrap it well, and refrigerate it for at least half an hour.

Separate one-third of the dough from the rest, and lightly roll out the larger piece on a floured surface so that it fits into an 8-inch tart pan with a removable bottom, pressing it up the sides. Don't worry if the dough falls apart; just patch and press it into the pan. Brush with the reserved egg white and set aside.

Meanwhile, mix the raspberry preserves with the currant jam. Grate in the zest of the lemon, enjoying the wonderful citric scent. Add the juice of the lemon, mix well, and pour the filling into the crust.

Roll out the reserved dough and make ½-inch strips.

Weave a lattice over the top of the jam; the dough will very likely break, but you can patch it, which will give your torte a pleasantly rustic quality. Brush with the remaining egg white and bake in a 350-degree oven for about 1 hour.

Sift a little confectioner's sugar over the torte as it comes out of the oven, and let it cool completely before serving.

Guests gone. Completely satisfying Xmas. Dishes still to do, but music's playing and there are roast beef bones to gnaw.

MY CHRISTMAS PRESENT TO MYSELF WAS A SEVEN-POUND DRY-AGED PRIME RIB ROAST. It was stunningly expensive, and as I ordered it I thought, with a touch of mordant humor, that by this time next year it would probably be beyond my reach.

Great beef has a clear mineral scent, and I knew, just from the aroma, that this cut was going to be good. Nothing could be easier to cook: I simply brought the meat to room temperature, sprinkled it with salt and pepper, put it into a 450-degree oven for 15 minutes, turned the oven down to 350 degrees, and roasted it for another hour and 20 minutes, until it reached an internal temperature of 125 degrees. Then I took it out and let it rest for 20 minutes before tackling the carving.

I paired the beef with potatoes au gratin, another extravagant classic. To counter all that richness, I served a side of sautéed spinach sharpened with anchovy and zinged with lemon peel. It was a perfect meal, and as I looked around the table I felt, for the moment at least, more lucky than lost.

POTATOES AU GRATIN

SHOPPING LIST

1½ cups cream

2½ pounds
boiling potatoes
(such as Yukon
Gold)

½ pound Gruyère
cheese (grated)

STAPLES

2 cups milk

2 cloves garlic
(smashed)

1 teaspoon salt

pepper

whole nutmeg

butter

Serves 6 to 8

The secret to these potatoes is that they're cooked twice. First you plunk them into a big bath of milk and cream that's been infused with just a touch of garlic and bring them gently to a boil. Then you dump them into a baking dish, grate a bit of fresh nutmeg over them, and sprinkle the entire top with Gruyère before putting them into the oven where they drink up all the liquid as the cheese turns into a crisp crust.

Pour cream and milk into a large pot. Peel the potatoes and slice them as thinly as you can, putting them into the pot as they are ready. Add the garlic, the salt, and a few good grinds of pepper and bring it all slowly to a boil.

Meanwhile, butter a gratin dish or a rectangular baking pan. When the milk comes to a boil, remove it from the heat and pour the contents into the buttered gratin dish. Grate a bit of fresh nutmeg over the top and cover with grated Gruyère cheese.

The baking is pretty forgiving; you can bake at anywhere from 300 to 400 degrees, depending on what else you have in the oven. The timing's forgiving, too; at the lower temperature it will take about an hour to absorb the liquid and turn the top golden, at 400 degrees it will take about 35 minutes.

Let it rest for at least 15 minutes—but this, too, is forgiving. If the potatoes have to wait an hour, they will be absolutely fine.

SAUTÉED SPINACH

SHOPPING LIST

2 pounds fresh
spinach

STAPLES

4 tablespoons
(½ stick) butter

4 cloves garlic
(minced)

1 lemon

1 tablespoon mashed
anchovies

salt

pepper

Serves 6

Wash the spinach really well and remove the ribs. If your spinach leaves are large, cut into smaller pieces. Whirl the leaves in a salad spinner until they're almost dry.

Put the butter in a large sauté pan with the garlic and the zest of the lemon, and wait until it's very fragrant. Add the anchovies, and poke and stir with a wooden spoon until they have disintegrated. Add the spinach and keep stirring, until the leaves are wilted but still tender and bright. Taste; add pepper, and more salt if the anchovies haven't contributed enough for your liking. Serve immediately.

Woke to winter wonderland, every tree dusted with a glittering filigree of silver snow. Almost unbearably beautiful. Perfect Xmas present.

I'd never seen hoarfrost before, and I couldn't stop staring. It was as if some snow fairy had waved a wand, outlining every outdoor object in a sparkling coat. Up close, each blade of grass was flocked with tiny icicles.

Nick and I went walking through the woods, following deer trails, looking around like wide-eyed children. The soft snow crunched beneath our feet, winter music, and we went farther and farther, thinking we might never see this again. We returned home breathless, red-cheeked, and happy, built a fire, and began to cook.

Few scents are as exuberant as that of a plump chicken roasting in its own juices. If you put some potatoes underneath to catch the dripping fat, add a couple of quartered onions, and throw in some whole cloves of garlic for good measure, the scent gets better still. (Even if nobody wants to spread the melted garlic onto bread, it perfumes the air in the most wonderful way.) All you need to make this dish a complete dinner is a small salad on the side.

ROAST CHICKEN WITH POTATOES

SHOPPING LIST
1 small chicken
  (about 3 pounds)
6 small potatoes

STAPLES
2 large onions
4 cloves garlic
olive oil
salt

Serves 3 or 4

Take the chicken out of the refrigerator 2 or 3 hours before you want to eat. Pat it really dry, inside and out. Remove all visible fat from the chicken; carefully lift the skin away from the breast and slide the fat underneath, where it will baste the breast and keep it moist.

Put the chicken on a rack in a pan and scatter some small peeled and quartered potatoes, a couple of large onions cut into 6 or 8 wedges each, and a few whole unpeeled garlic cloves underneath. Why waste all that lovely chicken fat? (If you roll the vegetables in a bit of olive oil before you throw them into the pan, they will taste even better. But you don't have to.) Generously sprinkle the chicken—and the potatoes and onions—with sea salt.

Preheat the oven to 450 degrees—high heat makes a crisper chicken—and cook the chicken for about 50 minutes. (A larger chicken will take a few minutes more.)

Remove the chicken from the oven and let it rest for 10 minutes before carving. Serve it with the crisp potatoes, onions, and garlic cloves, and the wonderful juices in the bottom of the pan.

Blue moon in the Berkshires. Pure magic. Filet of beef, very rare. Small icy oysters laid out on snow. Goodbye. Hello. New Year.

A FULL MOON ON A COLD, CLEAR NIGHT IN THE COUNTRY: NATURE WAS PULLING out all the stops, and I stared up at the second full moon of the month with enormous gratitude. It felt like a gift.

The day had been filled with gifts. Late in the afternoon the FedEx man drove up the hill with a box of oysters from Puget Sound. They'd been pulled from the ocean just the day before and I couldn't stop thinking about their journey. Here they were, still living creatures, on the other side of the continent in an entirely different climate.

We headed off to a potluck party, a filet of beef tucked into the backseat along with the box of oysters. The full moon lighted our way, and the icy roads turned the drive into an adventure. But all that ice had given me an idea.

On my way into the party I scooped handfuls of snow into the box of oysters. When we arrived I spread the snow across the platter and placed each just-opened oyster on the sparkling bed. The beef was rare, robust, delicious. The oysters were sweet, saline, sharp. I was with Michael, surrounded by friends, and as I raised a glass to the coming year, I was filled with hope.

FILET OF BEEF

SHOPPING LIST
3-to-4 pound whole
    filet of beef
1 tablespoon
    truffle salt
horseradish
tarragon

STAPLES
sour cream
pepper
lemon juice

Serves 6 to 8

This filet of beef is a wonderful dish for a potluck. Easy, too: the meat cooks in a trice, it's delicious cold, hot, or in between, and the recipe can be doubled or quadrupled to feed a crowd.

But I wanted something more. Pawing through the spice cupboard, I found an overlooked jar of truffle salt. It was a couple of years old, but when I opened it, the flavor literally leaped out of the jar, filling every corner of the kitchen. I patted the filet dry (this is important) and sprinkled it liberally with the truffle salt.

Preheat the oven to 450 degrees. Brown the filet in a pan that's lightly slicked with oil until all sides of the meat have turned a generous shade of brown, then put it in the oven for about 20 minutes (a meat thermometer should read 120 degrees). Let it rest for at least 15 minutes, at which point it will measure 130 degrees and be a lovely rosy rare. Leave it longer if you like. You can cut the filet into medallions and serve it as a hot dish, but I think it tastes best at room temperature.

Want an easy sauce? Stir a little horseradish into sour cream and add some chopped tarragon, a bit of freshly ground pepper, and a splash of lemon juice.

WINTER

New Year. Sunrise through the trees.
Sky silver, clouds shining gold.
Wild turkeys saunter past. Squeezing
pomegranates, drinking color.

WANDERING INTO THE KITCHEN ON THE FIRST MORNING OF THE YEAR, SLIGHTLY hungover and desperate for orange juice, I was struck by the sight of half a dozen turkeys strutting past the window. Their strangely syncopated gait and prehistoric appearance were so comically arresting that I was still watching as I reached into the refrigerator, and I ended up pulling out pomegranates instead of oranges. I'd never thought of making pomegranate juice, but I was thirsty enough to try. To my surprise, pomegranates squeeze as easily as oranges—their skin may be hard, but it's very thin—and I soon had a full glass of juice. On its own the tannic juice buzzed against my tongue, but cut with orange juice it turned out to be the perfect cure for a hangover.

POMEGRANATE SUNRISE FIZZ

Cut a pomegranate in half and squeeze it as if it were an orange. On its own, the color is extraordinary—like liquid garnets—but if you combine it with the juice of an orange, you end up with the color of a sunrise. Pour over ice and splash in a bit of soda water. (A jigger of vodka turns this into a perfect way to toast the sunset.)

Grating cheddar. Shredding scallions. Slicing shallots. Tangled onto buttered bread, melted into a crisp-edged puddle. Lunch!

REALITY. NICK WENT BACK TO SCHOOL AND MICHAEL AND I WERE ALONE IN THE country, contemplating winter. If I didn't get a job soon we'd be unable to keep both our New York apartment and our little summer house upstate. One of them would have to go. But which?

I'm a New Yorker, and the answer seemed obvious to me. But Michael had other ideas; he loves the quiet of the country, the peaceful panorama of the changing seasons, the closeness of our small community. Life upstate, he argued, would be less expensive. Though unconvinced, I agreed to attempt my first rural winter.

In the beginning everything seemed quaint, and the landscape provided its own excitement. One day, as Michael and I huddled over our computers at opposite ends of the house, I looked out the window to find a moose ambling up the driveway. "Come see!" I was so amazed I could barely find my voice, and the words came out in a hoarse whisper. We watched for almost half an hour as the magnificent creature made his slow way into the bare woods, head high, his enormous rack of antlers like the crown of some fantastic monarch. A moose so close to civilization? It seemed somehow significant, a sign of what to expect from a country winter, and I went into the kitchen to construct a celebratory little lunch.

I can't think of a single other simple dish that equals the everyday opulence of a grilled cheese sandwich. Rich, crisp, and chewy, a great grilled cheese requires no more than a few minutes. Michael and I sat staring out the window, hoping for the return of the moose, thinking how fine it was to be holding on to something so warm, so soft, so utterly delicious.

THE DIVA OF GRILLED CHEESE

SHOPPING LIST
leeks
scallions
¼ pound cheddar
  cheese
2 slices sturdy
  sourdough bread

STAPLES
shallots
1 onion (any color)
1 clove garlic
  (minced)
butter
mayonnaise

Makes 1 sandwich

Gather a group of shallots, leeks, scallions, and an onion red, yellow, or white—as many members of the allium family as you have on hand—and chop them into a small heap. Add a minced clove of garlic. Grate a few generous handfuls of the best cheddar you can afford (Montgomery is particularly appealing), set a little aside, and gently combine the rest with the onion mixture.

Butter one side of thickly sliced bread and heap as much of the mixture as possible between the slices. Spread a thin layer of mayonnaise on the outside of the bread (this will keep it from scorching on the griddle). Press the reserved grated cheese to the outside of the bread, where it will create a wonderfully crisp and shaggy crust, giving your sandwich an entirely new dimension.

Fry on a heated griddle or in a skillet about 4 minutes a side, until the cheese is softly melted.

Snow on the ground, fricassee on the stove, cats purring by the fire. Pretty perfect Sunday.

COUNTRY LIFE ASSUMED A TRANQUIL RHYTHM, AND I WAS SURPRISINGLY CONTENT. With few distractions, I began to write again, working on a short story, wondering if I might expand it into a novel.

Most days I'd take a break, driving into our little village and making friends with the butcher, the people at the cheese store, the cashiers at the supermarket. In the halcyon months of summer they have no time to talk, but in the slow languor of winter they were eager for conversation.

"Try these chickens." Jeremy Stanton, my country butcher, sources all his meat from local producers. "I've found a new farmer who's raising the most delicious birds I've ever tasted."

"At this price they'd better be."

His chickens were twice the price of even the most expensive supermarket sort.

"On me if you don't think they're worth it." He was already folding a plump bird into a sheet of brown butcher paper.

I drove home thinking about recipes, wondering what I might do. A light snow sprang up, the tiny flakes melting as they hit the windshield, running down the glass. That gave me an idea, and I stopped to buy a pint of the thick, almost golden cream that rises to the top of Jersey milk. I also bought some mushrooms, thinking how fine a fricassee would taste on a winter night.

I cut the bird into ten pieces, enjoying the clean scent rising off the meat, the firmness of the muscles. As the bird went sizzling into a pan of local butter, I chopped onions, realizing that everything in the dish had been raised within twenty miles of my kitchen. The scents rose around me, a seductive meld of wine, cream, and onion that reminded me of the food I ate when I was living on the Île d'Oléron in the sixties. Back then, French meat and produce offered a remarkable contrast to everything you could buy in American markets. I would have been incredulous to learn that one day we'd raise ingredients as good in the Hudson River Valley. Thinking how far American food has come made me feel very lucky to be exactly where I was.

CHICKEN FRICASSEE

SHOPPING LIST
1 chicken (cut into
    10 pieces)
1 medium carrot
    (diced)
1 stalk celery (diced)
1 cup white wine
½ pound
    mushrooms
    (quartered)

STAPLES
salt
pepper
5 tablespoons butter
olive oil
1 onion (diced)
flour
2 cups chicken stock
    (see recipe,
    page 301)
parsley
1 bay leaf
2 egg yolks
¼ cup heavy cream
1 lemon

Serves 4

Shower the chicken with salt and pepper.

Melt a couple of tablespoons of butter in a large casserole with a tablespoon of olive oil. Brown the chicken over medium-high heat, starting skin side down and not crowding the pot, about 5 minutes on each side, removing the pieces as they brown.

When the casserole is empty, add the onion, the carrot, and the celery to the pot and cook for about 10 minutes, until the vegetables are soft and fragrant, stirring occasionally to get all the brown bits. Stir in a couple of tablespoons of flour and cook, stirring continuously, until the flour has been absorbed by the fat in the pan. Add the white wine and stir until the liquid is slightly thickened. Add the chicken and the chicken stock. Add a few sprigs of parsley, salt and pepper, and a bay leaf. Bring to a boil, reduce to a simmer, partially cover, and cook for about half an hour, or until the chicken yields when you stick it with a fork.

Meanwhile, sauté the mushrooms in a couple of table-spoons of butter. Salt to taste and set aside.

When the chicken is ready, remove it from the pan. Discard the herbs and simmer the liquid gently for a few more minutes to reduce it.

Whisk the egg yolks into the cream and slowly add some of the hot liquid to temper it. Stir the mixture into the broth and, stirring constantly, let it cook gently for a minute or so. Add the mushrooms and the chicken. Add the juice of half a lemon and a tablespoon of butter. Your fricassee is ready.

Slate sky. Power out.
Ferocious wind. Fire blazing.
Cold ham, thick bread, chunky
applesauce. Hot coffee. Cream.

THE SNOW STARTED AND DIDN'T STOP. ICY WINDS BANGED AGAINST THE WINDOWS as if they wanted to come inside and warm themselves by the fire. The gale howled, the drifts mounted around the house. Three weather advisories warned us not to leave unless absolutely necessary.

Inside, the house was cozy. The small backup generator a friend had insisted we install meant that we had water, heat, and a few lights, but we lacked an oven. Concerned with conserving fuel—who knew how long it might be until the power returned?—we camped by the fireplace.

That first night I lit some candles and set out a small old-fashioned feast, feeling like a character in a Jane Austen novel. I sliced a loaf of sturdy bread and carved slabs of rosy meat from a leftover ham. I was moving through the dim kitchen when the fresh, autumnal scent of the Arkansas Black apples I'd stashed in the pantry came wafting toward me. They're great keepers, growing slowly darker over time as their fragrance becomes increasingly intense. Right now it struck me as an invitation to make applesauce.

I lit another candle, which made my shadow dance along the wall. As I stood at the fireplace, stirring apples, country life seemed very fine.

APPLESAUCE

SHOPPING LIST
6 apples
1 stick cinnamon

STAPLES
1 lemon
sugar

Applesauce practically makes itself. Peel your favorite apples, chop them into hefty chunks, and throw them into a pot with a splash of lemon juice, a bit of water, a stick of cinnamon, and a few spoonfuls of sugar. Let the mixture sputter slowly until it's soft enough to smash with a fork. Season to your own taste and remove the cinnamon stick before eating. Another bonus: the applesauce will keep for a couple of weeks in the refrigerator. When the power came back on and I had an oven, I turned the leftovers into this fantastically fragrant cake.

GINGERED APPLESAUCE CAKE
GLAZED WITH CARAMEL

Preheat the oven to 350 degrees. Butter and flour a 12-cup Bundt pan.

Break the eggs into a large bowl. Whisk in sugar and brown sugar. Add ½ tablespoon (or more) of freshly grated ginger and the applesauce. Whisk in the oil and vanilla and mix until it is smooth.

Put the flour into a small bowl. Whisk baking soda, salt, a few grinds of pepper, cinnamon, and ground cloves into the flour and stir gently into the applesauce mixture.

Pour the batter into the prepared Bundt pan and bake for about 45 minutes, until the cake bounces back when you press your finger into it.

Cool the cake for 15 minutes on a rack before turning it out and allowing it to cool. This cake is delicious all by itself— but even better with this sweet, sticky glaze.

GLAZE

Put the cream in a small heavy-bottomed pot. Whisk in the brown sugar, the corn syrup, and a pinch of salt and bring to a boil. Turn the heat down to medium and continue to boil for about 15 minutes, whisking every few minutes.

When the glaze has come together into a smooth, thick caramel, remove from heat and stir in the vanilla.

Put the cake, still on the rack, over a sheet of waxed paper. Carefully pour the glaze over the cake. (If you don't mind a bit of a mess, you can simply pour the glaze, less carefully, over the cake and let it drip onto the plate.)

So cold. Heavy snow-swollen sky.
Butter-toasted oatmeal,
rivers of thick cream, brown sugar.
Fresh orange juice; such fragrant hope.

COLD NOSE, COLD TOES, COLD FINGERS: GETTING OUT OF BED WAS TOO HARD. In-stead, I pulled the covers around me, reading the poems of Tomas Tranströmer, captured by this line: "The storm puts its mouth to the house and blows to get a tone."

It was blowing. Blowing. The weather had taken over, becoming the only thing that mattered. Michael and I were alone together on a mountain, and for the moment, everyday life consumed me. We were cut off from the world, intent on conserving as much energy as possible. My entire being was focused on feeding us and staying warm.

"You're liking country life, right?" Michael came into the kitchen wearing three sweaters. I handed him a glass of orange juice.

I nodded, thinking that the aroma of oats toasting in butter is one of the finest scents on earth. Michael built a fire, and as the flames began to capture the logs, it occurred to me that the oatmeal could also use a little spark. I tossed in a hand-ful of diced apricots, more for color than for flavor, but the sweetly sour tang of the fruit was like staccato notes in the bland cereal. A little sugar, a little cream . . . We took our bowls to the fireplace and sat hugging them, ready for whatever the weather was about to throw at us.

BUTTER-TOASTED APRICOT OATMEAL

SHOPPING LIST

1 cup steel-cut
  oatmeal
½ cup dried apricots

STAPLES

butter
1 teaspoon salt
brown sugar
cream

Serves 4

Begin by melting a dollop of unsalted butter in a small pan until it becomes fragrant and slightly golden. Toss in the oats and worry them about until they're glistening, have turned slightly brown, and are very fragrant; it should take about 5 minutes.

Add 4 cups of water and the salt; turn up the heat and bring to a furious boil. Turn the heat down very low, cover the pot, and cook until most of the water has evaporated; this process should take about half an hour. At the last minute, stir in a handful of chopped dried apricots, heap the oatmeal into warmed bowls, and top with a few crumbles of brown sugar and a generous drizzle of cream.

White world. Snow still falling.
Even the hawks have flown away.
Lemon soup, bright, soothing.
Somewhere the sun is shining.

FOUR DAYS IN AND THE SNOW SHOWED NO SIGNS OF STOPPING. THE ROADS WERE impassable. We lived with the light, rising with the sun and going to bed early. The thrill of country life was beginning to fade.

I sat staring glumly out at that frozen landscape, thinking about what I'd been doing this time last year. In late January we would have been working on the April issue. Succumbing to a fit of nostalgia, I got out the final April issue and began turning the pages. At that moment I would have given anything to be back in my office on Times Square.

Reaching an article called "Transformers," I remembered how it had come about. We'd been sitting around the big table in the conference room, talking about the foods of spring, when someone—who?—wondered how many different desserts you could make with three eggs and two lemons. The results were impressive—an entire range of cakes and puddings—but now my thoughts moved in a different direction. Why hadn't we come up with something savory? I went into the kitchen, pulled out a lemon, and held it in my hand.

I stood for the longest time simply staring down at that bright yellow ball, reveling in the color, allowing the oil to perfume my fingers. Then, almost unconsciously, I began grating the zest, concentrating on the scent, stopping every few seconds to inhale the aroma.

I found some chicken stock in the freezer and put it in a pot. The comforting scent filled the air as the broth began to melt, pushing the black cloud from over my head. I cracked four eggs, separating them one by one, wholly in the moment, focused on keeping the yolks from breaking. I relished the way the fragile orbs felt in my hands, savored the sensation of the whites trickling thickly through my fingers. By the time I began beating the yolks into the soup I was remembering the unpleasant parts of my old job—the tedium of budget meetings, the embar-

rassment of sales calls, the disappointment of cutting great stories to save space, the endless hours in airports.

The soup with its sunny color, smooth texture, and subtle flavor was extremely satisfying. I looked down at the last lemons sitting on the counter, considering other possibilities.

AVGOLEMONO

STAPLES
6 cups chicken stock
 (see recipe, page
 301)
⅓ cup rice
1 lemon
4 eggs
salt

Serves 6

Bring the chicken stock to a boil. Add the rice, lower the heat to a simmer, and cook for 20 minutes.

Meanwhile, grate the rind from the lemon into a bowl. Squeeze the naked lemon and add the juice to the rind.

Separate the eggs, dropping the yolks into the lemon juice. (Save the whites for another use.) Add a pinch of salt and beat the yolks into the lemon juice and rind.

When the rice is tender, whisk about half a cup of the hot stock into the yolks, then slowly pour the yolks into the soup, stirring constantly. Cook gently for about 5 minutes, or until the soup is slightly thickened. Pour into bowls and eat slowly. If snow is falling outside, so much the better.

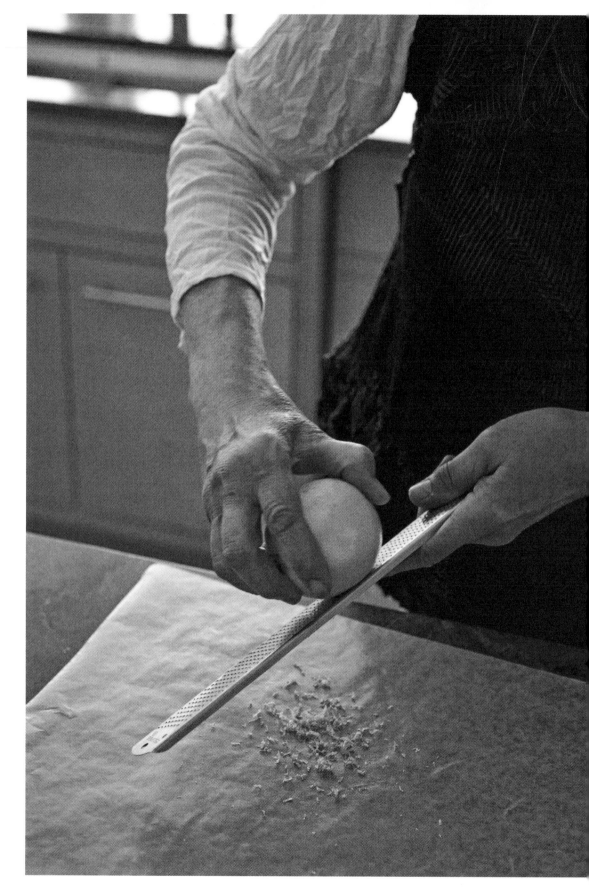

*Lemons. Again. Can't get enough.
Always thought you could make
panna cotta without gelatin.
Guess what? It works!*

THAT ARTICLE HAD JOGGED MY MEMORY. DURING MY FIRST YEAR AT *GOURMET,* A reader sent in a recipe for what she insisted was the most wonderful custard. The cooks had dismissed it; the recipe contained nothing more than lemons, cream, and sugar, and they said it was impossible to make custard without a binder of some kind, like eggs or gelatin.

Why had I never tried it?

Feeling like an alchemist, I worked deliberately, concentrating on heating the cream very slowly.

The result was more than I could have hoped for; it was the most delicate panna cotta I've ever eaten—a fragile custard that seemed held together by a wish. Excited, I went to the computer to tweet about it.

The return tweets were almost instant; responses came from all over the world, making me feel that I'd been joined by invisible companions. Then, in love with lemons, I made a lemon tart, just for fun.

LEMON PANNA COTTA

SHOPPING LIST
2 pints whipping
  cream

STAPLES
3 lemons
½ cup white sugar

Serves 6

Grate the zest from the lemons, being careful not to include any of the bitter white pith. Squeeze the lemons, add the zest to the juice, and set aside.

Pour the cream into a heavy-bottomed pot, stir in the sugar, and bring to a boil, stirring constantly and scraping the spoon across the bottom of the pot, for about 2 minutes. Remove from the heat and, still stirring, add the lemon juice and zest. Pour into ramekins or small bowls, cool, and leave to set in the refrigerator for at least 4 hours.

If you want to gild the lily, garnish with whipped cream and a sprig of mint.

TART LEMON TART

SHOPPING LIST
½ cup cashews (or
  unsalted almonds or
  hazelnuts)
¼ cup confectioners'
  sugar

STAPLES
¾ cup flour
salt
10 tablespoons (1¼
  stick) butter
3 tablespoons olive oil
5 large eggs, separated
4 large lemons
¾ cup sugar
2 teaspoons cornstarch

Begin by making a tart shell. If you have some nuts on hand—I like cashews in this crust, but unsalted almonds or hazelnuts are also excellent—carefully toast a handful, then grind them in a spice grinder or food processor with the flour, the confectioner's sugar, and a pinch of salt. Put the nut mixture into a bowl and cut in 4 tablespoons of butter with two knives until it is the size of peas. Stir in the olive oil and 1 egg yolk.

Form the dough into a disk, put it between two pieces of plastic wrap, and roll it out to an 11-inch round. Press the dough gently into a 9-inch tart shell with a removable bottom, and chill for half an hour. Bake in a 400-degree oven for about 15 minutes and allow to cool on a rack.

To make the filling, grate the zest from 1 lemon. Squeeze all 4 lemons and mix the juice with the zest. Put the lemon mixture into a heavy-bottomed non-reactive pot and whisk in the sugar and cornstarch. Whisk in 2 eggs plus 2 additional yolks.

Put the pot on the stove and turn the heat to medium high. Whisk constantly until the mixture begins to boil, then keep whisking for a couple more minutes until the mixture is smooth and thick.

Remove from the heat, add 6 tablespoons of butter (cut into pieces), and whisk the mixture until the butter has vanished. Spread into the tart shell and allow to cool. Put the tart in the refrigerator to chill for at least 2 hours.

The world is white. Clouds hug the house. Every color has vanished. Salvation: the riotous shades of January pudding!

THE RADIO WAS PROMISING THAT THE STORM WOULD SOON END. I WAS ALMOST sorry; the late January weather was so severe that it had pushed everything but survival from my mind. It seemed like weeks since I'd done anything but concentrate on keeping us warm and fed.

For the moment, though, we were still snowed in, and I was eager to try one more experiment. Scrambling through the cupboards in search of inspiration, I came upon a forgotten jar of raspberry jam. Somewhere in the back of my mind a memory stirred; didn't I have an old Irish recipe for January pudding somewhere?

I went to the ancient manila folder I've been carting around for most of my life. "Recipes to Try" is scribbled on the cover in the spiky handwriting of my sixteen-year-old self. There, among the torn-out pages of long defunct magazines (*McCall's, Sphere, Cuisine*), was a handwritten recipe given to me by a now forgotten friend.

"Before the advent of refrigeration, when fruit in winter was a rare treat," the friend had written, "steamed puddings like this were standard cold weather desserts. Although they've gone out of fashion, this one is worth trying when you want a little taste of the past."

JANUARY PUDDING

SHOPPING LIST
10 tablespoons
  raspberry jam

STAPLES
8 tablespoons (1 stick)
  unsalted butter
½ cup brown sugar
2 eggs
1 cup flour
½ teaspoon baking
  soda
1 lemon

Cream the butter with the brown sugar for 5 minutes, until light and fluffy. Beat in the eggs, one at a time, and then 2 heaping tablespoons of raspberry jam. Sift the flour with the baking soda and fold into the butter-egg mixture. Pour the pudding batter into a well-buttered 1-quart mold. Stand the mold in a pot with enough boiling water to come two-thirds of the way up its sides, turn the heat down to a simmer, cover the pot, and steam the pudding on top of the stove for 2 hours. The water should remain at a simmer, but check every now and then and replace evaporated water. (If you don't have a mold, use a small bowl. Cut a piece of parchment paper to fit snugly onto the top, butter it, and then cover it with two layers of aluminum foil securely tied with a string.)

You'll end up with a lovely, simple deep brown cake, and if you've used good jam, it will have great flavor. Serve it with a splash of cream, a dollop of sour cream, or a sauce made by stirring ½ cup of raspberry jam into a quarter cup of water, heating over a low flame until the jam has dissolved, and stirring in the juice of the lemon. Or simply eat the dessert on its own, reveling in the sheer simplicity of a cake that does not require an oven.

LA rain biblical: water pounding down. Streets turned to rivers. Came expecting sunshine and strawberries. Found <u>Waterworld</u> instead.

LATE IN JANUARY, I WAS INVITED TO Los Angeles by the ideas exchange organization Zócalo to participate in a panel celebrating the legacy of *Gourmet.* I said yes . . . and immediately regretted it. In the month we'd been upstate, I'd started letting go of the magazine, achieving a fragile sense of well-being. Was it foolish to risk this hard-won serenity?

I could not resist the lure of sunshine, and in the end I went. But the weather was not on my side. The plane landed in wind so strong I imagined angry gods flicking us around in a celestial game of badminton. Torrential rain pounded the pavement. The drive from the airport was a nightmare; every truck on the freeway spewed an enormous wake, erasing the road before me. Long before I reached the theater where the panel was taking place, I was ready to take the next plane home.

But when I walked out on the stage I felt a wave of good feeling sweeping toward me from the audience. They remembered the magazine with great affection, and one by one, people stood up to talk about articles that had touched them.

"Looking back," someone asked, "would you do anything differently?"

I thought about all the critiques that said we'd been too ambitious, that if we'd simply stuck to printing recipes the magazine would not have folded. I began to say that I would have done anything if it would have kept *Gourmet* alive. But the words stuck in my throat. I couldn't say them. I was proud of what we'd done. And so I shook my head and said, "I don't think there's any way I could have made a magazine that did not recognize that eating is an ethical act, that our food choices matter." It was the first time I'd said the words out loud. The audience clapped.

The next day, I went to the Hollywood farmers' market, feeling so optimistic that when the strawberries I bought turned out to be large, watery, and not very flavorful, I remained undaunted. I roasted them, which concentrated the flavor. Topped with ice cream, they were delicious—and a fine reminder that no situation is ever hopeless.

ROASTED WINTER STRAWBERRIES WITH ICE CREAM

SHOPPING LIST
1 pint large
 strawberries
mint
vanilla ice cream

STAPLES
4 tablespoons (½
 stick) unsalted
 butter
1½ tablespoons
 balsamic vinegar
white sugar

Buy a pint of the largest strawberries you can find, remove the stems, and set them, stem side down, in a baking dish. Brush them with melted butter. Mix the balsamic vinegar with an equal amount of water and put it in the bottom of the baking dish. Dust the berries with sugar and roast them in a hot (400-degree) oven until they slump into softness, about 8 minutes. Garnish with fresh mint and serve warm, with ice cream.

Sun coming up. Hawks hovering outside. Dancing in the kitchen with gnocchi and the blues. Good way to start a Sunday.

AFTER A WEEK IN THE GRAY RAIN OF LOS ANGELES, OUR LITTLE UPSTATE HOUSE FELT like an oasis. The sky was huge, the air clean. Knowing that the weather couldn't last, I went to the supermarket on my first day home, determined to be prepared. I piled lemons into my cart and bought huge bags of spinach so we'd have some sturdy greens. Four pounds of butter, three cartons of eggs, and every imaginable dairy product. Beef. Pork. Bacon. Flour, sugar, boxes of pasta. Let it snow, let it snow, let it snow.

Then I came home and made gnocchi. It seemed like the ideal dish for the middle of winter: clear and bright with the promise of spring.

SPINACH AND RICOTTA GNOCCHI

1 scant pound baby
  spinach
1 cup fresh ricotta
1 cup grated Parmesan
  cheese

3 tablespoons butter
1 shallot (minced)
2 egg yolks
1 lemon
fresh nutmeg
½ to ¾ cup flour
salt
pepper

Serves 4 to 6

Wash the baby spinach. (The beauty of baby spinach is that it's clean, so you don't need to wash it that well, and you don't have to remove the stems.) Blanch the spinach quickly in boiling salted water and drain it well. When the spinach is cool, squeeze it dry with your hands, as if you were wringing out a towel. Squeeze it again; you want as little liquid as possible in the spinach. Now chop it fine.

Measure out the ricotta and let it drain. Some ricotta contains a great deal of liquid, so allow some time for this process; you want the ricotta to be very dry.

Melt the butter in a large skillet. When the foam dies down, add the shallot and cook for about 5 minutes until it's fragrant and golden. Stir in the spinach, taste for salt, and cool.

Stir the cooled spinach into the drained ricotta, along with a cup of grated Parmesan, the egg yolks, the zest of most of the lemon, and a quick grating of fresh nutmeg. Fold in ½ cup flour until the mixture has the texture of stiff biscuit batter. If it's too loose, add up to another ¼ cup of flour to firm up the batter.

You can make the gnocchi immediately, bringing a large pot of water to a boil, seasoning it generously with salt, and reducing the heat to a rolling simmer. Use two spoons to form little oval dumplings out of the batter, and drop them into the water 8 or 9 at a time. When the water comes back to a boil, cook for about 3 minutes; the gnocchi will be floating on the surface of the water. Scoop them out with a slotted spoon and repeat the operation until all the gnocchi are cooked.

If you have the time, however, it's easier to pat the batter out into a long roll, about an inch in diameter, wrap it in plastic, and put it in the refrigerator to season for a few hours. When you're ready to cook the gnocchi, simply cut off little rounds and poach them as above. (Since the batter is cold, they'll take a bit more time to cook—about 5 to 6 minutes, depending on how large you've made them.)

You now have some options. You can serve the gnocchi naked, with just a bit of melted butter on top. You can serve them with a simple tomato sauce and a sprinkling of Parmesan. Or you can take them one step further and make a gratin by putting the gnocchi into a buttered baking dish and drizzling them with melted butter. Top with a shower of grated cheese and put them in a preheated 400-degree oven for about 8 minutes or until they're lightly browned and the cheese has melted.

Surreal. Trees etched in white. Edges banished. Unearthly silence. Birds hiding. The world's dropped away. And snow keeps coming.

———————

THE SNOW CAME BACK, CLOSING IN AROUND US, AND AGAIN WE WERE UTTERLY alone. Flakes swirled from the sky, a silent white world, hugging the house in a soft embrace. The cars vanished into huge humps. The driveway became impassable. Michael built a fire and we settled in to enjoy it.

Then I made a pot of stew.

Stews are slow food in every sense. You can throw one together, but a hurried stew is never as good as one that's been carefully constructed.

I turned on Bessie Smith and went into the kitchen looking forward to a few fine hours. I removed a two-pound chuck roast from the refrigerator and slowly cubed it, concentrating on the feel of the knife sliding through meat as I calibrated the cut. (If you begin with precut stew meat it's likely to be odd bits left over from different muscles in the animal, and they'll each cook differently.)

I began building the stew, layering in the onions, the vegetables, the aromatics. I poured in the wine, admiring the rich round scent that rose around me. As it cooked, I polished my copper pots, watching the stew, keeping it at a slow simmer.

When the copper was shining I mixed a batch of bread dough, leaning into the knead. Leaving it to rise, I peeled potatoes and washed lettuce, carefully drying every leaf. The cats were curled up in the window, and every once in a while Stella let out a purr, just loud enough to let me know that she approved of the life I was living.

BEEF, WINE, AND ONION STEW

SHOPPING LIST

2 carrots

fresh thyme

1 tablespoon tomato
    paste

2 pounds beef chuck
    (cubed)

¾ cup cognac

1 bottle red wine

1 stalk celery

1½ pounds cremini
    mushrooms
    (quartered)

2 pounds small red
    potatoes

STAPLES

onions

butter

2 strips thick bacon

garlic

parsley

olive oil

salt

pepper

flour

bay leaf

Serves 4 to 6

Take as many onions as you feel like chopping and throw them into a casserole with a bit of butter and the bacon, cut into little squares. Add the carrots, cut into whatever size you consider edible. Cook the vegetables together until they are fragrant and just a bit golden.

Add a few cloves of garlic, smashed, to the mix, and any herbs you happen to have on hand; thyme is nice, as is parsley, although personally I'd stay away from big flavor bullies like tarragon and rosemary. When all has turned soft, add a squirt of tomato paste (it adds a touch of sweetness), stir for a minute or so, and put the entire contents of the pot into a bowl to wait.

Melt a splash of oil and a pat of butter in the same pot. While it heats, take the beef, cut it into stew cubes, and pat it dry. (Dry meat ensures better caramelization.) Salt and pepper the cubes, then toss them in a bag with a bit of flour and shake until they look like they've been dusted with snow. Cook the beef in flights—it hates being crowded in the pan—until beautifully brown, and then set it aside with the onions.

When all the beef has browned, deglaze the pan with a bit of cognac. Return the beef and vegetables to the pot, cover them with most of a bottle of decent red wine, and throw in the celery and a bay leaf. Simmer very gently, partly covered, for 3 or 4 hours. (Make sure the liquid remains at a lazy burble; if the stew cooks too quickly, the beef will get tough.) You could finish the stew now and serve it. But it will be better if you allow it to cool and then put it in the refrigerator overnight; a stew appreciates a little time to rest.

The next day, remove the layer of hard fat that has risen to the surface, along with the celery and the bay leaf, and very gently reheat the stew over a low flame.

Just before serving, sauté the cremini mushrooms in a nice amount of butter for about 10 minutes, adding salt and pepper at the end. Toss them into the stew and taste it. If it needs salt, pepper, or more wine, add it.

I like this stew with plain boiled potatoes and a loaf of sturdy bread.

*Anybody have a banana bread recipe
that you love? I've got a bunch
of black bananas, but haven't
made bb in years. Suggestions?*

I WONDERED IF I HAD TIME FOR ONE MORE FORAY TO THE MARKET BEFORE YET AN-other storm cut us off from the world, but when I started down the hill, the driveway was so icy that I quickly gave up.

The sky grew very dark. Quickly, before the power failed, I sent this tweet into the universe, hoping to connect with my community of cooks. The outpouring of answering recipes was immediate. Astonishing. Humbling. Sitting on a chilly hill in rural New York, I was receiving recipes from thousands of miles away.

Banana bread, it turns out, is the kitchen sink of cakes: the ingredient that some-one, somewhere, does not consider an appropriate addition simply does not exist.

Fruit. Nuts. Spices galore. Half the recipes included chocolate, and every pos-sible permutation of coconut, from toasted shreds to Coco Loco mix. There were even a few flowers.

Boozy banana bread is also very popular. Richard Bertinet wrote from Bath to say that he always adds a measure of dark rum. Chez Pim likes a glug of Jameson's. And lots of people consider bourbon a banana bread essential.

It was exciting and a little overwhelming; in the end I reverted to the recipe I've been using most of my life. This is what I think banana bread should be: simple, innocent, easy.

BANANA BREAD

Preheat the oven to 325 degrees.

Cream the butter with the brown sugar and white sugar. Beat in the eggs.

Mash the bananas and squish them into the butter mixture, along with the vanilla.

Whisk the flour with the baking powder, baking soda, and salt. Add that to the banana mixture, alternating with the buttermilk (you can also use yogurt).

Pour the batter into a greased loaf pan and bake for about an hour.

Early NY morning: conversations with sidewalk strangers. Familiar fog of crowded coffee shop. Toasted corn muffin, crisp, sweet, buttery.

IN TOWN FOR A WRITERS' CONFERENCE, I STROLLED THE FRENZIED STREETS, STARING at passing people as if each one was a gift. I said hello to doormen, petted people's dogs, and when my feet began to freeze, I turned in to the nearest coffee shop, took a seat at the counter, and ordered a toasted corn muffin. It's a peculiarly New York treat, the soft, sweet muffin split and toasted on a hot griddle until the top is crisped, the butter melted.

I was inhaling the vanishing scent of the classic New York coffee shop, that mixture of milky coffee, yesterday's burgers, onions, and wet newspaper, when I realized the woman next to me was tugging timidly at my sleeve.

"Ruth?" she said. I turned to look. A stranger, surely. She reached for her satchel and diffidently pulled out a copy of *Gourmet;* it was still wrapped in its plastic mailer.

"It's the last issue," she said, obviously embarrassed. "I couldn't bear to open it, so I kept it for a day when I needed cheering up. I got fired yesterday, and I was just about to open the issue. But now . . . Would you mind?" She handed me a pen. "I think I'll just ask you to sign it, and keep it for another day. You look like you're doing okay."

I patted her arm. "I have a feeling that you're going to be fine, too."

I signed the issue and we ate our muffins in companionable silence. Each bite was pure comfort. I left first and, remembering Newark airport, asked the cashier to put my neighbor's breakfast on my bill.

NEW YORK CORN MUFFINS

SHOPPING LIST
1 cup cornmeal
1 cup buttermilk
1 cup corn kernels

STAPLES
1 cup flour
6 tablespoons white
  sugar
2½ teaspoons baking
  powder
½ teaspoon salt
¼ teaspoon baking
  soda
6 tablespoons butter
2 eggs

Makes 1 dozen muffins

Mix the flour with the cornmeal. (I prefer stoneground.) Whisk in sugar, baking powder, salt, and baking soda.

Melt the butter. Allow it to cool, then stir in buttermilk along with 1 egg and 1 additional egg yolk. Stir into the dry mixture. Toss in the corn kernels. (You can use frozen corn, and there's no need to defrost it.) The dough will be lumpy; don't worry about that.

Divide the batter into a well-greased muffin tin and bake at 400 degrees for about 20 minutes. Cool for 5 minutes before turning the muffins out.

I like these best served the way they are in old New York coffee shops: split horizontally, brushed with butter, and toasted on a griddle or in a pan.

Bacon and marmalade sandwich at Prune. Strangely delicious. Took half home and then, couldn't help myself, ate it on the subway.

ON THE SECOND DAY OF THE CONFERENCE, I MET A GROUP OF *GOURMET* REFUGEES for lunch at Prune. We hadn't seen one another in a few months, and it felt fine to be spending time together again in one of our favorite downtown restaurants. When I ordered the weirdest dish on the menu, Doc Willoughby, who was now the editor of *Cook's Illustrated Magazine,* gave me one of his sly grins. "Do you think other people actually order this?" he asked.

I looked around the table at my former colleagues, thinking what fun it was to be surrounded by food people again. We had instantly relaxed into our old easy relationship, and when the sandwich arrived we passed it from one hand to the next without a word. It was so delicious that by the time it got to me there was nothing left. We ordered a second, and then a third. I liked it so much that I stopped to buy bacon on my way home, thinking I'd cut the sandwiches into dainty squares to make hors d'oeuvres for my guests. "How'd you ever think of this?" asked Michael when he took a bite.

MY VERSION OF PRUNE'S BACON & MARMALADE SANDWICH

SHOPPING LIST

8 strips bacon
orange marmalade
4 slices pumpernickel
  bread

STAPLES
butter

Serves 2

It's a genius combination. Extremely simple. But unless you get the right ingredients, it doesn't work. You need a sweet, feminine apple- or maple-smoked bacon, not the more manly porkier sort. And you must stop the cooking before the bacon crisps; this recipe requires floppy strips of bacon.

You also need good pumpernickel bread, the deeply brown kind. And the strongest, meanest orange marmalade you can find.

Toast your bread. For each sandwich, butter one slice generously and spread orange marmalade on the other slice. Fry the thick-cut bacon, drain it, put 4 slices into each sandwich, and cut into small squares.

The entire city smells like curry.
Passing the fourth halal chicken cart,
I can't resist. Spicy, tangy, irresistible.
The taste of now.

WHEN I WAS AT *GOURMET* I VISITED THE HALAL CART ON THE CORNER OF SIXTH Avenue and Forty-Third Street at least once a week, taking perverse pleasure in riding the Condé Nast elevators with my fragrantly curried lunch. I especially enjoyed watching the *Vogue* fashionistas shrink away from me, terrified the scent might contaminate their clothes.

I think of that each time I pass one of those carts sending its curried cloud into the air. That day, though, as I watched a man pushing saffron-colored cubes of chicken around a grill, I had another thought: why don't I go home and make my own version?

FOOD CART CURRY CHICKEN

SHOPPING LIST

1 pound chicken
  thighs (boneless,
  skinless)
1 tablespoon curry
  powder
fresh oregano

STAPLES

½ onion
3 tablespoons olive oil
1 lemon
¼ teaspoon coriander
  seeds
2 cloves garlic
  (minced)
¼ teaspoon paprika
½ teaspoon ground
  cumin
salt
pepper
vegetable oil

Serves 4

Cut the chicken thighs into bite-size chunks, and slice the onion into thin rings.

Make a paste by combining the olive oil with 1½ tablespoons lemon juice, the coriander seeds, the garlic, the curry powder, a sprig of oregano, the paprika, the cumin, and a teaspoon of salt in a spice grinder or a blender. Give it a whirl, then grind in copious amounts of black pepper.

Put the onions and chicken into a plastic bag, pour in the marinade, and squish it all around so the onions and chicken are thoroughly coated. Marinate in the refrigerator for at least 4 hours or overnight.

Sprinkle with more salt and pepper. Slick a heavy pan or wok with 2 tablespoons of vegetable oil and cook the onions and chicken for about 5 minutes, tossing every minute or so. It will splutter a bit, and it will smell so delicious you'll be snatching pieces from the pan.

Serve over white rice. I always asked for my chicken without the white sauce they have at the carts, but if you must have it, combine equal parts of mayonnaise and Greek yogurt, then add a dollop of sugar, salt and pepper, and a splash of vinegar. Personally, I think a righteous red hot sauce is far more delicious.

Cold shadows on the mountain.
Stark branches. Huge moon. In here
there's a fine fire and we're about to
eat the world's best rice pudding.

"I'm looking forward to getting back to the country," I said to Michael as we drove up the Taconic State Parkway.

"Who are you trying to convince?" he replied. "Me or yourself?" I wasn't quite sure.

It was late when we arrived, the sky thick with stars, the moonlight reflecting off the snow. The air was so clear it seemed ready to shatter when we got out of the car.

We went inside and lit a fire; the house seemed to gather us in, welcoming us home.

I poured myself a glass of wine, curled up in a big chair, a cat on either side of me, and began poring through the stash of old cookbooks I'd bought on one of my city strolls. I was especially intrigued with *Cooking à la Longchamps* with its evocation of a long-gone New York. It was a time of "Crabmeat Exquisite," "Abalone Steaks in Rhine Wine Sauce," and gnocchi that were called "Baked Cream of Wheat with Parmesan." I was intrigued, but I had no desire to actually make any of these dishes. Then I got to the rice pudding.

Longchamps was famous for this dish, which was served in little brown custard cups, with a pitcher of cream to pour over the top. I used to love it. Was it really as good as I remembered?

I went into the kitchen and began rummaging around to see if I had the ingredients. The only rice I had was basmati, but I couldn't see why that wouldn't work.

It was even better than I remembered. So good, in fact, that we turned it into dinner. Pure guilty pleasure.

LONGCHAMPS RICE PUDDING WITH RAISINS

SHOPPING LIST
½ cup raisins
1 cup heavy cream
  (divided)

STAPLES
¾ cup long-grain
  basmati rice
zest of 1 lemon
¾ cup sugar
⅛ teaspoon sea salt
1 quart whole milk
4 egg yolks
1 teaspoon vanilla
sprinkling of
  cinnamon

Serves 6 to 8

Preheat the oven to 425 degrees.

Put the basmati rice in a bowl filled with water. Stir the rice with your fingers, then pour out the water. Keep repeating the process until the water runs clear.

Put the rice in a pot with 3 cups of water, bring to a boil, lower to a simmer, cover, and cook for 10 minutes. Drain.

Meanwhile, put the raisins in a small saucepan, cover with water, bring to a boil, and simmer for 10 minutes. Strain and set aside. Add the grated lemon rind.

Stir the sugar, a pinch of salt, and the milk into the drained rice. Bring to a boil, then reduce to a gentle burble, stirring frequently with a wooden spoon for 25 minutes until the mixture is the consistency of thick porridge. Remove from the heat.

Whisk the egg yolks with half a cup of the heavy cream. Stir 1 cup of the rice mixture into the egg mixture, then pour it all slowly back into the saucepan with the rice, stirring, until everything is thoroughly blended.

Add the raisins and vanilla. Pour the pudding into a small gratin pan or a pie plate. Whip the other half cup of cream, spread it over the top, sprinkle with cinnamon, and bake in a 400-degree oven for 8 minutes or until the top is golden.

Eat warm or cool, with more cream.

Ice blue afternoon. No sun. No color.
Even the birds are still. Thai noodles.
Sweet. Spicy. Slippery.
A tiny trip to the tropics.

SHORT DAYS, COLD WEATHER: EVEN IN THE BEST OF TIMES, MID–FEBRUARY ISN'T easy. The holidays are a distant memory, and spring seems very far away. But this year, lacking the distraction of a job, this horrid in-between season was especially difficult. Out there, in what I was coming to think of as "the real world," people were doing big things, thinking big thoughts, living big lives. I felt marginalized, and hard as I tried to concentrate on the now, I couldn't help thinking about the life I might be living.

I do, however, have the great good fortune to have a partner who's exquisitely attuned to my darker moments. As I sat at my computer pretending to work, Michael called out, "What's for lunch? Could we have Thai noodles?"

I never would have made them for myself. But now I went into the kitchen and opened a package of rice noodles, thinking, as I always do, how lovely the brittle white strands are. I ran hot water over them, watching them become soft and pliable. I peeled shrimp and pounded peanuts. I measured out fish sauce and began squeezing limes, the scents strong and insistent, anchoring me in the moment. I minced garlic.

Then I began to cook, watching the shrimp slowly turn pink as they lent their lovely color to the oil. I sprinkled in the chiles, tossed them with the rice sticks, and poured in the liquid. The scent—sweet, strong, and salty all at the same time—

seized every sense. I watched the noodles slowly absorb the liquid, then added the eggs, tilting the pan and watching them spread into thin, floppy sheets.

Captured by the cooking, I had a fleeting thought that I'd spent too many years trading time for money. Was I better off now? I added the peanuts, gave the noodles another turn, and the thought flew away. I squeezed more lime juice, stirred it in, put the noodles on a platter.

These noodles might not impress anyone standing on the banks of the Chao Phraya River. But on a cold New York mountain on a grim afternoon, this Americanized version of Thai noodles brought me to my senses.

THAI-AMERICAN NOODLES

SHOPPING LIST
8-ounce package very
   thin rice vermicelli
   (sometimes called
   rice sticks or rice
   vermicelli)
½ pound shrimp
4 scallions
¼ cup Asian fish
   sauce
2 limes
½ cup peanuts
½ pound ground
   pork
Sriracha sauce
cilantro

STAPLES
3 cloves garlic
¼ cup sugar
¼ cup white vinegar
2 eggs
red chile flakes
peanut oil

Serves 4

Soak 6 to 8 ounces of the thinnest rice noodles in hot water for about 10 minutes, or until they go limp. Drain and set aside.

Peel the shrimp and dry them well. If they're big, cut them in half.

Dice the whites of the scallions, and slice the green parts into confetti. Smash the cloves of garlic.

Mix the sugar with the fish sauce and the white vinegar. Squeeze in the juice of 1 lime.

Put the peanuts into a plastic bag and hit it with something heavy—a rolling pin works well—until the peanuts are crushed.

Assemble all of this next to the stove, along with the ground pork, the eggs, and some crushed red chile flakes.

Working quickly, heat a large wok and film it with peanut oil until it shimmers. Add the shrimp, toss them just until they're no longer transparent, and turn them onto a platter. Add a bit more oil to the wok, toss in the garlic, and stir; add the whites of the scallions, the chile flakes, and then the pork, stirring until it's no longer red. Throw in the drained noodles, give a couple more stirs, and pour in the fish sauce mixture. Cook, at high heat, about 7 minutes, until the noodles have absorbed all the liquid. Push them aside and crack one egg into the bottom of the wok, breaking the yolk and tilting so that it forms a sheet. When it has set, mix it into the noodles, breaking the sheet into little pieces as you go, then repeat with the other egg. Toss it all about, add the shrimp and scallion greens, and toss once again. Turn out onto a platter and top with crushed peanuts.

Serve with lime wedges, fresh cilantro, and Sriracha sauce.

Pork, chiles, oranges: perfect antidote to endless winter. Yesterday's stew perfuming every corner of the house with its cheerful scent.

As this new reality began to sink in, I began thinking about all the other lives I might be living. On this particular afternoon I retreated into a Berkeley reverie. I had moved to "the People's Republic" when I was in my twenties, sharing a kind of commune, intent on becoming a writer. Living on the tiniest amount of money, I sacrificed everything in order to have time to write.

I was cooking in a restaurant, but I rose early every morning, writing in the dark before going off to work. When my shift was over I walked home and sat at my desk late into the night, tapping on the typewriter keys. It was Berkeley, it was the seventies, the Vietnam War was finally over, and the entire town was filled with hope.

Our restaurant, a collective, was intent on trying new things. One day, making the daily produce run, I encountered my first tomatillo. I picked it up, marveling at its papery husk, wondering how it tasted. I bought one, cut it open, and discovered that it had an intriguingly sexy sourness. I'd play that up, I thought, stew the strange green orbs in orange juice and dark beer. Cilantro, another new acquaintance, would make a perfect substitute for parsley. I threw in a lot of garlic, too; in those days, no Berkeley person could get enough of what we called "the stinking rose."

The stew was a hit with our customers, and I've been making it ever since. The flavors are deep and slightly elusive, with none of the heaviness of most long-cooked dishes. But what I like best is that each time I make it, I'm reminded of a time when tomatillos and cilantro were completely new and nothing seemed impossible.

PORK AND TOMATILLO STEW

Serves 6

Begin by cutting the pork shoulder, butt, or loin into 2-inch cubes. Sprinkle them with salt.

Remove the husks from the tomatillos, wash the sticky surface off, and quarter them. Put them into a pot with the tomatoes, the dark beer, and 1½ cups of fresh orange juice. Let that stew for half an hour or so, until everything has become tender.

Brown the pork in a casserole, along with 8 to 10 whole cloves of peeled garlic, in a few tablespoons of grapeseed or canola oil. You'll probably need to do this in batches, removing the pork as it browns.

Put the onions into the now empty casserole, along with the cilantro and jalapeños. Add salt and pepper to taste, and be sure to scrape the bottom, stirring in the delicious brown bits.

When the onions are translucent (about 10 minutes), put the tomatillo mixture along with the pork and garlic back into the casserole, turn the heat to low, partially cover, and cook very slowly for about 2 hours.

Squish the garlic cloves into the stew with the back of a spoon, add a cup or so of cooked black beans (or a can of drained beans), and cook for 10 more minutes.

Serve over white rice.

Stir the juice of a lime into a cup of sour cream and serve as a garnish.

Ice storm. Electricity out. Stove not working. Worse weather on its way. What will happen to my bread dough?

THE STORM RAGED, BUT I DIDN'T MIND; I WAS FEELING MORE OPTIMISTIC. WHAT I did mind was that the electricity had deserted us while my dough was rising, and I didn't know what to do. It might be days until I had a working oven. Should I throw the dough out?

I tossed the question into the Twitterverse and the responses came roaring back. "Don't throw it out!" at least a dozen people tweeted. "Just keep punching the dough down."

Convinced that it was a lost cause, I did it anyway. What did I have to lose? The electricity was out for three days, and by day two I was noticing a change. The dough was capturing wild yeasts with great abandon, and before long it began to smell like fine champagne. I could hardly wait for the power to be restored.

As soon as the lights came on, I shaped the dough and preheated the oven. When the loaf had risen for the final time, I put it into the oven. Almost at once a cascade of complex and exciting aromas began to fill the air. The loaf emerged fat and brown, with a dense crumb and a gently sour character. It was far more intense than anything I'd made before—and it lasted for days without getting stale.

I've been using Jim Lahey's brilliant recipe, from his book *My Bread,* for years because it's so easy, and the results so satisfying. But after the storm I changed the recipe, adding a second and sometimes a third and fourth rise. The addition of time gives the bread considerably more character.

JIM LAHEY'S NO-KNEAD BREAD

SHOPPING LIST
3 cups bread flour
instant yeast

STAPLES
salt
cornmeal

Put the flour into a bowl with 1½ teaspoons of salt and ¼ teaspoon yeast. Stir in 1⅓ cups cool water (the mixture will be rather sticky), cover it with a plate, and leave it to rise in a cool place for 18 hours, until it's doubled in size. Punch it down and allow it to rise again until it's doubled; it will take less time. Do this at least one more time. More is better.

Nudge the dough gently out of the bowl onto a floured surface and shape it into a loose ball by folding the edges in. Sprinkle a towel with cornmeal, set the dough on the towel, put the towel on a plate, and wrap it loosely up around the dough. Allow the dough to double once more; it should take only about an hour this time.

Meanwhile, turn the oven to 475 degrees and set a cast iron Dutch oven or other covered casserole in it to heat up. When the dough has doubled, very carefully remove the casserole from the oven with sturdy oven mitts, remove the cover, and quickly turn the dough in; it may land slightly cockeyed, but don't worry.

Cover the pot and set it back into the oven. Bake for 30 minutes, remove the cover, and bake for another 15 minutes or so, until the loaf has turned a deep golden caramel color.

The scent of the baking bread will be almost shockingly delicious, but you're going to have to control yourself. You need to let the bread cool on a rack for at least an hour before eating it. But once that hour has passed, this bread, with some cold, sweet butter, will be one of the best things you have ever tasted.

Subtle sponge cake from antique cookbook. An ancient flavor. No fat. Great texture. Gently sweet. Backbreaking before Edison. Easy now.

THE DREAD WAS GONE. FOR NOW. BUT WOULD IT COME BACK? I FELT THE WAY I HAD when I was at boarding school, surfacing from the tidal wave of homesickness. It was weeks before I was able to believe the forlorn feelings were gone for good.

I was writing, but I was wary. Not wanting to take any chances, I stopped every few hours to go into the kitchen. I baked bread, rolled pasta, whipped up the occasional soufflé in an attempt to stave off whatever lurking misery was out there waiting to pounce on me again.

When I ran out of ideas I flipped through old cookbooks, looking for inspiration. On this February morning I found it in a nineteenth-century issue of the *Boston Cooking School Magazine:* a recipe for a cake requiring no fat and no leavening. It is, essentially, a soufflé with a bit of flour whisked in. Mary J. Lincoln, the principal of the school (and Fannie Farmer's teacher), called this "a genuine sponge cake." She did not mince words. "You will look far to find a better sponge cake than this when properly made and baked."

Working the recipe out was absorbing; things were so much more complicated before measurements were standardized. And as I ground the sugar in the food processor, I wondered how Mrs. Lincoln managed to get her sugar extra fine.

The result was surprising: a fluff of a cake with a very airy texture. In more clement weather it would make a perfect foil for custard, whipped cream, or fruit. But it is delicious all by itself, or with a sprinkling of brandy.

MRS. LINCOLN'S GENUINE SPONGE CAKE RECIPE (IN HER OWN WORDS)

"The weight of the eggs in sugar, and half their weight in flour. This enables you to make a cake of any size you desire. The usual proportion for one loaf, by measure, is four large or five small eggs, one cup of fine granulated sugar, one cup of sifted pastry flour, and the grated rind and juice of half a lemon. Beat yolks till thick and very creamy, add sugar, and beat till light colored; add lemon. Beat whites till stiff and nearly dry, and fold them in with care, so as not to break down the bubbles, sift in the flour lightly, and fold over (not stir) till just barely covered. Bake in a moderate oven from forty to fifty minutes."

MY TRANSLATION

SHOPPING LIST
1 cup cake flour

STAPLES
4 eggs
1 cup sugar
1 lemon

In Mrs. Lincoln's day this would have been quite a project, requiring a very strong arm. In this time of electric mixers, it requires very little effort. One note: if you want to make a picture-perfect cake, you must use extra-fine sugar. Don't have any? Simply grind regular sugar in a food processor until it has the texture of very fine sand.

Preheat your oven to 350 degrees and very carefully separate the eggs. The egg whites are your only leavening here, so you want to make sure that you don't get a single drop of yolk in with the whites.

Beat the yolks in a stand mixer until they're thick and creamy; it should take about 5 minutes.

Grind the sugar in a food processor until it's very fine and beat it into the egg yolks for 2 more minutes, or until the mixture is fluffy. Mix in the zest of the whole lemon and the juice of half the lemon.

In a separate, extremely clean bowl, beat the whites with clean beaters until very stiff and almost dry, 1 to 2 minutes. Stir one-third of the whites into the batter with a spatula, then gently fold in the rest.

Sift the cake flour on top of the batter through a strainer and carefully fold into the batter, just until the flour has disappeared.

Pour into an ungreased 10-inch tube pan with a removable bottom and bake for 40 to 50 minutes until golden and a cake tester comes out clean. Cool on a rack for 10 minutes. Run a knife around the outside of the cake, remove the bottom of the pan, and cool completely on a rack.

Cabin fever. Reality required.
Scrambling through the refrigerator,
craving color. The simple green
pleasure of parsley!

A NIGHT OF TERRIBLE DREAMS BROUGHT ALL THE DAYTIME DEMONS BACK, AND I dragged miserably around the house feeling as if nothing good would ever happen again. I tried to write, but I was too jumpy. I went into the kitchen, opened the refrigerator, and stared glumly inside.

A bunch of parsley caught my eye, and I grabbed it. As I ran it under a stream of running water, its bright color winked at me like a promise of spring, a sign that things *would* get better.

SALSA VERDE

SHOPPING LIST
1 bunch flat-leaf
   Italian parsley
½ cup almonds

STAPLES
2 shallots
3 cloves garlic
red wine vinegar
¼ cup capers
1 lemon
high-quality extra-
   virgin olive oil

I BEGAN CHOPPING PARSLEY, THE MERE MOTION A RELIEF AS I brought my knife down again and again, reducing the frilly little leaves to tiny slivers as they shot their chlorophyll aroma into the air.

I threw some almonds into a pan and toasted them, waiting for the moment when their fragrance hit that peak just before they scorched. Leaving them to cool, I chopped shallots and garlic, reducing them to shreds. I covered the chopped shallots with red wine vinegar.

Then I attacked the almonds, leaning into the task, reveling in the crack of the nuts falling apart beneath my knife. Feeling better, I opened the refrigerator again to see what else I might throw in. Capers! I soaked them to remove the salt. I squeezed a lemon. And then I started to build the salsa verde.

Tasting as I went, I put half the parsley in a bowl and added half of the shallots, capers, garlic, and almonds. I kept tasting and adding ingredients, thinking that the heap of parsley looked like nothing so much as grass cuttings. The thought made me laugh, and I realized that the gloom had gone. I stirred in olive oil and squeezed in lemon juice, and it began to resemble a shimmering green pool. Tasting again and again, it hit me that this kind of cooking is a lot like writing; you can keep tweaking it forever, but at some point you have to decide that you are done.

When I reached that point, I made a little nest of salsa verde and filled it with a fried duck egg. It made a delicious little lunch, but I think I would have been grateful no matter how it tasted; all that chopping had exorcised my demons.

Power still out. Storm raging.
Running out of food. What can I cook
with this sad cabbage?

THE WEATHER WAS EPIC THAT LAST WEEK OF FEBRUARY; ONE DAY IT SNOWED AN
inch an hour. I tried remaining cheerful, but I'm a social creature and I'd been
shut away too long. Even my kitchen activity was becoming limited: it's hard to
be creative when there's nothing left to cook.

"You'd rather be back in the city." Michael, who remained annoyingly unfazed
by country weather, found me rooting glumly through the refrigerator.

I nodded; the people staying in our apartment were due to leave on the first of
March.

"So we'll go back," he said. Instantly cheered, I turned back to the refrigerator,
found a head of cabbage, and decided to make my grandmother's favorite dish.

MY GRANDMOTHER'S CABBAGE

NANNY WAS NOT MUCH OF A COOK; TO MY KNOWLEDGE THIS WAS THE ONLY DISH
she ever attempted, which probably explains why I have such affection for it.

I shredded the cabbage into ribbons the width of wide noodles, enjoying the satisfying crunch of the knife moving through the crisp vegetable. I sprinkled the shredded
cabbage with salt, covered it with a plate, and plunked some cans on top to weight it
down. Then I put it in the refrigerator for a few hours. (Overnight would be better.)

The cabbage sat in the cold all day, shedding liquid. At last I removed it, put it in a colander, and began squeezing it, removing as much liquid as I could.

I melted a stick (8 tablespoons) of unsalted butter and cooked the cabbage for a half hour, until it was limp and soft. Then I boiled a package of egg noodles, drained them, and tossed them in with the cabbage, stirring it around as I added a little salt and a lot of pepper.

We were just finishing our meal when the power came on, and when we looked out the window, the snowplow was nosing up the hill. We could leave!

Cheered by the thought of New York, I used the last of our dairy supplies to make one spectacular cheesecake.

BIG NEW YORK CHEESECAKE

SHOPPING LIST

1 package Famous
  Chocolate Wafers
1½ pounds cream
  cheese
1 pint sour cream

STAPLES

1⅜ cups sugar
salt
8 tablespoons (1 stick)
  butter (melted)
4 eggs
2½ teaspoons vanilla

Serves 8 to 10

Cheesecake is about the easiest thing you can possibly bake, a completely foolproof recipe that relies on supermarket staples. Most people adore it: at *Gourmet,* cheesecake was our most requested recipe. Show up anywhere with one of these and you'll be welcome.

Preheat the oven to 350 degrees.

To make the crust, crush chocolate wafers until you have about a cup and a half (that will take about 6 ounces of wafers). Mix in a quarter cup of sugar, a pinch of salt, and the melted butter. Using your fingers, pat this mixture into the bottom and sides of a 9-inch springform pan, making it even all around. Put the pan into the freezer for 15 minutes (it will keep here, covered, for a couple of months). Bake for 10 minutes, just to crisp the crust. Remove the pan and turn the oven down to 300 degrees.

Beat the cream cheese with a cup of sugar, the eggs, and 1½ teaspoons of vanilla until you have a completely smooth mixture. Pour it into the crust and bake for about 50 minutes, or until the cheese is set on the edges but still a bit wobbly in the middle. Remove the cake from the oven (leave the oven on) and cool for about 10 minutes on a wire rack.

Meanwhile, mix the sour cream with 2 tablespoons of sugar and 1 teaspoon of vanilla. Spread this mixture evenly over the cooled cake, then return it to the oven for about 12 minutes until the glaze is glossy and set.

Cool completely, then chill for at least 8 hours.

*How to be a great houseguest:
friend who stayed at our place
left good Parmigiano, bacon,
and eggs in the fridge for us.*

"USED ALL YOUR SUPPLIES," OUR DEPARTING FRIEND HAD SCRIBBLED ON THE EGG carton. "Didn't want to leave the cupboard bare. Your carbonara recipe has gotten me through a lot of hard times."

Still, I didn't expect to be making my standard fallback dinner quite so quickly. That first day back I was interviewed for a television show; my only job was to add context to a profile of the chef José Andrés, but the interview plunged me back into a world of hairdressers, makeup, wardrobe, and limousines. It was dizzying, and when Anderson Cooper began asking questions, I found myself talking fast, my mind racing as I turned into a completely different creature than the woman who'd been quietly cooking on the mountain.

"How are you feeling, after *Gourmet*?" one of the producers asked when the cameras were turned off. It was kindly meant, but it brought all the old feelings—failure, fear, inadequacy—roaring back.

They called a limo to take me home, and I sat in the back, feeling the adrenaline that had fueled me for the cameras leak away. Lacking the energy to go to the store, I was grateful to know I had everything for carbonara. I stood at the stove cooking up this fast, familiar dish. The eggs hit the hot pasta and I tossed madly, watching them begin to cook, knowing it was time I found a job.

SPAGHETTI ALLA CARBONARA

SHOPPING LIST
¼ to ½ pound bacon

STAPLES
salt
1 pound spaghetti
  (dry, or see pasta
  recipe, page 30)
garlic
3 eggs
Parmesan cheese
pepper

Serves 4

Bring a pot of water to a boil, salt it well, and toss in the spaghetti. Most brands of commercial spaghetti take about 10 minutes, which is all the time you'll need to make the sauce.

Cut anywhere from a quarter to a half pound of bacon into small pieces and brown them in a large skillet with a couple of whole peeled cloves of garlic. (The garlic is mainly for the pleasure of the fragrance.)

Break the eggs into a big bowl.

Grate a generous amount of Parmesan cheese (about half a cup).

Cook your pasta al dente.

Drain the pasta and immediately plunk it into the bowl with the eggs, tossing frantically so the hot pasta will cook them. Remove the garlic from the bacon and then add the bacon, along with as much of the fat as your conscience will allow. Toss. Add the cheese. Toss again. Add salt to taste.

Grind a good amount of pepper over the pasta and serve. You will instantly understand why this quick, easy dish has given so much comfort to so many people.

Gray day in the city. Dogs running joyous circles in the park. Drinking coffee with cream. Eating matzo brei. Happy to be here.

———

FOR THE NEXT COUPLE OF WEEKS I DID THE DUE DILIGENCE I SHOULD HAVE DONE when the magazine first closed. Michael was out of town doing research for a book, so I scheduled lunches with editors, met with colleagues, put out feelers for teaching jobs. In between I wandered the streets, drinking in the color, trying to appreciate the noisy chaos of New York. Then I'd return to the apartment and make myself the one dish that's even more comforting than carbonara.

MATZO BREI

Matzo brei is basically Jewish French toast, with the matzo standing in for the traditional leavened bread. The difference is that you use water in place of milk as the soaking liquid—and you smash the matzo into pieces and scramble like crazy.

Begin by breaking a matzo into a strainer set over a bowl to catch the crumbs. Remove the strainer from the bowl and run it under the tap, soaking the broken crackers. Drain them well, turn them into the bowl, and beat in an egg.

Melt as much butter as you can bring yourself to use in a skillet, wait for the foam to subside, toss in the eggy matzos, and scramble for a few minutes until some of the bits are crisp little nubbins and others are as soft as clouds. Salt to taste. This dish has a simple goodness that always makes me feel better.

Bitter cold. Walkers greet like lost voyagers in the tundra. Warm rye bread hidden beneath my coat. Thick white bean soup. Restored.

HUNGRY FOR FOOD SHOPS, I SPENT MY TIME BETWEEN APPOINTMENTS DRIFTING IN and out of bakeries, produce markets, cheese shops, and fish stores, slowly gathering food. I was feeling fragile those first few weeks in the city, and for the most part I relied on comfort cooking.

This is one of the most consoling dishes I know, a sturdy soup I first tasted in a tiny Tuscan hill town. When we rented a stone cottage heated only by wood, our kind landlady greeted us with a pot of soup simmering on the stove. All night we could hear it humming softly to itself. In the morning, we could see our breath in the room, and I braved the cold to bring big bowls of the fragrant soup back to bed. It was Christmas Day, and just as we began to eat, the bells in the villages up and down the mountains began to ring.

TUSCAN BEAN SOUP

SHOPPING LIST
1 pound dry white
    cannellini or navy
    beans
1 nice meaty ham
    bone
2 stalks celery
1 carrot

STAPLES
2 onions (halved)
bay leaf
parsley (optional)
salt
peppercorns
Parmesan cheese
olive oil

Serves 4

Pick over the beans, wash them well, cover them with a lot of water, and let them sit overnight.

In the morning, drain the beans and add about three times as much water as you have beans. Add the onions, the ham bone, the celery, the carrot, and perhaps a bay leaf and some parsley. Throw in a small handful of salt and a few peppercorns. Bring to a simmer, partially cover, and cook until the beans are completely soft. How long this takes will depend on the age of your beans; it could be anywhere from 1 hour to 3. Don't be stingy with the heat; you definitely don't want crunchy beans.

Remove the vegetables and the ham bone. Puree about half of the beans and stir them back into the pot so you end up with a chunky puree. Taste for seasoning. If you're so inclined, strip the meat from the bones, chop it up, and stir it back into the soup.

I like to serve this soup with a sprinkling of grated Parmesan and a drizzle of olive oil.

Cold sake-steamed chicken, straight from the refrigerator. Pearly flesh smooth as satin. Cats twine hopefully around my ankles. Think not.

A FAMOUSLY HARD-DRIVING MAGAZINE EDITOR TOOK ME TO LUNCH, PUSHING HER food around the plate as she offered me a job. She'd obviously allotted an hour and a half for the meeting, and 80 minutes into the meal she put her fork down and called for the check. Exactly 90 minutes after entering the room she was making her exit. I said I'd think about the job—and stayed to finish my lunch.

I walked slowly home. The job would pay well. And I would be miserable. This woman was famous for last-minute changes, making her staff work all night when she pulled an issue apart. She ran a notoriously unhappy office. Should I take the job? I knew instinctively that I needed to go into the kitchen to consider her proposition.

I wanted to lose myself in a recipe, to make something that demanded my total attention. I stopped at the butcher's and peered into his glass case, thinking that the simplest dishes require the most intense concentration.

Chicken, I thought, *that's what I'll cook:* there is such a fine line between good enough and great. I left the shop with an excellent bird tucked beneath my arm.

At home I made myself a cup of ginger tea and sat down, inhaling the fragrant steam. Then I went into the kitchen, unwrapped the chicken, and rinsed it really well. I dried it, and then dried it again, inside and out, feeling the way the bones moved beneath the plump pearly flesh. I rubbed it with salt and set it on a plate, breast side up. I put the plate on a rack and put that inside a large casserole with a tightly fitting cover.

I mixed ½ cup of sake with 1½ cups of water, poured in enough of the mixture to reach the bottom of the plate, and brought the liquid to a boil, watching it the entire time. Just as the first bubble rose to the surface, I covered the pot, turned the heat down, and left the chicken to steam gently.

I made another cup of tea and sat quietly for 45 minutes. Then I began checking for doneness, making a cut in the breast, looking for clear-running juices. (Unless you're using a very large chicken, it should be done in under an hour.)

I turned off the flame and allowed the bird to relax in the covered pot for half an hour. This is not a dish that wants to be hurried: yank it right out of the steamer and the flesh will seize and toughen.

Meanwhile, I began washing rice beneath running water, swishing my hands through it, enjoying the way the water gradually became clear. I put that on to cook so that the rice would be ready at the same time as the chicken.

The aromas in the kitchen were clean, pure. I thought of spare Japanese temples, the clear sound of bells. I removed the bird from the steamer and reduced the liquid to create a simple sauce. (You could also serve it with ponzu or soy sauce, but in this case, less is more.)

I'd been concentrating completely, which rewarded me twice. The chicken was the smoothest, most tender bird I'd ever cooked. And the slow quiet time in the kitchen had calmed me so completely that I sat down to dinner as refreshed as if I'd been visiting a spa.

I knew, with absolute certainty, that I would turn the job down.

The Bowery, frantic with hip activity.
The pulsing frenzy of Chinatown shops.
Cheese in Little Italy. Walking NY
is a constant pleasure.

THAT DECISION OFFERED ME RELEASE, AND I BEGAN WRITING EASILY IN THE MORN-
ings. The afternoons I spent exploring the city. One day I got off the subway in
Chinatown and made my way into one of the mysterious medicinal shops, gazing at dried seahorses, deer horns, and great whorls of ginseng. Next door, in the
fish shop, live shrimp were doing comical somersaults in their tank.

The fishmonger pointed. "Very good," he said encouragingly. I nodded and
asked for a pound, watching him scoop them from the water with a net. I was
thinking about the pasta I'd learned to make in Venice that gets its intensity (and
bright orange color) from a fast stock made of shrimp heads.

I added a pound of sparkling squid, faintly lavender in the late afternoon light,
and then some gleaming mussels. Carrying my parcels, I went home and began to
cook.

The secret to this dish is simple: you finish cooking the pasta in the aromatic
seafood broth so that the pasta becomes one with the sauce. This is not spaghetti
with sauce on top; it's spaghetti with sauce inside each strand. The seafood on top
is delicate and delicious, but here it's merely a garnish. You could add some grated
Parmesan if you like, but it would be decidedly un-Italian; Italians frown upon
mixing seafood with cheese.

SPAGHETTI ALLO SCOGLIO

SHOPPING LIST

20 cherry tomatoes
1 bunch flat-leaf
  parsley
1 large carrot
1 pound mussels
1 pound squid
¾ pound medium
  shrimp
1½ cups dry white
  wine

STAPLES

garlic
1 onion
olive oil
1 pound dry spaghetti
salt
pepper
red pepper flakes

Serves 4

Start by prepping the vegetables:

Cut the cherry tomatoes in half. Chop a cup of the parsley. Mince a couple of cloves of garlic. Peel the carrot and chop it coarsely. Chop the onion. Set it all aside.

Now prep the seafood:

Scrub the mussels and set them aside. Clean the squid, carefully removing the ink sac and inner shell, and cut the body into quarter-inch rings; set aside. Remove the heads and shells from the shrimp, being careful to conserve everything, including the beautiful orange fat.

Next, make the stock:

Put the shrimp heads into a pot with the carrot, onion, a handful of the chopped parsley, and a small pour of olive oil. Cook, covered, over medium-low heat, stirring lazily every once in a while, for about 15 minutes. Toss in the shrimp shells, ¾ cup of the white wine, and 4 cups of water and simmer very gently for about an hour and a half to make an intense stock. It will turn bright orange from the fat in the shrimp heads. Strain the liquid into a bowl and set aside.

Heat a couple of tablespoons of olive oil and the garlic in a deep heavy skillet. When the garlic is fragrant, add a pound of mussels and the remaining ¾ cup white wine, cover the pan, and cook until most of the mussels have opened. This should take only about 3 to 5 minutes. Snatch the mussels out as they open, putting them in a colander set over the stock bowl. Discard any mussels that refuse to open.

Meanwhile, cook a pound of spaghetti in well-salted boiling water until the strands have barely lost their stiffness, about 5 minutes. Drain in a colander.

Put the cherry tomatoes in the skillet that held the mussels, along with a cup of the shrimp stock, and some more chopped parsley, and let it simmer for a few minutes until the tomatoes get soft. Stir in the not-quite-cooked spaghetti and simmer until the pasta has absorbed all the liquid (about 3 minutes), adding more stock as needed to make the pasta almost al dente. Add the squid and shrimp and cover, cooking for a couple of minutes or just until the shrimp turn rosy and the squid loses its translucence. Stir in the mussels and a bit more parsley, add salt, pepper, and red pepper flakes to taste, and serve immediately.

Shopping at Fairway on Friday: as
exhilarating as a bumper car ride.
We careen around the olives, crash
into the coffee. Messy, crazy, fun.

STANDING IN LINE WAITING TO PAY, A WOMAN LOOKED INTO MY CART AND PICKED up one of my thin Asian eggplants. She studied it critically. "What are you going to do with those?" she asked.

I didn't really know; I'd bought them because they were there, and because they were so beautiful. But I made up a recipe on the spot.

"I'm going to make an Asian eggplant salad," I said boldly. "I'm going to char them and marinate the flesh in a mixture of fish sauce, lime, chiles, and garlic."

I love charring the skin off eggplants, love watching the skin blister and blacken as I turn them over the gas jet. I like the feel of the flesh when it collapses in on itself, and the way the skin lifts off, revealing the gray pulp underneath. But what I love most about cooking with eggplant is their complete docility: no other vegetable is so content to abandon itself to your will.

ASIAN EGGPLANT SALAD

SHOPPING LIST

1½ pounds long,
  thin Asian or baby
  eggplants
3 tablespoons fish
  sauce
1 lime
cilantro
mint leaves

STAPLES

2 tablespoons brown
  sugar
1 clove garlic (minced)
1 teaspoon chile flakes

*Serves 6 as an
appetizer*

Prick the eggplants all over with a fork and singe them over the burner of a gas stove, turning constantly, for about 10 minutes until the skin is black and blistered. Allow to cool.

Carefully peel the skin away from the eggplant (this can be fussy, and you want to get all the skin off). Pull the eggplant into strips and lay them in a shallow bowl.

Mix the fish sauce with the juice of the lime, the sugar, and couple of tablespoons of water. Add the minced garlic and chile flakes. Pour over the eggplant and marinate in the refrigerator for a few hours. When ready to serve, garnish with a few leaves of chopped cilantro or mint.

This makes a fine appetizer, or a perfect little side salad when you're serving Asian food. Sometimes, at lunch, I'll just eat the eggplant over rice.

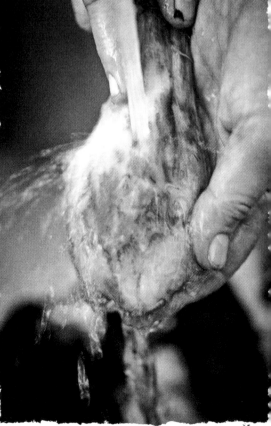

Chelsea afternoon. The High Line,
almost sunset. Man chants poetry.
Scent of coffee in the air. Butcher shop:
lovely roasts displayed like jewels.

IN THE CITY, SURROUNDED BY CEMENT, IT'S EASY TO BE OBLIVIOUS TO THE SMALL changes taking place around you: trees beginning to bud, early flowers peeking out of the ground. An artisanal butcher shop brings it all back, connecting you to the seasons.

"The young lambs have arrived," the butcher said when I walked in. "They've just culled the herd."

"Spring" lamb has become a year-round marketing term for conventional meat; factory animals can be harvested in any month. But when animals are allowed to live with nature, spring is the lambing season, the time of rebirth. When you buy humanely raised meat, lamb really is the first sign of spring. And there is nothing quite like it.

Pastured lamb has a sweetness that factory lamb lacks. I think it tastes best rare, but this is the meat that takes the worry out of roasting: it's delicious at any temperature. The only way to ruin young lamb is to serve it with that sticky sweet mint sauce that comes in a jar. Fresh mint sauce is another thing altogether; it's the perfect counterpoint to lamb, and a fine way to say farewell to winter.

ROAST LEG OF LAMB
WITH FRESH MINT SAUCE

SHOPPING LIST

1 small leg of lamb
  (6 to 7 pounds,
  trimmed of all
  visible fat)
1 bunch rosemary
1 bunch mint

STAPLES

4 cloves garlic
2 tablespoons olive
  oil
salt
pepper
2 tablespoons sugar
½ cup cider vinegar

Serves 6 to 8

Preheat the oven to 350 degrees.

Cut 2 cloves of garlic into slivers, make 8 small slits in the lamb on each side, and wiggle a sliver of garlic and a sprig of rosemary into each slit. Massage the lamb all over with olive oil, shower it with salt and pepper, and let it sit out of the refrigerator for a few hours to come to room temperature.

Place the lamb on a rack on top of what's left of the bunch of rosemary. Toss a couple of whole cloves of garlic into the bottom of the roasting pan.

Roast, uncovered, for 1¼ to 1½ hours, or until an instant-read thermometer inserted away from the bone registers 125 degrees.

Remove from the oven and allow to rest for 20 minutes before carving.

Make the mint sauce as soon as the lamb goes into the oven. Wash a bunch of fresh mint. Pull the leaves off the stems and pack them into a 1-cup measure. Chop them coarsely, enjoying the lovely scent. Toss them with the sugar and pour a half cup of boiling water over them. Mix in the cider vinegar and let the sauce stand, allowing the flavors to develop.

Very old lady begging in the subway.
Gave her money, muffins, coffee. Tears.
Home to play with puntarelle.
Contradictions of the city.

I climbed onto the subway, clutching the precious head of puntarelle I'd just found at a downtown market, so engrossed in considering how I might prepare it that I almost bumped into the old woman begging on the steps, crutches clamped beneath her arms.

It was her age, I think, that stopped me, more than her gender. How would it feel to be old and so alone you have to stand in the subway begging for food? I gave her the contents of my wallet, then went back upstairs to buy her a cup of coffee and a blueberry muffin.

"God bless you," she said, taking them from me. To my intense relief, the train came thundering noisily into the station just then, and I was able to make an apologetic gesture, turn, and run for it.

But the image of that woman stayed with me as I put the puntarelle on the counter at home. This is a strange vegetable; when you peel away the dark green strands you find a heart composed of small bulbs that resemble stubby white asparagus spears. Cut them off, cut them open, and you find that they are hollow.

Where does she sleep? I wondered. *Does she have no family?* I cut the bulbs into long thin strips and put them in ice water, still haunted by the memory of the old woman.

An hour later the strips had curled in upon themselves like pinwheels. I drained them, put them in a bowl, and set them aside while I made an anchovy sauce.

I mashed a clove of garlic in a mortar with a pestle until it had all but disappeared, added 4 anchovy filets, and smashed them into a paste. I grated in a fair amount of pepper, then slowly drizzled in a quarter cup of olive oil and a few tablespoons of powerful red wine vinegar.

I poured the sauce over the puntarelle and ate slowly, pretending that I was in Rome on a rainy spring day.

This vegetable has a reputation for being bitter, but the bulbs are not; they're delightfully crisp, juicy, and rather gentle. It's the leaves that are bitter, and with the image of the old woman in the subway still in my head, I decided that I could not waste them. I blanched them for a minute in a pot of salty boiling water, then dropped them into a bowl of ice water for another minute or so. I put a good dollop of olive oil into a pan, added the drained leaves and a couple of cloves of smashed garlic, and sautéed them for about 10 minutes, adding salt and pepper.

At the very last minute I grated some Romano cheese over the top and tossed the greens with a dusting of crisp bread crumbs. It was a perfect contrast to the crisp, cold salad.

I understood exactly why this is, to Romans, the first taste of spring. It mirrors the season: hot and cold, sweet and tart, crisp and soft. It is everything but predictable.

Winter returned the next day, bringing a short, grudging snow shower. I still couldn't get the woman out of my mind. I made some chili, packed it in a thermos, and went back to see if I could find her. But, like the weather, she had moved on.

Rain-soaked streets. Misty air. Van Morrison pours from passing car. Café au lait, lemon pudding cake, blood orange juice. Happy to be home.

IT WAS THE FIRST OF APRIL, ALMOST SIX MONTHS SINCE *GOURMET* HAD CLOSED, AND I'd turned down the one full-time job I'd been offered. I needed to find something else, and I needed to do it fast.

That night we gathered for another *Gourmet* reunion, meeting in the same cheap and cheerful Chinese restaurant where we'd gotten so drunk in the fall.

Although I was in turmoil, there was comfort in being together, and we ate like wolves, drinking so much bad wine that by the end of the evening every one of us was singing along with the silly karaoke machine. We toasted those who'd moved to exotic places—Prague, Paris, Santa Fe—saluting those who'd opted for other kinds of work. Our drinks editor was in Texas, thinking about opening a bar. Our creative director was at a handbag company, and one of the food editors was opening a pastry shop. Nobody was getting rich, but almost everyone was making do.

As we packed mountains of leftover food into little white boxes, someone asked our former travel editor if he missed all the free trips. "Checking in to a different hotel every night isn't all it's cracked up to be," Bill replied. He turned to me. "But I bet you're missing all those expensive meals; when was the last time you were without an expense account?"

It stopped me cold. I did the math. "Nineteen seventy-eight."

I love restaurants, and for thirty-two years I'd been able to eat anywhere I wanted, anytime, on someone else's money. I spooned the last of the fried rice into a box and closed the flaps. "I've been so happy in the kitchen," I said, the words coming slowly, "that I haven't even thought about fancy restaurants."

"Really?" Bill stared at me. "Then maybe you should be writing a cookbook instead of looking for another job."

We walked to the subway to-gether, handing off the leftovers to the first panhandler who approached. "When we were at *Gourmet* you never stopped talking about want-ing to coax people back into the kitchen," he said as we rode uptown. "Maybe a cookbook is how you're meant to do it now?"

We said goodbye and I climbed the subway stairs in a kind of daze, his words echoing in my ears. It had started to rain, a pleasant drizzle that made the sidewalks sparkle. I passed

Fairway, still bustling at midnight, the store's bright lights and friendly clatter an open invitation. I went in; perhaps I'd bake when I got home.

I stood among the produce, dreaming of pies. But in this in-between season, nothing tempted me, and in the end it was the lemons I lingered over. Lemon pudding cake would make a perfect late-night project.

This recipe can't decide what it wants to be. You toss a bunch of ingredients into a pan and they separate themselves into opposing parts while they're in the oven. What emerges is a layered dessert that's part cake, part soufflé, part pudding. A perfect snack, in fact, for someone in an extreme state of indecision.

LEMON PUDDING CAKE

STAPLES

2 large lemons
3 large eggs
1⅓ cups milk
¾ cup sugar
salt
¼ cup flour

To begin, preheat the oven to 350 degrees and grate the zest from the lemons until you have a heap of yellow fluff. When you're done, squeeze the juice. You should have something close to a half cup.

Carefully separate the eggs. The whites should go into a very clean bowl, the yolks in with the lemon juice and zest. Whisk the milk into the lemon mixture, and slowly add a half cup of sugar, a dash of salt, and at the end a mere quarter cup of flour. If you've used good spring eggs, the mixture will positively glow with color.

Using clean beaters, beat the whites until they hold soft peaks. Beat in a quarter cup more sugar, continuing until the whites turn sleek and glossy and hold stiff peaks when you pull the beaters from the bowl. Whisk a quarter of the whites into the yolk mixture, then gently fold in the rest of the whites. Pour into a buttered 8-inch square glass pan or a deep-dish pie plate.

Boil some water in a kettle. You're going to bake the cake in a water bath, so you'll need a second baking dish, large enough to leave a couple of inches all around the first. Set the large empty pan in the oven, put the pan holding the cake in the center, and carefully pour boiling water all around it, about halfway up, being careful not to splash any water into the cake itself.

Bake for about 45 minutes, until the cake is puffed and golden, but still pudding on the bottom. Remove from the water bath and cool on a rack. This is best served while still a bit warm; by day two, lemon pudding cake loses much of its luster.

Good night. Hot kimchi, slicked with chiles. Smoky, sweet grilled beef in crisp lettuce. Sake. Slow stroll home down electric streets.

———————

NICK CAME HOME FOR THE WEEKEND AND WE WANDERED CHINATOWN AND LITTLE Italy together, noses pressed against the windows, trying to decide what kind of food to eat. We kept walking, talking, putting off dinner until we reached Koreatown, where the air is always pungent with garlic. Suddenly we were famished, and we turned in to a little restaurant where they brought us huge platters of meat to grill ourselves.

On a chilly night, nothing is more satisfying than bulgogi. We seared the sweet, salty, garlic-drenched beef, sparked it with spicy kimchi, smoothed it with spoonfuls of rice, and wrapped it in cool leaves of lettuce. It wasn't fancy or expensive, but that meal was delicious fun; there was no place else on earth I would rather have been. "You know," Nick pointed out as we walked out the door, "you could easily do this at home."

BULGOGI AT HOME

Mix the soy sauce with the sesame oil, sugar, and a few good grinds of black pepper. Mince the garlic and ginger and throw them in, too. Mince the scallions and add them to the mix.

Take a pound of beef of some sort—you could use just about anything, but skirt or hanger steak is traditional—and slice it across the grain as thinly as you possibly can. (This will be easier if you put it in the freezer for a half hour or so ahead of time.) Plunk it into the marinade and leave it to soak up the flavors for at least 15 minutes (an hour is better).

Meanwhile, separate the leaves of the lettuce, put a pot of rice on to cook, and rummage through your cupboards to see what would go well with this sweet, salty meat. You're going to wrap the beef and rice into little lettuce packets, and many accompaniments suggest themselves: kimchi is a good start; Sriracha is imperative in my mind; sliced cloves of raw garlic would be nice, as would some sliced chiles, onions, or toasted sesame seeds.

Heat a wok or frying pan, slick it with a bit of oil until it begins to shimmer, and quickly sear the drained meat on both sides. It should take 3 or 4 minutes. Pile it onto a platter. On another platter arrange leaves of lettuce, heaps of kimchi, sliced onions or scallions, chiles, and shards of raw garlic. Put out a fragrant heap of warm rice and a bottle of Sriracha.

Now everyone gets to help themselves, wrapping the beef into lettuce bundles with whatever ingredients suit their fancy. What makes this dish so appealing is the way each bite tastes slightly different from the last. It's wonderful fun when you've gathered a small group but equally satisfying when cut down to an indulgent and solitary supper.

Early morning Manhattan, a private world. Sun rises. Sidewalks sparkle, clean. Semis prowl like dinosaurs. Coffee in the air. People smile.

I'D GONE OUT FOR A FRESH LOAF OF BREAD, INTENDING NOTHING MORE IMPRESSIVE than toast. But it was a beautiful day, and the good feelings on the street were so infectious that I came home eager to cook.

French toast, I thought, wondering how I might make it my own. I opened the refrigerator, saw the maple syrup, and decided to incorporate its sneaky sweetness right into the bread. What I love best about cooking is the adventure of combining ingredients, hoping they'll play well together, combine into delicious new flavors.

Ever since that night in Chinatown, I'd been seriously considering a cookbook. For the past six months, cooking had been my lifeline, and I was grateful for everything I had learned in the kitchen. Most cookbooks, I thought as I reached for an orange and began to squeeze it for juice, are in search of perfection, an attempt to constantly re-create the same good dishes. But you're not a chef in your own kitchen, trying to please paying guests. You're a traveler, following your own path, seeking adventure. I wanted to write about the fun of cooking, encourage people to take risks. Alone in the kitchen you are simply a cook, free to do anything you want. If it doesn't work out—well, there's always another meal.

I threw the juice into a bowl and then, as an afterthought, grated in the rind as well. Why not? A splash of rum, I thought, unconsciously thinking out the recipe in Twitter form. Golden toast crisped in butter. Thick. Soft. Hint of orange. Touch of maple. Egg rich. Cinnamon dusted. So good.

As I turned on the gas, the kitchen began to fill with exuberant scents: browning butter, dark maple, the rich sweetness of rum. Hovering about it all was the joyous scent of citrus. The toast slices puffed up, fat and sassy, and I put them into the oven to finish cooking. *If the recipe works,* I thought, *I'll put it in the cookbook.*

FRENCH TOAST

SHOPPING LIST
1 loaf brioche (or challah) bread
1 orange
maple syrup
bourbon or rum
confectioner's sugar

STAPLES
6 eggs
cream or milk
nutmeg
cinnamon
butter

Serves 4

Remove the ends from a solid loaf of brioche bread (you could also use challah) and slice the loaf into 8 fairly thick slabs, about an inch each.

Whisk the eggs with a quarter cup of fresh orange juice, 4 tablespoons of maple syrup, a couple of tablespoons of cream or milk, and a bit of grated nutmeg and cinnamon. Grate in the rind of the orange. Toss in a hefty dollop of bourbon or rum as well.

Melt a tablespoon or so of butter in a large, heavy pan over medium heat.

Preheat the oven to 425 degrees.

Beat the egg mixture well, then dunk one of the slices of bread into the egg mixture, pressing on it so it absorbs the liquid. Turn it over and dunk it again. Squeeze it gently, so it doesn't drip, and put it into the hot pan. Repeat with 3 more slices of bread. Cook for a couple of minutes, until the bottoms are golden; turn and cook the other sides for half a minute or so. Put these slices on a baking pan and repeat with the remaining 4 slices of bread, wiping the pan, if necessary, between batches.

Put the baking pan with the French toast into the oven for about 8 minutes. Sprinkle with a bit of confectioner's sugar, just because it looks so pretty, and serve with more maple syrup.

On the river, tiny sailboat drifting by.
Spry old man doing pushups. Geese
nibble grass; I savor eggplant and
arugula sandwich, bite by bite.

SPRING HAD ARRIVED, AND THE WHOLE CITY SEEMED HAPPIER. OR MAYBE IT WAS just me? I was thinking about recipes all the time now, and as I walked across the park, noticing the tiny green buds on the trees, I remembered the eggplant and arugula sandwiches I used to buy at an overpriced (and long gone) restaurant. I'd always been impressed by how much flavor they'd managed to elicit from a few simple ingredients.

On an impulse I went home and attempted to replicate the sandwiches, packed one up, and went for a walk along the river. A flock of geese flying north swooped down for a little snack, and I sat on a bench to watch them. Just as I bit into my sandwich they wheeled upward, filling the sky above me.

EGGPLANT AND ARUGULA SANDWICHES

SHOPPING LIST

4 Japanese or baby
  eggplants
2 ficelles
1 bunch arugula

STAPLES

3 tablespoons bal-
  samic vinegar
3 tablespoons olive oil
salt
pepper
unsalted butter

Makes 2 sandwiches

Preheat the oven to 425 degrees.

Slice eggplants lengthwise into strips and lay the strips side by side on an oiled baking sheet.

Mix equal parts of balsamic vinegar and olive oil in a shallow dish. Brush the oil mixture across the top of each slice of eggplant. Sprinkle them very lightly with sea salt, grind some pepper over the top, and put them in the hot oven for about 10 minutes. Turn them over, brush them with the vinegar and oil mixture, and roast the other sides for another 8 minutes or so. Cool.

Cut the ficelles in half and spread them generously with unsalted butter. (If you can't find ficelles, use baguettes, but cut each lengthwise into two skinnier loaves; the proportion of bread to filling is important in this sandwich.)

Lay the eggplant slices on the bread and top with arugula leaves. The charm of this sandwich is the simplicity of the way the flavors marry; the peppery arugula underlines the slight bitterness of the eggplant, and the sweetness of the balsamic vinegar sets it off. Eggplant is usually the chameleon of the vegetable kingdom, so accommodating that it often disappears. Here it finally has a chance to star.

Man at next table alone, anxious. Dials. Fidgets. Sweats. Swivels. An hour. Pretty woman sidles in. Apologetic smile. Wine. Salmon. Big kiss.

———

A FRIEND IN FROM OUT OF TOWN INVITED US OUT TO EAT. "PICK A PLACE," HE SAID. "Anyplace. I'm on an expense account." I should have been excited by the prospect of a fancy restaurant, but what I'd told Bill was true: I would rather have stayed home. Spring was coming, and the shops were filling with young English peas, with shad roe, with rhubarb, and the kitchen called. Yet as we walked into the restaurant I found myself inhaling deeply, thinking that few scents are as heady as this mingled aroma of food, flowers, and money. The maître d' bowed us to a table, and I settled into the banquette and surveyed the room.

"Poor guy." Michael was looking at the man in the next booth, dapper in his Zegna suit. He was nervously checking his watch every few minutes, clearly worried that he'd been stood up. When the date finally arrived, the man looked so elated I think he would have happily dined on cardboard. But he ordered salmon, pushing the food into his mouth with relieved abandon. Looking over, I saw that the fish was farmed and overcooked, and I felt sorry for him. Wild salmon is so much better, and not just for the diner.

That sad salmon made me remember the best salmon I've ever tasted, a gorgeous Copper River salmon I'd cooked in Seattle. It was a wild, majestic creature wrapped in gleaming silver scales, and I'd wanted to do right by it. Greg Atkinson, formerly the chef at Canlis, showed me two little tricks that are worth passing on.

SALMON WITH RHUBARB GLAZE

SHOPPING LIST
1 pound rhubarb
6 wild salmon filets
  (about 6 ounces
  each)

STAPLES
sugar
salt
pepper
olive oil

Serves 6

Cut the rhubarb into half-inch pieces and cook over high heat with ⅓ cup sugar and a couple of tablespoons of water, stirring, until the rhubarb starts to fall apart (about 5 minutes). Strain it and set the rhubarb aside while you cook the fish.

Greg sprinkles his salmon with a little bit of sugar mixed into the traditional salt and pepper; the result is a slightly caramelized crust. Mix ¾ teaspoons each of salt, pepper, and sugar. Pat the filets with paper towels to dry them, then dust both sides with the mixture. Oil a large cast iron or nonstick skillet and heat it until it's very hot. Put the salmon in, skin side up, and cook for about 4 minutes, then turn the filets over and cook 3 minutes more. Brush with the glaze and serve.

Slicing rhubarb, ruby fruit falling
from the knife, fresh green scent
rushing upward. Outside a purple
finch flies past the window.

RHUBARB IN THE STORE IS LIKE ROBINS ON THE LAWN; THE FIRST TIME I SEE IT I begin wondering what's happening upstate. I may be a relentlessly urban person, but springtime in the country is such a hopeful time. I wanted to go upstate and watch the world waking up from winter.

The last of the snow was still melting in the woods, but the house was sitting in sunshine. Seriously into the cookbook now, I went to the market and gathered stalks of rhubarb until they were spilling from my arms. I carried them into the kitchen, and just as I made the first cut, a small reddish bird flitted past the window; I felt as if nature was smiling in at me.

I cooked the rhubarb into a tangy sauce and stirred it into thick yogurt, staring out the window, hoping the purple finch would reappear. Maybe tomorrow. Meanwhile, I sliced more rhubarb and put it in the freezer. Come winter, when the wind was howling around the house, it would be a fine reminder of this lovely spring day.

Rhubarb is as forgiving as it is beautiful. It takes very little work to turn it into something wonderful: cut it up, toss it with a bit of sugar, and cook it on top of the stove or in the oven. That's it. The only thing to watch for is the green leaves, which are mildly poisonous. They won't kill you, but they'll give you a miserable couple of hours.

RHUBARB SUNDAES

SHOPPING LIST
2 pounds rhubarb
1 orange
1 vanilla bean
  (optional)
vanilla ice cream or
  yogurt

STAPLES
¼ cup sugar
1 knob fresh ginger
  (optional)

Buy the reddest stalks of rhubarb you can find. Slice them into casual pieces—a half inch or so—and put them in a pot with the zest and juice of an orange and the sugar. If you like, grate in a bit of ginger, or scrape in the seeds of a vanilla bean. Cook over medium heat until the fruit relaxes and slumps into a sauce; it shouldn't take more than 10 or 15 minutes. Cool it down and stir the rhubarb into thick yogurt, or leave it warm and dollop it onto cold vanilla ice cream.

*Too beautiful. Spring breeze whispers
outside, outside. Grilled chicken,
cucumber salad, radishes on the lawn.
Sunshine. Lemonade. So rare.*

INCREDIBLE WEATHER! NINETY DEGREES IN THE FIRST WEEK OF APRIL. PEOPLE MUT-
tered about global warming, but after the ferocity of winter, this early summer
seemed like an incredible blessing, an omen, a sign that the bad times really were
over. I brined the chicken with a light heart and went outside to light the grill.

GRILLED CHICKEN

SHOPPING LIST
½ cup kosher salt
6 pounds chicken
  parts

STAPLES
¼ cup sugar
⅓ cup olive oil
1 lemon
garlic
balsamic vinegar
salt
pepper
chile pepper flakes
  (optional)

Serves 6

It's funny; people spend days agonizing over the Thanksgiving turkey they eat once a year, but they spend almost no time
thinking about how to grill chicken—something that most of
us do with great regularity. But what's good for the big bird is
also good for the small one: if you're going to subject the poul-
try to heat this intense, it helps to brine it beforehand.

The brine: Dissolve the sugar and the kosher salt in 4 quarts
of really hot water in a large bowl. Bring it to room temperature,
add the chicken parts, and refrigerate for 4 to 8 hours.

Pat the chicken dry and allow it to come to room temperature before grilling.

Grill the chicken over moderately high heat until cooked
through; it should take about 10 to 15 minutes. As soon as the
chicken comes off the grill, plunk it into a vinaigrette, which
will give you moist, delicious meat.

You can use any sort of vinaigrette, but a fairly basic one would be a mix of ⅓ cup olive oil with ¼ cup of lemon juice, a smashed clove of garlic, a dash of balsamic vinegar, salt, pepper, and perhaps a sprinkling of chile pepper flakes.

Eaten with the fingers (and plenty of napkins), this messy, smoky chicken tastes wonderful anytime. But it never tastes quite as good to me as it does on the first hot day of the year.

Red breakfast for a sunny morning: sparkling salmon roe on sour-cream-slathered buckwheat blini, ice-cold Kishu triangles, blood orange juice.

EASTER WAS EARLY, AND FRIENDS WERE COMING FOR THE HOLIDAY WEEKEND. WE aired out the house, made the beds, built a fire in the grate. Wanting to greet them with something special, I went off in search of inspiration. In the market the salmon roe sparkled up at me, and I thought of blini. In the next aisle I found blood oranges; their deep magenta hue would be the perfect accompaniment.

I love making blini, love the warm, yeasty aroma in the kitchen and the earthy taste of buckwheat. But authentic Russian recipes involve a complicated rigmarole of separating eggs, whisking in sour cream, and then allowing the batter to rise twice, if not three times. My simplified version offers the joy of blini with a lot less work.

BUCKWHEAT BLINI

SHOPPING LIST
¼ cup buckwheat
  flour
1 teaspoon yeast
salmon or trout roe

STAPLES
½ cup flour
1 tablespoon sugar
½ teaspoon salt
4 tablespoons
  (½ stick) butter
1 cup milk
2 eggs
sour cream

Mix the flour and the buckwheat flour. Add the sugar, salt, and yeast.

Put the butter and milk into a small pot and cook until the butter has melted. Cool it to the point that when you stick your finger in it is warm, but not hot, then whisk the milk mixture into the flour mixture. Cover with a plate or plastic wrap, and set it in a warm place to rise. When it is about doubled (about an hour and a half), whisk in the eggs.

You can use it now, or store it in the refrigerator for a day or so; it's better on the second day, but be sure to give it a good stir before you heat your griddle.

Russians like their blini large; they say you should slather them so abundantly with butter that it runs down your arms as you eat. But I also like them small. Cook them on a butter-brushed pan about a minute on each side, and keep them cozy in a 200-degree oven until the batter is entirely used up.

Serve them warm, topped with lots of sour cream and generous dollops of salmon or trout roe.

Grass green. Sun shining. Radiant Easter morning. Pink deviled eggs. Saffron yolks. Set on a turquoise plate.

IT WAS THE YOLKS. AS THE DAYS GOT WARMER, MY NEIGHBORS' HENS BECAME MORE generous with their eggs. Each time I cracked one open, that bright orange flash of color made me smile.

When I saw the Easter egg dye in the supermarket it gave me an idea. Would it be possible to dye the egg whites instead of the shells? What to use? When I passed the canned beets I thought how beautifully their fuchsia hue would frame those marigold yolks. I'd hard-boil some eggs and give it a try.

But first, a small digression on hard-boiling eggs. Fresh eggs are impossible to peel, so begin by allowing your eggs to age in the refrigerator for a week or so. When you're ready to cook them, take them out of the refrigerator an hour ahead of time; cold eggs have a tendency to crack in hot water. Put them into a pot large enough to hold them in a single layer (so they heat evenly), and cover them with cold water. Crank up the heat so the pot comes quickly to a boil, cover the pot, turn off the heat, and leave it alone for exactly 12 minutes. Now rush the eggs into a large bowl of ice water; this will keep that unattractive green ring from forming around the yolk.

PINK DEVILED EGGS

SHOPPING LIST
1 jar pickled beets
Sriracha sauce
sweet pickles

STAPLES
1 dozen eggs
mayonnaise
mustard
salt and pepper

Makes 1 dozen

Once your eggs are boiled and peeled, put them into a bowl with the juice from a can of pickled beets; add a bit of water if the eggs aren't completely covered.

Before long the eggs will begin to turn a vibrant shade of pink. Leave them in the refrigerator overnight, and the whites will be the most beautiful color, a dazzling contrast to the marigold color of the yolks. (Leave them in the beet juice for more than 18 hours, however, and the yolks will turn pink as well.)

Deviled, the eggs become even more impressive. I mashed the yolks with some mayonnaise, a bit of mustard, and salt and

pepper and added a splash of Sriracha. Then I piled the deviled yolks back into the pink eggs. At the end, just for color, I topped each one with a little triangle of sweet pickle. They were gorgeous—and delicious. But it was that bright blue plate that sent them over the top.

Sturdy spears of asparagus march through the market, soldiers of spring. They round me up, call my name. Yes, please.

———

ON THIS MID-APRIL MORNING THE TABLES AT THE FARMERS' MARKET WERE HEAPED with fat, bold spears of asparagus, more purple than green. I snapped off an end and took a bite; it was stunningly sweet, more akin to corn than the grassy supermarket stalks. I had to buy them.

Asparagus has become as ubiquitous as tomatoes, strawberries, and watermelon; skinny stalks, flown from all corners of the earth, are now a supermarket perennial. But, like those out-of-season fruits, they're attractive to the eye yet disappointing to the mouth. They need all the help you can give them.

In-season asparagus, however, needs nothing more than a bit of heat. I cut off

the very bottoms, laid the spears into a large skillet, added some water, brought it to a boil, and cooked the asparagus until softened just a little. For my very fat spears it took about 8 minutes, but the timing depends on their girth and your taste; some people like asparagus more al dente than I do. Then I piled the spears onto a platter, plopped a pat of butter on top, and let it gently melt. Finished with a tiny splash of good balsamic vinegar, they made lovely finger food.

Sawdust on the floor. Clean mineral tang.
Calico purrs. Neighbors swap recipes.
Serious men cut serious meat.
Easter at the local butcher's.

I STOPPED IN AT THE BUTCHER'S, LOOKING FOR SOMETHING TO MAKE A SPECIAL meal. The paperback version of my memoir *For You, Mom. Finally.* was about to come out, and I was leaving on book tour. Again. It would be three weeks until I was back in my kitchen.

"I just got a pig from your favorite farmer." Jeremy came struggling out of the cooler with a quarter of an animal slung over his shoulder. "I could cut you off a few ribs for a roast."

I looked at that lovely meat, thinking it had so much beautiful white fat that it would not need brining. On the other hand, a good brine makes even a juicy piece of pork even more delicious. I'd brine it, roast it with some crisp potatoes and a pile of asparagus. It would make a memorable dinner, one my family would remember when I was on the road.

PORK ROAST

SHOPPING LIST

⅓ cup kosher salt
fresh rosemary
5-rib pork roast
  (about 4 pounds)

STAPLES

3 tablespoons sugar
3 cloves garlic
  (minced)
black peppercorns

Serves 6

Combine 2 quarts of very hot water with the kosher salt, sugar, garlic, and a couple of stalks of rosemary. Throw in a handful of black peppercorns and stir until the salt and sugar have dissolved.

Put the bowl of brine in the refrigerator, and when it's cooled down, add the pork roast, cover, and refrigerate for 2 days.

About 4 hours before you want to eat, take the meat out of the brine and drain it. (Discard the liquid.) Let the meat rest at room temperature for at least an hour. Then pat it dry and brown it on all sides in a heavy cast iron skillet. Place the roast on a rack, fat side up.

Cook in a 350-degree oven until a meat thermometer reads 140 (about an hour and a quarter). Remove the roast, tent it with foil, and allow it to stand for 30 minutes before carving.

CRISP AND EASY POTATOES

SHOPPING LIST

3 pounds Yukon Gold
  potatoes
fresh rosemary or
  thyme (optional)

STAPLES

salt
olive oil
pepper
garlic (optional)

Serves 6 to 8

Generously salt a lot of water and bring it to a boil.

Peel the Yukon Golds (or any nice heirloom potato) and cut them into cubes (about an inch on each side). Boil them in very salty water until they are just starting to go soft, about 12 minutes. Drain them well and turn them into a large bowl.

While the potatoes are still hot, toss in generous lashings of olive oil, turn them about, taste them, and season with as much salt and pepper as you like. You could, if you want, stir in some smashed garlic, crushed rosemary, or chopped thyme at this point. But I often like to leave them unadorned, so that the dominant experience is texture. The crisp exterior acts like a frame for the fluffy, soft, yielding interior.

Put them on a baking sheet and cook them in a hot (400-degree) oven for about 40 minutes, stirring once halfway through, until the edges get crisp. You can turn the oven down at this point and keep them in a 250-degree oven for another half hour or so.

Book tour: Portland. Garnet-hued
carpaccio. Diced apricot, arugula,
scattered Parmesan. Sprightly,
surprising, deeply delicious. Le Pigeon.

I CLIMBED OFF THE PLANE IN PORTLAND TO FIND MY ESCORT HOLDING OUT A BAG of just-picked hazelnuts. "I've just got time to take you for the best espresso in Portland before your first reading," she said. "And maybe for a little taste of this really great Thai food cart." It was the start of a memorable book tour for *For You, Mom. Finally.* The eating never stopped.

My favorite meal was at Le Pigeon, where we sat at the counter watching the chef, Gabriel Rucker. He makes bold, uncompromising food, and I liked everything he fed us. I was still thinking about the cookbook, and the dish I took the most careful notes on was a salad made of thinly sliced raw duck breast and apricots. It was elemental and elegant at the same time, and I'd never tasted anything quite like it. I planned to make my own version once I was back home.

DUCK CARPACCIO

SHOPPING LIST
1 moulard duck
  breast (about
  ½ pound)
1 apricot
1 small bunch
  arugula

STAPLES
2 tablespoons salt
2 tablespoons sugar
pepper
Parmesan cheese
balsamic vinegar

*Serves 4 to 6 as
an appetizer*

Feeling squeamish about feeding my friends raw duck, I decided to quickly cure it. The result is remarkable, firming the breast and lending duck an entirely new character.

Remove all the fat (easy) and sinew (slightly fussy work) from the duck breast. Mix the salt and sugar with a fair amount of ground pepper, rub the mixture all over the duck, wrap it in plastic, and allow it to cure in the refrigerator for 12 hours.

Rinse off the brine and dry the duck well. Slice the duck breast, against the grain, and then dice it. Chop a firm apricot and a few leaves of arugula and mix them together, along with a few thin shards of Parmesan cheese that you've crumbled with your fingers. Drizzle on a few drops of good balsamic vinegar.

Oyster morning. Raining in Portland.
Woke with the memory of lemons and the
mysterious flavor of crisply fried
kumamotos. Satisfied.

IN THE PANTHEON OF GREAT FOODS, FRIED OYSTERS ARE VERY NEAR THE TOP. WHEN I find good ones, I have a hard time stopping. And the ones I ate that night in Portland were very much like eating clouds.

FRIED OYSTERS

SHOPPING LIST
1 pint (about 16)
   oysters
1 pint buttermilk
2 cups cornmeal

STAPLES
2 cups flour
1 teaspoon salt
vegetable oil

Serves 2 to 4

You could shuck your own oysters, but unless you're really an expert, that makes the entire process a whole lot harder. I open my own oysters to eat on the half-shell, but when I'm frying oysters, I buy them preshucked.

Carefully drain the oysters and soak them in the buttermilk for about 10 minutes.

Line a baking sheet with waxed paper or a Silpat pad. Mix the cornmeal with the flour and the salt. Pick up each oyster and shake it a bit, allowing the buttermilk to drip off, before plunking it into the cornmeal mixture; toss it about so it's coated on all sides and place it on the lined baking sheet. Do the same with the next oyster, and the next . . .

In a deep pot, heat at least 2 inches of neutral vegetable oil—I would not use a strongly flavored oil like olive or

peanut—until it registers 375 degrees on a candy thermometer. (Don't be impatient; this could take a while.) Pick up an oyster, shake it to remove excess breading, and plunk it into the oil. Fry for about a minute and a half, until just golden, then remove with a slotted spoon and set on paper towels to drain. You should be able to fry 6 to 8 oysters at a time. Bring oil back to 375 degrees before adding a new batch of oysters.

Sprinkle with salt and serve with plenty of fresh lemons. Some people like tartar sauce or rémoulade with their oysters, but I think that masks the delicate flavor.

Dreamed rainstorms. Woke to sunshine in Portland and the sharp, spicy memory of the food at the khao man gai cart.

THE NEXT MORNING, KAREN TOOK ME ON A TOUR OF PORTLAND'S FAMOUS FOOD carts. We ate sweet fried egg sandwiches and tart rhubarb pie. We had manly burgers and delicate chicken sandwiched into bread between layers of lemon confit. But the dish I still dream of is the chicken rice, khao man gai, made by a young Thai woman who spiced it with such precise sharpness that it brought back the memory of my first halcyon night in Bangkok. It was one of the first dishes I tried to re-create when I was back in my kitchen again.

KHAO MAN GAI

SHOPPING LIST

4 scallions

1 bunch cilantro

1 small chicken

1–2 jalapeño chiles, sliced

½ cup fermented black beans

3 cucumbers

STAPLES

salt

1 knob fresh ginger

3 shallots (peeled and chopped)

vegetable oil

2 cups jasmine (or Thai or basmati) rice

3 cloves garlic (peeled and chopped)

½ cup brown sugar

¼ cup dark soy sauce

¼ cup thin soy sauce

⅓ cup white or cider vinegar

Serves 4

Bring a large pot of water (about 3 quarts) to a boil along with ½ teaspoon of salt and any aromatics you happen to have on hand (scallions, a piece of ginger, some stalks of cilantro). Add the whole chicken, breast side down; bring back to a boil, reduce the heat to a gentle simmer, cover, and cook for 20 minutes. Remove the pot from the heat, turn the chicken over, and allow it to stand in the water, covered, for another 45 minutes. Take the bird out of the pot and let it cool.

While the bird cools, reduce the chicken stock by bringing it back to a boil and allowing it to boil furiously for about 15 minutes. Meanwhile, sauté a good handful of chopped shallots in a bit of oil until fragrant, then rinse the rice well, add it to the pan, and cook it until the rice is dry. Add 4 cups of the chicken stock, with its fat, to the pan. (Save the remaining stock for another use.) Bring it to a boil, cover, reduce the heat to low, and cook for about 20 minutes, until the rice has absorbed the stock.

While the rice is cooking, make the sauce. There are dozens of versions of khao man gai sauce—even more if you consider that this is just the Thai version of Chinese Hainan chicken rice. Mine is slightly unconventional, because I cook it briefly, but I love the way the flavors come together.

Chop the peeled ginger in a casual fashion until you have a third of a cup. Put it in a blender with the chopped garlic and the whole jalapeño (including the seeds). Rinse the fermented black beans and add them to the mix, along with the brown sugar, dark soy sauce, and thin soy sauce. (In a pinch, you could use ordinary soy sauce.) Add the vinegar and whiz it into a coarse puree. Pour it into a small saucepan, bring it to a boil, and cook it for a mere half minute. Allow it to cool, then taste. Do you want it hotter? Add another chile pepper. Sweeter? More sugar. Or perhaps you want the notes to be slightly more sour, in which case you could add more vinegar. The sauce, incidentally, will keep for a very long time in the refrigerator. You can also freeze it.

Strip the chicken from the bones—it will be very tender and silken—and tear it into nicely manageable strips. Serve it over the rice, along with lots of sliced cucumbers, cilantro, and that wonderful sauce.

Just landed. Perfect San Francisco night. Cool breeze. Lights shimmer on the water. Scent of jasmine. So happy to be here.

LEAVING PORTLAND WOULD HAVE BEEN DIFFICULT HAD I NOT BEEN ON MY WAY TO San Francisco and a few more days of fantastic food. At the Ferry Building I indulged in gloriously messy Korean tacos, a joyful jumble of sweet meat, salty seaweed, spice, scallions, and fragrant rice. I bought a bacon-laced hot dog zinged with kimchi and topped with a crisp curl of chicharron, and ate it as I walked along the bay. One night, in the invitingly casual atmosphere of Zuni, I sat staring at the big wood-burning oven eating sweet, slippery anchovies with sharp shards of Parmesan, the flavors framed by the ancient taste of olives, the textures empha-sized by the crunch of celery. And on my last afternoon I sat on the waterfront reveling in the sheer briny simplicity of just-opened oysters naked on ice.

But what I remember best is a salad a friend made for me. She called it Fergus Henderson's beetroot salad, but it reminded me of the borscht my grandfather used to love, magically transformed into a solid. The color vibrated, a vivid magenta that seems the perfect recipe in early spring when you're yearning for something really bright.

This is my version of Henderson's recipe.

BORSCHT SALAD
(À LA FERGUS HENDERSON)

SHOPPING LIST

3 beets
1 green apple
½ small red cabbage
1 orange

STAPLES

1 small red onion
1 tablespoon balsamic
  vinegar
4 tablespoons olive oil
salt
pepper
sour cream

Serves 6

Peel the raw beets and grate them. (You might want to use rubber gloves, or your hands will be magenta for quite a while.) Peel and grate the apple and stir that into the beets.

Slice the cabbage as thinly as you can. Do the same with the red onion. Toss them with the beet/apple mixture.

Squeeze an orange and measure out 2 tablespoons of juice. Mix it with the balsamic vinegar and olive oil, then toss with the beets. Season with salt and pepper to taste. Spoon onto 6 plates and top each serving with a dollop of sour cream.

Sitting on the roof of my car.
Sunshine. Warm tacos. Spiced pork.
Ferocious salsa dripping down my arms.
The grungy joy of Yuca's. L.A.!

———————————

MY FRIENDS TEASE ME BECAUSE I'M INCAPABLE OF SPENDING SO MUCH AS AN HOUR in Los Angeles without hitting a taco stand. Other people want tacos al pastor or carne asada, or bean and cheese burritos. I want the great Yucatecan pork, cochinita pibil.

In the Yucatán they marinate huge pieces of pork in a wonderful red spice mixture, wrap it in banana leaves, and bury it in a pit to cook very slowly for many hours. It makes a wonderful dish for a crowd—and the leftovers give you great tacos for days.

This easy home version doesn't require a yard or a pit, but it does require a trip to a Latino grocery store for the achiote and frozen banana leaves. It also requires a bit of forethought; the pork needs to marinate for at least 12 hours, to soak up the flavor of all those spices.

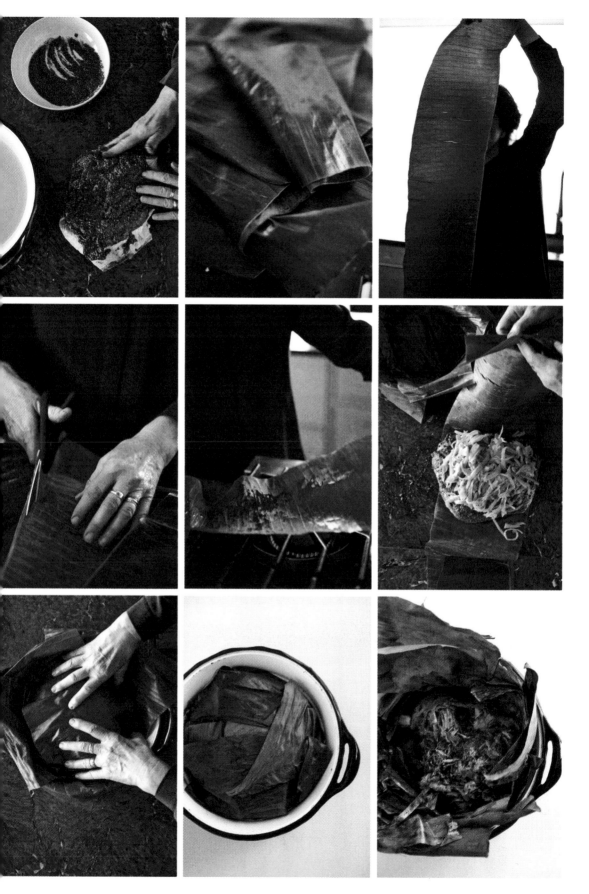

SPICE-RUBBED PORK COOKED IN BANANA LEAVES (COCHINITA PIBIL)

*Serves 8 to 10,
with some left over
for tacos*

Put the spices into a grinder with 2 teaspoons of salt; whirl to a fine powder. This may take a bit of time; achiote seeds are rather hard and dense. Add garlic cloves and vinegar. Whirl again. Add the juice of the 2 limes.

Smear the deep red paste onto the pork shoulder, cover well, and marinate overnight in the refrigerator.

The next day, remove the pork from the refrigerator and the banana leaves from the freezer. Preheat the oven to 325 degrees.

Peel the onions, cut them in half, then slice them lengthwise into matchsticks. Sauté them in a bit of olive oil until they turn translucent. Meanwhile, slice the peppers into strips (use rubber gloves for the hot ones). Add the pepper strips to the onions, sprinkle in salt and pepper to taste, and sauté them until they've all gone limp and tender, about 15 minutes. Set aside.

By now the banana leaves should be defrosted (it takes about half an hour). Remove them from the package, unfold them, and cut off the frayed edges and the thick middle spine with kitchen shears. To make them soft and pliable, quickly run each leaf across a gas burner, matte side toward the flame. I love watching the way the color change ripples across the leaves, turning them shiny in a matter of seconds.

Line a large Dutch oven with banana leaves. Then put the pork on a banana leaf, top with the onion-pepper mixture, and wrap the package well, tucking in the ends. Cover the pot.

Cook for 3 to 4 hours.

Serve with white rice, black beans, and pickled onions. The meat will fall off the bone, and I like to pass it around, still shrouded in the aromatic banana leaves (which are not edible), so that diners can tear off their own pieces of pork. There's always lots of flavorful jus in the bottom of the casserole, and I pour that off and pass it in its own little bowl as gravy for the meat and rice.

PICKLED RED ONIONS

STAPLES

2 red onions

6 tablespoons
  vinegar

¼ cup sugar

2 teaspoons salt

Slice the onions into fairly thin rings.

Put 4 cups of water into a small pot and stir in the vinegar, sugar, and salt, then bring the liquid to a boil. Add the onions, bring back to a boil, and simmer for 2 minutes. Allow the onions to sit in the liquid for an hour, then drain.

These will keep for a week or so in the refrigerator.

Tripped. Fell. Emergency room.
Mitch made farewell food: steak,
French fries, spinach. Far too much
red wine. Heading home.

It was just a little stumble in a restaurant in L.A., and I refused to admit that anything was wrong. All night I hobbled stubbornly in and out of parties; at midnight I was in a celebrity-packed pop-up restaurant in an iffy part of town.

But the next morning I was unable to stand. The friends I was staying with took me to the emergency room and brought me back in a wheelchair; I'd shattered a bone into five pieces. The book tour was over.

I would have been miserable if I'd been in a hotel. But I was with friends, and we ended up having a very merry evening. "Let's make French fries," said one friend. "They won't fix your foot, but they'll make you feel better." To my surprise, they did.

FRENCH FRIES

SHOPPING LIST

5 large russet potatoes

STAPLES

salt

1 quart vegetable oil

Serves 4

There are some things that anyone who has thoughts of French-frying a potato needs to know. In the first place, you have to use russet potatoes, which are high in solids and very low in moisture. Peel the potatoes and quickly cut them into sticks about a half inch wide. The moment they're sliced, put the potatoes into a bowl of ice water and walk away for half an hour, allowing them to shed their starch.

Remove the potatoes from the water. Dry the potatoes well. Now dry them again.

Heat a lot (if you're going to try conserving oil, don't bother frying) of neutral oil such as canola, safflower, even good old Wesson in a deep pot. Leave at least 3 inches of air at the top—the potatoes will bubble up and you don't want them leaping out of the pot. Use a candy thermometer and heat the oil to 300 degrees. Cook the potatoes, in batches small enough to allow them floating room, until they go limp and begin to be translucent. This will take from 6 to 8 minutes. Skim them out of the oil and spread them on paper towels to drain for at least 10 minutes (or up to 2 hours). This step not only cooks the potatoes, it also steams off much of the water inside them, so they will stay crisp on the second fry.

Reheat the oil until it reaches 375 degrees. Fry the potatoes, again in small batches, for another couple of minutes. When they become golden, scoop them out, drain them on paper towels, toss them with salt, and run to the table while they're still piping hot. Crisp and salty, with an earthy sweetness, they'll improve anybody's mood.

Fever dreams from the recovery room. Hot bread topped with cold sweet butter. Caviar. Clams. Eric Ripert's wicked sea urchin pasta.

AFTER THE INEVITABLE OPERATION, THE DOCTOR INSISTED THAT I STAY IN BED WITH my foot above my heart. It would be at least two months until I could cook again, and right there in the recovery room I began hallucinating food.

All the dishes I loved best came to visit, whirling around my bed as I sent out tweet after tweet about these fantasy foods. They are obviously the ravings of a person under the influence of morphine.

I consoled myself by reading recipes. But the memory of that very first fantasy—Eric Ripert's sea urchin pasta—stayed with me, and it was one of the first things that I cooked when I was finally able to stand.

SEA URCHIN PASTA

SHOPPING LIST

½ cup (1 tray) sea
   urchin roe
chives
salmon or trout
   caviar

STAPLES

8 tablespoons
   (1 stick) butter
salt
1 tablespoon finely
   grated Parmesan
   cheese
pepper
4 ounces dried angel
   hair pasta
½ lemon

Serves 4

Your sea urchin roe will preferably be from Santa Barbara (Atlantic sea urchin has an entirely different flavor). You can find it in some fish stores and most good Japanese markets, where it's sold in trays (a tray will give you the ½ cup you need).

Puree the sea urchin roe in a spice grinder or a blender. Eric puts it through a sieve; I think that's too much work.

Melt a stick of unsalted butter in a small saucepan, whisk in a tablespoon of water, and turn the heat down to its lowest point. Very slowly whisk in the pureed sea urchin, about a tablespoon at a time. Season with just a touch of salt. Eric adds espelette pepper at this point; I prefer it without.

Turn the sauce into a bowl. Stir in a few chopped chives and the finely grated Parmesan. Taste and add salt and pepper if you like.

Toss with the angel hair pasta, very gently cooked. Squeeze a bit of lemon juice over the pasta and toss again.

Eric serves this topped with Osetra caviar. I like to top each of 4 tiny first-course servings with a couple of shining beads of salmon or trout caviar, although the true sea urchin addict might want to top it with a single little roe.

In the recovery room, still dreaming food.
One luscious peach, velvet skin, perfumed
flesh, juice singing in the mouth.
Watermelon with cream.

A PERFECT PEACH IS ONE OF THE RAREST FOODS ON EARTH, ONE OF THE MOST DELICIOUS, and one of the most universally acknowledged. Watermelon sundaes, on the other hand, are decidedly underappreciated. Too few people are aware of watermelon's affinity for cream. Nothing sets off a smooth dish of vanilla ice cream like a few crunchy chunks of cold watermelon. When I was in the recovery room, I found myself yearning for those sweet, fresh flavors.

Fluffy pink clouds outside my window.
Tart pleasure of apricot pie.
Stella's soft purr. World at my fingertips.
Stuck in bed: not so bad.

———————

ANY PERSON IN POSSESSION OF A CAT WILL INSTANTLY UNDERSTAND HOW THRILLED mine were by my misfortune. Day after day they snuggled against me, delighted to discover that I had finally given up my ridiculous human habits. Elegant Stella barely left my side, purring in contented approval. Fat Halley was happy, too, although he thought a few cans of cat food stored beneath my pillow would have greatly improved the situation. He resented having to jump down from the bed each time he felt the need for a snack.

People were also incredibly kind. Neighbors showed up with books, games, and all my favorite foods. "I found fresh apricots," said one friend, walking in with a pie. "I know how much you like them. I used your recipe."

Apricot pie always makes me happy. I love the way the tart apricots lean into the crumble, tempering the sweetness. I love the way they sink into softness in the oven without losing their integrity. And I love their bright sunny color. The fact that this is one of the easiest pies on earth doesn't hurt; you don't even need a knife. Simply pull the fruit apart with your fingers, discard the pits, and pile the fruit into the shell.

APRICOT PIE

SHOPPING LIST
pastry for a 9-inch
  pie
2 pounds apricots

STAPLES
¾ cup brown sugar
8 tablespoons
  (1 stick) butter
  (melted)
¾ cup flour
salt
nutmeg

Begin with an unbaked pie shell (you could even use a frozen one) and fill it with fresh apricot halves (it will hold about a pint, or 2 pounds).

Preheat the oven to 425 degrees. Make a streusel topping by mixing the brown sugar into the melted butter, stirring in the flour and a pinch of salt. Grate some fresh nutmeg in, spoon the topping over the fruit, and put the pie on the bottom rack of the hot oven.

After 10 minutes turn the oven down to 375 degrees and bake for another hour or so, until the top is golden and the aroma so wonderful that everyone is standing hopefully in the kitchen, forks at the ready.

Pink sky. Wispy clouds. Green lawn.
Curious deer peer through window.
Coffee, waffles, crossword puzzle.
Breakfast in bed. Helpless.

"YOU CAN DO IT," I'D TOLD MICHAEL THE NIGHT BEFORE. "YOU CAN MANAGE waffles. They aren't all that difficult." I handed him the classic Fannie Farmer recipe and gave him a pleading smile. "I've been craving waffles." He looked dubious.

I'd been lying in bed thinking about foods I really liked, and suddenly these waffles—crisp, light, yeasty—floated into my mind. There are easier waffle recipes, but they're little more than pancakes with dents. These, in contrast, seem like the result of an amazing alchemy that turns a few ordinary ingredients into something ethereal.

"All you have to do is mix up the batter tonight," I pleaded. "Leave it on the counter to rise. Then in the morning you just stir in a couple of eggs and heat up the waffle iron."

"I think I can manage that." Michael went off to the kitchen, and the cats, sensing an opportunity, jumped off the bed and followed him hopefully down the hall.

FANNIE FARMER'S CLASSIC
YEAST-RAISED WAFFLES

Sprinkle the yeast over ½ cup warm water in a large bowl and wait for it to dissolve. While it's starting to foam, melt the butter in a saucepan, add the milk, allow it to just gently warm itself up, and add it to the yeast mixture.

In another bowl, whisk the salt and sugar into the flour. Add this to the liquid and whisk until smooth. Cover the bowl and let it stand overnight at room temperature.

In the morning, beat in the eggs and baking soda, stirring well.

Ladle ½ cup of the thin batter into a very hot waffle iron and cook until the waffle is crisp. Start looking after about 3 minutes, and if it's not golden, let it cook another minute or two. If you have an old-fashioned waffle iron that cooks on top of the stove, turn it over and cook the other side for a couple of minutes.

One of the great attributes of this batter is that it keeps for a few days (in the refrigerator), so you can have waffles every morning for almost a week if you're so inclined. These waffles also make spectacular ice cream sandwiches, especially if you make them individually and wrap the warm waffles around very cold ice cream.

One week in bed; many more to go. Tedious. But Nick just called to say he's coming home to cook before exams. Feeling lucky.

"I KNOW DAD'S DOING HIS BEST." TWO WEEKS INTO MY ORDEAL, NICK WALKED IN with his friend Gemma and four enormous bags of groceries. "But we thought we'd come help."

I could hear them in the kitchen, clanging pots, banging pans. Together they produced a small mountain of food: fried rice, pasta, salads . . . We feasted all weekend. One of their greatest triumphs was these short ribs, accompanied by nothing more than a salad with blue cheese dressing.

THREE-DAY SHORT RIBS

SHOPPING LIST

½ bottle robust red
  wine
2½ pounds short
  ribs (separated)
2 carrots (diced)
1 celery stalk (diced)
fresh thyme
2 tablespoons
  tomato paste

STAPLES

flour
salt
pepper
olive oil
1 onion (chopped)
2 cloves garlic
  (smashed)
2 cups chicken stock
  (see recipe, page
  301)

Serves 4

Pour the red wine over the short ribs and let them luxuriate together overnight in the refrigerator. In the morning, pour the wine into another bowl and pat the ribs dry. Dredge them in a mixture of flour, salt, and pepper, then pour a good glug of olive oil into a large casserole and brown the ribs in batches, removing each one from the pot when it looks deliciously crisp.

Add the onion, carrots, celery, and garlic to the pot and cook them for about 15 minutes, watching as the vegetables become soft and fragrant. Return the ribs to the pot; toss in a sprig of thyme, the chicken stock, and the reserved wine. Bring to a boil, cover, and put into a 350-degree oven for an hour and a half.

Turn the meat and cook for another 45 minutes. By now you should be able to wriggle the bones out. Do that, throw the meat back into the pot, remove the sprig of thyme, allow the stew to cool, cover, and refrigerate overnight.

The next day, remove the hard layer of fat that has floated to the surface of the pot, and reheat the ribs and the sauce. Remove the ribs and boil the sauce down to about 2 cups. Stir in the tomato paste, taste for seasoning, and serve. It's not a lot of meat, but it's extremely satisfying on a pile of mashed potatoes.

BLUE CHEESE DRESSING

SHOPPING LIST

¼ cup blue cheese

STAPLES

garlic
salt
pepper
olive oil
cider vinegar

This wicked salad dressing is a bit much for tender greens, but spicier greens have the stamina to stand up to it. It also tastes terrific on a crisp, juicy wedge of iceberg lettuce.

Smash about a quarter of a clove of garlic in the bottom of a bowl. Add salt and pepper and mix until the salt has been absorbed into the garlic. Add a handful of blue cheese (my favorite is Carles Roquefort, which seems to have a special affinity for greens, but any good blue will do) and mix and smash until it has turned into a paste. Pour in olive oil (about 4 tablespoons) and mix well. I especially like cider vinegar with this, but a good white wine vinegar will do very nicely. (Red wine vinegar, on the other hand, does not get along well with blue cheese.) Pour a couple of tablespoons in and mix again. Taste and keep adjusting until you're satisfied.

Quiche for a cool night.
Crisp. Creamy. Flaky.
Airy. One perfect bite.
Chablis, very cold. A gift.

"Is there anything you'd really like me to make for you?" Nick asked. I studied him, wondering if I could ask him to attempt something as complicated as quiche. Then I remembered that I'd already done the hard part: I had an extra pastry crust stored in the freezer, ready for an impromptu meal.

A CUSTARD IN A CRUST

SHOPPING LIST
1 premade
   pie crust
¼ pound
   Gruyère cheese
1 cup heavy cream

STAPLES
3 eggs
salt
pepper
nutmeg

Serves 6

"Quiche?" Nick looked worried. "Isn't that hard?"

"The hardest part of making quiche," I told him, "is blind-baking the crust."

"What's that?"

"You take the empty crust, pierce it all over with a fork so it doesn't buckle, cover it with tinfoil, and fill it with weights. There's a bag of beans that I use as weights, sitting next to the pie pans. All you have to do is put the weighted crust into a hot (four twenty-five) oven for twenty minutes, then remove the foil and the weights and put the crust back into the oven for another eight minutes or so, until it turns golden. Don't worry if it slumps a little in the pan. It always does and it won't matter. Then you let it cool on a rack while you make the filling."

Nick went out to the kitchen and I could hear cupboards opening and tinfoil crackling. An hour or so later he came back into the bedroom triumphantly carrying the empty crust. "What now?" he asked.

You can put anything into a quiche: the custard is fine all by itself, but strips of bacon, bits of leftover ham, sautéed onions, vegetables, grated cheese—virtually everything tastes good married to a custard and a crust.

"I think there's some Gruyère cheese. Grate some and scatter it over the bottom of the prebaked crust. If there's some kind of leftover meat or vegetable, you can shred it and add that as well. Or not. Then whisk three eggs with a cup of cream and a little salt and pepper. Grate a little nutmeg on top and stick it in the oven."

"How long do I bake it?"

"About thirty-five minutes. Maybe forty. At 375 degrees."

I heard Nick and Gemma out in the kitchen, murmuring as they cooked. Then I began to smell the fine scent of softly melting cheese. Suddenly Nick was back, looking worried. "It's been in there half an hour. How will I know when it's done?"

"You'll see. The custard will rise and get really golden. When it looks like it can't possibly go any higher, you'll know it's done."

He went back into the kitchen and I heard a shout, "Now!"

He sounded elated, and I knew exactly how he felt. There's nothing quite so spectacular as a just-baked quiche before the custard deflates. He and Gemma came into my room triumphantly bearing a gorgeous golden dome. The four of us finished every morsel, which made me a bit sad; leftover quiche is delicious.

Damp earth. Tiny birds flit through
soft rain. Fire lit. Beans burble, slowly.
Quiet scent of baking bread.
Light begins to fade.

———————

AND THEN IT WAS TIME FOR NICK TO LEAVE. BEFORE THEY WENT BACK TO SCHOOL, he and Gemma baked a loaf of bread and made a big pot of hummus, going to the trouble of using dried chickpeas and removing every husk. The result was warm, soft as velvet with the seductive smoothness of whipped cream. It was one of the nicest presents anyone's ever given me.

Here's the thing about hummus: when you make it at home, and make it right, it bears very little resemblance to the stiff, gritty stuff you buy in grocery stores. But the humble dish is a fair amount of work—a true labor of love.

FABULOUS HUMMUS

Begin by going through a cup and a half of dried chickpeas—the smallest ones you can find—rejecting small stones and broken peas. Wash them, put them in a bowl with enough water so they can double in volume, and stir in a tablespoon of baking soda. (Baking soda creates an alkaline environment that allows water to penetrate the chickpeas more easily; it makes an enormous difference, giving you a hummus that's extremely smooth.) Let them rest overnight.

In the morning, drain the chickpeas, rinse them, and put them in a large pot. Add about 5 cups of water (the water should be a couple of inches above the beans) and ¼ teaspoon of baking soda, and bring the water to a boil. Turn the heat down, cover, and cook over low heat until the chickpeas are very soft; it should take about 2 hours. If the water cooks away, add more. Drain, but reserve the cooking liquid.

Rub the chickpeas between your fingers under cold running water, shedding the skins. It takes a while, but it's a meditative process that I find enormously pleasurable. Don't rush it.

They should be cool now, which is important. The starch crystals in the chickpeas break down more easily when they're warm; this is not a good thing, since it will make the puree pasty.

Put the chickpeas in a food processor with the garlic, the juice of the lemon, a quarter cup of the cooking liquid, and the raw (uncooked) tahini. Buy the best tahini you can find, organic if possible. Some of the commercial brands have a terrible metallic taste. You might want more tahini; a traditional recipe uses about half a cup, but I find that makes the sesame flavor too dominant. Process the chickpeas for 4 or 5 minutes, until they are smooth and creamy, with the dreamy texture of just-made frozen custard. The paste should be very soft and smooth. If it's too thick, add more liquid. Add salt to taste.

Now's the fun part. You have just created a lovely canvas. Top it with a glug of good olive oil, some chopped parsley, or a smattering of ground cumin. Or toast some pine nuts in butter and top the hummus with those. Add cayenne, zatar, chopped onions, or some pomegranate seeds. Be creative, or just revel in the best hummus you've ever had.

Today I will stop mourning my Epicurean Cat. An elegant portly fellow, he lived to eat. Favorite foods: turkey, tuna, anything smoked. RIP.

IT HAPPENED SUDDENLY, THE WAY it does with older animals. One day Halley was stalking the dust-balls under the bed; the next he was listless, unable to move.

He was seventeen, a ripe old age for such an overweight animal, and I should have been expecting it. But the timing was terrible, and I lay in bed, missing his weight on my legs and the humming vibration of his purr.

In normal times I would have cooked for consolation. Instead I spent my time composing a little ode.

Fat Cat

Halley, Halley, epicurean cat,
Named for a comet, but grown very fat.
Eating's his joy, his thrill, his pleasure.
It's what he does when he's at his leisure.
He absolutely loves to eat
And he's always expecting a major treat.
When other cats call and beg him to play
Halley twitches his ears and turns away.
He'd like to go, if only he could
But he hates to think he'd miss something good.
You never know what will land on the ground,
A morsel of tuna, or even a pound
Of that aged ham with the wonderful smell.
After all, you never can tell,
When a morsel of chicken or a drop of ice cream
Will fall to the floor—a cat can dream.
Salmon, perhaps, or apricot pies
Or even that sausage she sometimes buys.
Strawberries, steak, macaroons, caribou.
It could be a slice of honeydew.
The world is filled with so much to savor,
Wonderful textures, fabulous flavor,
And what a terrible waste, how sad,
To refuse a tidbit you've never had
Only to find at a future meal
That it does, after all, have some appeal.
Halley licks his paws and smooths his fur,
Curls up his tail and begins to purr.
His world has no trouble, no worry, no strife,
He's discovered the key to a happy life.
You can take his advice with the greatest of ease:
When it comes to food, just say, "Yes, please."

Storm skies. Thunder, lightning, hammering rain. Black coffee, very strong. Fried eggs, smoldering salsa. Burnt toast. I want to cook!

I LONGED FOR THE FEEL OF A KNIFE IN MY HAND, THE HEFT OF WATER SPLASHING into a pot. Yearned for the joyous sizzle, burble, and hiss that are the ever-changing soundtrack of the kitchen. I missed the daily transformations: fruit ripening, dough rising, bread toasting into golden slabs. I'd always thought of these elemental pleasures as minor diversions, but now I understood that they're the glue that holds my life together.

I lay there unable to move, reading about disasters in the far corners of the world. What could I do? Write letters, send checks. But there will never be a time when terrible trouble is not stalking the earth, and I began to see how important it is to appreciate what you have.

For too long I'd been waiting for the wonderful. But there is so much joy in everyday occurrences: a butterfly in the sun, the first crisp bite of an apple, the rich aroma of roasting meat. Maybe I had to break my foot to open my eyes, but I finally understood why cooking means so much to me. In a world filled with no, it is my yes.

SUMMER

Hot. Hawks dance in the air.
Grass prickles. Warm peanut butter
and jam on thick white bread.
Summertime picnic. Feel about five.

Was it odd that I chose the easiest option when I was finally able to make myself a meal? Not really. What I most wanted at that moment was to taste my newfound freedom. Balanced precariously on crutches, I fixed myself a sandwich, carried it outside, lowered myself onto the lawn, and took a giant bite.

PB&J

SHOPPING LIST
organic peanut butter
excellent strawberry
  jam
bread from a
  Pullman loaf

STAPLES
butter
waxed paper

Makes 1 sandwich

Peanut butter was not a staple in my mother's house, and I remember my very first taste. Soft, sticky, sweet, salty . . . I took one bite and then another; all the good things in the world had just landed in my mouth. I was, I think, four.

Later, when I got to elementary school, I looked longingly as the other kids opened their lunch boxes to reveal pristine white sandwiches. So neat. So pure. So minimal. I did my best to hide the hefty affair Mom had packed for me, a ziggurat of ham still skewered with cloves, precariously balanced between mismatched caraway-studded slices of rye. As a further indignity, my sandwich traveled inside a wrinkled brown bag, the price of the fruit it had once contained scribbled across the front in gaudy grease pencil.

When I reached second grade, Mom decreed that I was old enough to make my own lunch. For the next two years I opted for peanut butter and jelly every day, delighting in the spare perfection of my sandwich and the exotic tumble of flavors. After all these years, peanut butter and jelly still tastes like liberty to me.

The trick, as in all sandwiches, is in the proportions. I like a thin layer of butter, a thick layer of good crunchy peanut butter (never the industrial kind), and a thinner layer of excellent strawberry jam. (In a pinch, raspberry will do, but any jam that is not red is simply wrong.) I consider this to be one of the few legitimate uses for commercial white bread (the other being as a vehicle for classic Texas barbecued brisket).

If you're going to eat immediately, cut off the crusts and zap the sandwich in the microwave for about 8 seconds. This will melt the ingredients into a texture so sexy you'll barely recognize the innocent sandwich of your childhood. It will also transform the flavors, marrying them into perfect harmony.

If you're saving your sandwich for later, pull out a roll of waxed paper and wrap your sandwich right. Listen to the musical crinkle as you fold it around the sandwich. Appreciate the smoothly seductive texture of the sheet. Pick it up and look at the way it diffuses the light. Waxed paper is so lovely that when I have nothing more pressing to worry about, I've been known to fret over its inevitable demise.

Strawberry morning. Sunshine and butterflies. Clean air. Flour, butter, cream: the scent of a very fine future. Everything seems possible.

HOBBLING OUT TO THE KITCHEN, I SLIPPED HESITANTLY ONTO THE LITTLE SCOOTER that had just arrived. I'd rented it online, lured by ads promising that it would zip me effortlessly around the house. I'd been skeptical, but it liberated me, allowing me to begin working on the cookbook in earnest. As I pulled out the flour and reached for a bowl, the thought of a summer in the kitchen flooded me with pleasure. I measured ingredients, delighting in the downy softness of the pastry flour whispering through my hands. I reveled in the crack of an egg and stopped to listen for the sound of the oven expanding as it slowly gathered heat. On this almost-summer morning, biscuits, cream, and small ripe strawberries seemed like a celebration.

STRAWBERRY SHORTCAKE

SHOPPING LIST
2 cups pastry flour
3 cups heavy cream
3 pints strawberries

STAPLES
1 tablespoon baking
  powder
½ teaspoon salt
2–3 tablespoons
  sugar

There are about a million different ways to make biscuits. The simplest method I know is to begin with 2 cups of pastry flour, mix in 1 tablespoon of baking powder and ½ teaspoon of salt, and then gently stir in 1¼ cups of heavy cream. (If you use all-purpose flour, you'll need an extra 2 tablespoons of cream.) Knead it all together, pat it out, and cut it into 8 little rounds. Brush them with cream, put them on a baking sheet (leaving some space between them), and bake at 425 degrees for about 15 minutes.

With a 2¼-inch round cutter, this makes a dozen biscuits. If you don't have a biscuit cutter, don't worry; you can use the rim of a glass, or even a sharp knife if you want to cut them into triangles or squares.

While the biscuits are baking, put a bowl and the beaters of an electric mixer into the refrigerator to chill.

Allow the biscuits to cool on a rack. Meanwhile, whip 1½ cups of cream with the cold beaters in the cold bowl just until it holds soft peaks. Add 2 or 3 tablespoons of sugar—the sweetness is up to you—and whip a bit more. Do not overbeat the cream.

Slice the strawberries and sprinkle them with a bit of sugar; taste until you've got the balance right. (If the weather's been fine, the strawberries will need no help, but if it's been a rainy season, the berries will be less flavorful and you'll probably want more sugar.)

Cover the bottom of each biscuit with sliced berries. Spread on a bit of whipped cream. Put the top on, slather it with more whipped cream, and decorate with the remaining berries.

IF YOU'RE INCLINED TO GO FOR SPECTACULAR INSTEAD OF EASY, HERE IS THE BEST biscuit recipe I know. It comes from my friend Nancy Silverton, who asked me to test it for her. "Are you aware," I asked when I was done, "that there's almost half a stick of butter in each of these biscuits?"

Her response was, "Yep."

So be warned. These are a lot of work. Your fingers will freeze. Your oven will smoke. Your fire alarm will go off. On top of that, they contain an unconscionable amount of butter. On the other hand they are, hands down, the best biscuits I've ever tasted. One bonus: you can keep unbaked biscuits in the freezer and simply cook one up whenever you're hit with a need for serious excess.

BUTTERY FLAKY FANTASTIC BISCUITS

SHOPPING LIST

2 cups buttermilk

flaked salt

STAPLES

2½ cups (5 sticks)
  unsalted butter

5 cups flour

2 tablespoons plus
  2 teaspoons baking
  powder

1 teaspoon baking
  soda

1 tablespoon kosher
  salt

1 tablespoon sugar

Makes 12 biscuits

Freeze the butter until it is completely solid, and then grate it (using the largest hole of a standing grater) onto a piece of waxed paper or aluminum foil. This will take longer than you think, and you will have to stop from time to time to let your fingers thaw. Put the grated butter back into the freezer for at least half an hour.

Meanwhile, mix the flour, baking powder, baking soda, salt, and sugar in a large bowl.

Toss the dry ingredients with the refrozen butter and put the bowl into the freezer for another 5 minutes. Then shake the buttermilk well and gently mix it in, using your hands, until the dough coalesces into a solid mass.

Now comes the hard part: you are going to treat the dough like puff pastry. And you're going to need a ruler. Begin by turning the dough out onto a counter and molding the shaggy mass into a 10x7 rectangle.

Fold the dough into thirds, beginning by folding the left side over the middle. Then take the right side and fold it over that, so you have a tall rectangle. Now rotate the dough so that the long side is parallel to the table edge and roll it out with a rolling pin into another 10x7 rectangle.

Fold the dough as before, rotate, and roll it out again.

Do this two more times. After the final turn, roll the dough out to measure 12 inches by 10 inches; it should be ½ inch thick. Cut off the shaggy edges so you have a sharp, clean rectangle. Cut this into 12 biscuits.

Put the biscuits on a baking sheet and freeze them solid, for at least 2 hours.

Preheat the oven to 425 degrees. Line a baking sheet with parchment paper.

Place the biscuits on the baking sheet. Brush the top of each biscuit with melted butter and sprinkle with a bit of flaked salt.

Bake the biscuits for 10 minutes. Turn the heat down to 400 degrees, rotate the pan, and bake another 15 minutes until the biscuits are golden.

Electric summer night. Wind in the trees. Smoke rising. Rare burgers. Sweet onions. Slaw. Righteous Rhône. Berries with cream. Friends.

My attempt at a dinner party. As the guests came trooping in, they couldn't hide their disappointment. They'd been anticipating something more exotic.

But I was not about to let them down. As far as I'm concerned, a great burger is one of the glories of American cuisine, and this is an extremely extravagant burger. This is basically chopped steak served between buns.

I love the taste of aged beef, but the only way I know to buy aged ground meat is to order it online from a fancy butcher. Instead, I buy aged steak with a fair amount of fat, mix it with some ordinary chuck steak, and then chop it myself. I enjoy watching the meat change from a solid chunk of vibrant red into a fluffy pink pile, and the results are completely pleasing: a juicy burger with the mineral taste that comes from aging. It's a fair amount of work—you have to sharpen your knife really well (two sharp knives are even better) and get it very cold—but the chopping is extremely satisfying

Grilled meat is great, but these burgers are best in their purest form. Reluctant to mask the fine mineral funk of aged beef with the smoke from a grill, I cooked the burgers in a very hot pan, making them to order. Then I watched my guests' faces as each one took a bite. Awe. Excitement. Pleasure.

HAMBURGERS

Begin by buying prime, well-marbled beef, and the best chuck you can find.

Cut the meat into 1-inch strips (including the fat), toss it with a teaspoon of salt, cover the meat, and let it sit in the refrigerator overnight. You can leave it for up to 24 hours.

Working quickly so the cold meat doesn't get warm, remove some of the beef from the refrigerator and chop it with a very sharp knife. Each time you remove more beef from the refrigerator, resharpen your knife. When the meat is chopped, cup your hands and lightly shape the meat into four ¾-inch patties. Be gentle: you don't want to compress the meat. Shower the burgers with salt and cook them on a grill or in a very hot cast iron skillet. Do not press down on the meat; flip only once. I like them cooked about 3 minutes a side, but the doneness is up to you. Once you've removed your burgers from the fire, allow them to relax for about 5 minutes before serving.

I sometimes bake my own buns, but it's probably more work than it's worth. I've found potato buns to be best, because they tend to have the most height; the optimal proportion is about 50 percent meat to 50 percent bun.

Condiments: my feeling is that you've made a fabulous burger, so you don't need much else. I'm a fan of a single slice of red onion and some classic ketchup. When tomatoes are at their best, they're a fine addition. If you must use lettuce, go for the crisp crunch of iceberg.

Living with the light on this lovely long day. Warm pancakes, tart apricot jam. Iced mint tea. Perfect summer start.

WHY SHOULD SOME OF THE WORLD'S FINEST FOODS BE SERVED WHEN PEOPLE ARE too sleepy to appreciate them? The morning meal is sadly undervalued, and I decided to celebrate the solstice by serving breakfast for dinner. I set a long table on the lawn and told my guests they were welcome to show up in pajamas.

The menu included some of my favorite morning foods: shirred eggs, crisp bacon, and warm pancakes. But the pièce de résistance was the jam I cooked up just as the guests were arriving; it was still warm when they spread it on their toast.

We started in sunshine and watched the light slowly fade around us. Bourbon splashed into iced mint tea. Toasts were offered. Darkness fell, and just as the stars came out, a single bright light went shooting across the sky. Hello, summer!

FRESH APRICOT JAM

SHOPPING LIST
2 pounds apricots
1 vanilla bean

STAPLES
1¼ cups sugar
1 lemon

I love apricots, love their tart sweetness and sunny color. And I love the way their flavor, elusive when they are eaten raw, intensifies as they cook.

I have yet to encounter an unappealing apricot, but our local ones, just picked, are in a class by themselves. The first day they appear in the market, I buy as many as I can carry, eat the first few, and turn the rest into jam.

Jam's easier than you think—especially if you make it in fairly small batches and forget about the bother of canning.

Begin with the heaviest-bottomed pan you have and make a syrup by stirring a quarter cup of water into the sugar and bringing it to a boil. Turn the heat down and simmer, stirring until it's clear.

Add a pound of apricots that you've pulled apart with your fingers, and cook slowly until the apricots disintegrate. When they've started turning into mush, add another pound of halved apricots and the vanilla bean. Cook until the apricots are soft and have reached a consistency that you find pleasing. Be sure to stir often so the jam doesn't scorch.

Remove the vanilla bean, slice it the long way, and run a knife along the inside edge to remove the seeds. Stir them into the jam. Add the juice of half a lemon, stir well, and cook another few minutes. This will keep well in the refrigerator for a few weeks.

MY PANCAKES

STAPLES

8 tablespoons
  (1 stick) butter
1 cup milk
2 large eggs
1 tablespoon
  vegetable oil
1 cup flour
4 teaspoons baking
  powder
4 teaspoons sugar
1 teaspoon salt

Serves 4 to 6

These pancakes are so good that when we tested pancake recipes for the first *Gourmet Cookbook,* my recipe won by a landslide. Little wonder: breakfast is a kind of religion to me, the one meal I always cook for my family. When Nick was small, I woke him every morning with a glass of fresh orange juice and a question: "What do you want for breakfast?" For many years the answer was, "Pancakes, please." I can make these almost literally in my sleep.

Melt the butter in a heavy skillet. Meanwhile, in a large bowl, whisk together the milk, eggs, and vegetable oil. Add the butter. Put the buttery skillet back on the burner, ready for the pancakes.

Whisk the baking powder, sugar, and salt into the flour. Whisk in the egg mixture and stir just until combined. Add a bit more milk if you think it's too thick.

Pour some batter into the skillet. The size is up to you; sometimes I make them tiny for children, sometimes I make them ludicrously large. Watch as the bubbles appear in the batter, grow larger, and then pop and vanish. When they've all popped, carefully flip the pancake and cook the other side, about a minute.

Rush the pancakes to the table as each one is finished. You

want them hot, sweet, salty, and a little bit crisp. You want the memory to linger as your family moves through the day.

(The batter will keep in the refrigerator for a couple of days; thin it by adding a bit more milk.)

Fried chicken on the lawn. James Taylor, Carole King, Yo-Yo Ma. Crisp, cold wine. Light fades; starry night. Ice cream. Friends. Tanglewood.

ALL THROUGH JUNE I STUMBLED AROUND ON CRUTCHES AND NEGOTIATED THE kitchen on my scooter. It worked well enough, but I was grateful to graduate to a walking cast in July; now I could go anywhere!

My new mobility made me giddy, and when Michael suggested we spend the Fourth of July at Tanglewood, I threw myself into creating a picnic. Deviled eggs. Potato salad. Brownies. An enormous batch of fried chicken.

Focused on the food, I paid no attention to the program; any music would have made me very happy.

We arrived to find a raucous crowd basking in the early-evening sun. As we searched for a spot to spread our blanket, we kept running into friends, stopping every few feet to share food, wine, and conversation. I was still oblivious to the program when we finally found a spot, and when the music started I was gnawing on a chicken leg. But as the first few notes floated into the air, I dropped my food, startled, and looked down at the program. James Taylor. Carole King. Yo-Yo Ma. I sat up and began to pay attention. And it all came back.

In my senior year of college my parents gave me a trip to Israel as a Christmas present. I'd been looking forward to a holiday at home with friends, and I left with fairly bad grace. The charter expedition they'd purchased included a two-day bus trip to various tourist sites, and when I discovered that my fellow travelers consisted largely of old ladies, I grew even grumpier.

There was only one familiar-looking person on the tour, another young woman with frizzy hair and hippie clothes. The organizers put us in the same room, and that first night we stayed up talking, sharing secrets the way you do with sympathetic strangers you know you'll never see again. She said she was a songwriter, which seemed very cool, and that she had two children, which did not. She wasn't much older than me, and I could not imagine having that much responsibility. As I poured out my romantic troubles I regarded my roommate with more than a little awe.

We spent a couple of fascinating days together—even the old people turned out to be interesting—and as we waved goodbye we promised to stay in touch. Of course we never did, but sometimes, when I was sitting in my classes, I'd think about my friend at home with her children and wonder how she was doing.

A couple of years later a friend gave me a beautifully wrapped album as a birthday present. I pulled the paper off: *Tapestry.* I'd heard the music, of course, and loved it, but when I looked down at the picture on the cover, I saw my roommate from Israel staring back at me.

Now, watching the sun go down over Tanglewood and the stars begin to appear, the music called forth my teenage self and I recalled how miserable I'd been. Carole King launched into "You've Got a Friend," and James Taylor joined in. Then Yo-Yo Ma began to play, and the music soared over our heads, floating into the night sky, taking away the teenage pain along with the last of my sorrow about *Gourmet.* Failure doesn't last forever. The sad young mother could end up being Carole King. The future is filled with surprises. There's always another chance.

I stood up, amazed again by my mobility, and began packing up the leftover brownies, salad, and eggs. All that remained of the chicken was a single drumstick, and I put it in my mouth, savoring the flavor; it was crisp, juicy, salty.

REAL FRIED CHICKEN

SHOPPING LIST
1 fryer chicken
  (cut into 8 pieces)
3 cups buttermilk

STAPLES
kosher salt
2 onions (sliced)
1 cup flour
cayenne pepper
pepper
1½ teaspoons salt
2 cups vegetable
  shortening or oil
8 tablespoons
  (1 stick) butter

Serves 4

Ask the butcher to cut your chicken into 8 pieces. Shower them with kosher salt and put them in the refrigerator (uncovered) for about an hour. This quick brine will draw off some of the liquid and concentrate the flavor of the meat.

Rinse off all the salt and plunk the chicken into a bowl with the buttermilk and the onions. Leave it to luxuriate in this bath in the refrigerater overnight; the buttermilk will transform the flesh, making it almost silky. Meanwhile the onions will leave behind a hint of their own perfume.

Paper bags are becoming an endangered species, but if you have one, fill it with the flour, a shake of cayenne pepper, a few grinds of pepper, and the salt. If you don't have paper, a sturdy plastic bag will do. Give it a good shake, then add one of the pieces of damp chicken and shake well so it's covered with flour. Set the chicken on a rack or a plate and repeat until all your pieces are covered with flour. Allow the chicken to dry for about half an hour.

Melt the shortening (I like using coconut oil, but any vegetable oil will do) in a large skillet (cast iron if you're lucky enough to have one) with the butter. Allow it to get very hot. Add as much of the chicken as you can fit comfortably without crowding, turn the heat down to medium-high, cover, and cook for 10 minutes. Turn the pieces over, cover again, and cook for another 10 minutes. Drain on a rack; if you don't have one, torn-up paper bags or paper towels will serve almost as well.

Cook remaining chicken in the same fashion. Add salt and pepper. Great hot—but just as good eaten cold.

Damp earth. Picking purslane.
Tiny birds flit through soft rain.
Quiet scent of baking bread.
Light begins to fade.

IN THIS HOPEFUL NEW MOOD I FOUND THAT MY EYES WERE OPEN WIDER THAN THEY usually are, making me see things I normally overlook. Walking out to the car one morning I stared at the green leaves struggling up through the paving stones in the walkway and dancing along the edges of the driveway. Bending down to take a closer look, I saw that these were no ordinary weeds; they were purslane.

Purslane is a gift. If it wasn't so ubiquitous, waving up from the cracks in city sidewalks to offer itself to every passing person, we would surely give it more respect. It's a wonderful vegetable: the little jade leaves are tender and succulent, with a faint citric tang and the tiniest pepper back-note. I've never seen purslane in a supermarket, but it is increasingly available in farmers' markets. If you don't see it, ask: many farmers consider these delicious greens an annoying weed, but they'd be happy to know there was a market for them.

I went back into the house to get a basket. Then I walked along the driveway, picking purslane as I contemplated the possibilities. In the end I gathered enough to make two of my favorite dishes.

MOROCCAN PURSLANE SALAD

SHOPPING LIST
purslane
olives (any kind)

STAPLES
garlic
salt
pepper
lemon juice
coriander
cumin
olive oil

Wash your purslane really well; it has a sneaky tendency to secrete grit in places that are easy to overlook. Chop it and steam it for about 20 minutes, along with a whole clove of garlic for each cup of purslane.

Drain the purslane, mash the garlic into the (much reduced) vegetable, and season it with salt, pepper, and lemon juice. I like to add a bit of coriander, or perhaps some cumin and paprika. Stir in a slosh of olive oil and embellish with pitted olives. If you have some preserved lemons, a bit of the chopped skin adds a lovely tang.

PURSLANE TACOS

4 tomatillos
1 small green chile
purslane
queso fresco or
  crumbled feta
corn tortillas

½ small onion
1 clove garlic
oil
salt
pepper

Serves 2 to 4

Begin by making a quick green salsa. Peel the papery husk off the tomatillos, wash them, and toss them into a blender with the chile, onion, and garlic. Whirl them into a thin liquid.

Take a big heap of purslane, wash it well, chop it, and boil it for about 10 minutes. Drain.

Slick a skillet with oil and add the salsa. Bring it to a boil, turn the heat down, and add the purslane. Add salt and pepper to taste. (Many Mexican cooks add cumin as well, but I prefer it without.) Cook it down until it's thickened.

Sprinkle some queso fresco or feta across the top and serve wrapped in warm tortillas.

*Grilled beef at sunset. Smoke spirals
to the sky. Charred red onions.
Crisp potatoes, lemon-edged.
Purslane salad. Dark falls. Moon rises.*

AFTER RAIN, SUNSHINE. I WOKE TO A DAY SO BRIGHT I COULD ONLY THINK OF grilling. I'd asked Michael to stop at the butcher's to get a steak, and when he returned with top round, I stared at the humble cut with dismay. Michael looked so crestfallen that I hurriedly adjusted my face.

"Good idea," I said. "We'll let it marinate all day. If it turns out well, I'll put it in the cookbook. I'd like to have an inexpensive steak alternative."

Michael's a great grill master, but he cooked this meat with special care. It was rare, juicy, and filled with flavor, and it had a satisfying chew.

"Putting it in the cookbook?" Michael asked. When I replied in the affirmative, he looked so smug I couldn't help wondering if he'd planned it all along.

MICHAEL'S GRILLED LONDON BROIL WITH RED ONIONS

SHOPPING LIST
2 pounds top round,
  London broil, or
  flank steak

STAPLES
4 cloves garlic
  (chopped)
5 tablespoons
  balsamic vinegar
3 tablespoons
  olive oil
salt
pepper
3 small red onions

Serves 4 to 6

The point of London broil (which is really a method, not a cut of meat) is to marinate a tough piece of beef to tenderize it. Begin by making a marinade of the garlic, balsamic vinegar, olive oil, and a good amount of salt and pepper. Mix it well, plunk the meat into it, and let it sit in the refrigerator for at least 4 hours; 8 hours is better.

Meanwhile, cut the onions into slices and throw them into the marinade as well.

When you start your fire, take the meat and onions out of the refrigerator and let the meat come to room temperature.

Meanwhile, sauté the onions (reserve the marinade) over medium-low heat in a lightly oil-slicked pan for about half an hour.

When the fire is at a steady medium heat, dry the meat well and grill it for 6 minutes a side for medium-rare meat. Let it stand for 10 minutes.

While the meat is standing, turn the heat up under the onions, pour in the marinade, and boil it down into a delicious sauce.

Cut the steak crosswise, against the grain, into thin slices, holding the knife at a 45-degree angle. Top with the onions and their sauce and serve.

CRISP, LEMONY BABY YUKONS

SHOPPING LIST
3 pounds baby Yukon
  Gold potatoes

STAPLES
3 cups chicken stock
  (see recipe, page 301)
1–2 lemons
2 cloves garlic
  (smashed)
olive oil
sea salt

Serves 6

Preheat the oven to 400 degrees.

Put the chicken stock into a medium-sized pan and stir in the zest of a lemon or two and the smashed garlic. Add the potatoes, bring to a boil, cover, and cook for about 12 minutes.

Drain the potatoes, reserving the lemon zest from the stock, and allow them to cool a bit. Put them on a sheet pan that is liberally covered with olive oil. Gently flatten each potato, using the back of a chef's knife, a rolling pin, or a small skillet. Drizzle with olive oil, sprinkle with sea salt and the lemon zest, and put in the oven for about 20 minutes, until the potatoes are crisp. Sprinkle with lemon juice and a bit more salt.

Misty dreamy day, soft green, tender gray. Scarlet breakfast in bed. Lobster claws in cream, on buttered toast. Strawberry orange juice.

WANDERING THE FARMERS' MARKET IN THE SECOND WEEK OF JULY, I WAS SURPRISED to discover a young man who'd driven a truck filled with just-caught lobsters over from the coast. I peered in to take a look: unlike supermarket lobsters, whose murky maroon shells tell you they've been out of the ocean too long, these were shining creatures, their shells the deep blue-black of mussels. I could not resist.

Boiled lobster is the perfect summer dinner. So easy: you plunk the lobsters into a furiously boiling pot of water, salty as the sea, and wait until they turn bright red; they're done when an antenna pulls easily away from the body when you give it a tug. (For a 1½-pound lobster this should take 10 to 12 minutes.)

I used to like butter with my lobster, but I no longer require anything more than a small splash of lemon. We ate them with our hands and teeth, pulverizing the shells, sucking out every morsel of meat. Michael and I are completely compatible lobster consumers; he likes the tails while I prefer the tomalley and the knuckles. But we always save the claws for morning, so we can share this spectacularly luxurious breakfast.

CREAMED LOBSTER CLAWS ON TOASTED BRIOCHE

SHOPPING LIST
1 cup half-and-half
12 ounces cooked
  lobster meat
6 slices brioche
  or challah

STAPLES
4 tablespoons
  (½ stick) butter
1 small onion
  (minced)
2 tablespoons flour
½ cup milk
salt and pepper
Worcestershire sauce
cayenne pepper
1 lemon
paprika

Makes 6 small servings

Melt the butter in a small skillet, and when it foams add the onion. Wait until it's turned translucent, then whisk in the flour. Add the half-and-half and milk, very slowly, allowing the sauce to thicken as you whisk it over gentle heat; it will become quite thick after about 5 minutes. Add salt and pepper to taste, a small dash of Worcestershire sauce, just a pinch of cayenne pepper, and as much leftover chopped lobster meat as you're lucky enough to have saved from dinner.

Just before serving, squeeze in a few drops of lemon juice, taste for seasoning, and serve on buttered, toasted brioche or challah, sprinkled with a dash of paprika.

Outdoor shower. Water splashing onto mint. Hot coffee in the sunshine. Sour cherry crostata. Summer. Happy.

———

"You really want them all?" The woman who runs my favorite farm stand seemed startled by the sheer quantity of my purchase. "You'll be pitting for days, and it's such an awful job."

"I'm working on a cookbook."

That seemed to satisfy her, but it was just an excuse; my sour cherry obsession cannot be rationally explained. I simply love them. They're not for eating out of hand, but their fragile flesh and slightly surly sourness make the most wonderful tarts. I like knowing that they're waiting in the freezer, ready to bring back summer in any kind of weather.

Pitting sour cherries is not nearly as onerous as people pretend. They're so soft you need nothing more than a paper clip. Simply unfold it once, so you have a little piece of wire with a hook on each end, and use that to flip out the pits. This wonderfully messy work provokes a Tom Sawyer moment; friends who show up invariably plead to help.

Most recipes call for too much sugar, which overrides the appealing tartness of these cherries. But this crostata teeters on the border between sour and sweet. An added bonus: unlike so many pastries, this tastes better on day two (provided it lasts that long).

SOUR CHERRY CROSTATA

Working with pastry dough can be difficult in the heat of summer. And this one, being soft, is challenging. Unlike regular pie dough, however, this cookie-like pastry is very forgiving and no matter how much you handle it, it won't get tough. If it gets too soft, simply put it back in the refrigerator for 5 minutes to let it cool off. It will become much more accommodating.

Mix 1½ sticks of soft butter with ⅓ cup of the sugar in a stand mixer until fluffy.

Break the egg into a small dish and beat it; reserve a bit to wash the pastry later, and add the rest of the egg to the butter. Toss in the vanilla.

Grate the rind of the lemon into the flour. Add a pinch of salt and slowly add the flour to the butter–egg mixture until it just comes together. Divide into 2 disks, wrap in waxed paper, and put in the refrigerator to chill for half an hour.

Meanwhile, make the cherry filling by removing the pits from the fresh sour cherries; you should have 4 cups once the pits are removed. (You could also use 4 cups of frozen pitted sour cherries; do not defrost before using.)

Melt the remaining butter (3 to 4 tablespoons) in a large skillet. Add the cherries, ½ cup of sugar, and the juice of half the lemon and stir gently, just until the liquids come to a boil. Don't cook them too long or the cherries will start to fall apart.

Make a slurry of the cornstarch with 3 tablespoons of cold water and stir it into the boiling cherries. Cook for about 2 minutes, stirring, just until the mixture becomes clear and thick. Allow to cool.

Preheat the oven to 375 degrees and put a baking sheet on the middle shelf.

Remove the pastry disks from the refrigerator. Roll out the first one, between two sheets of plastic wrap, to a round about 12 inches in diameter. Now comes the tricky part: invert it into a 9-inch fluted tart pan, with high sides. The dough will probably tear. Don't worry, just patch it all up, pat it around the bottom and up the sides of the pan, and put it back into the refrigerator to rechill.

Roll out the second disk in the same manner, put it onto a baking sheet (still on the plastic wrap), remove the top sheet of plastic, and cut this into 8 or 10 strips, about 1 inch wide. Put the baking sheet into the refrigerator to chill for a few minutes.

Remove the tart shell and the strips from the refrigerator. Pour the cherry filling into the tart shell. Now make a lattice of the strips on the top, crisscrossing them diagonally. Don't worry if they're not perfect; no matter what you do, the tart's going to look lovely when it emerges from the oven. Brush the strips with the remaining beaten egg, sprinkle with sugar, and put into the oven on the baking sheet. (You need the sheet to keep cherry juices from spilling onto the oven floor.) Bake for about 45 minutes, until golden.

Cool for 1 hour, on a rack, before removing the side of the tart pan. Allow the tart to cool completely before serving.

The indigo bunting is back! Crisp cold watermelon on a dew-damp lawn. Sour cherry lemonade. Rainbow colors of a summer morning.

———

I'VE NEVER BEEN A BIRD–WATCHER, BUT WHEN I WAS STUCK IN BED, GAZING OUT the window, I found their antics endlessly entertaining. I even bought a bird guide for the sheer pleasure of reading the names: wood thrush—purple finch—red-winged blackbird.

But the indigo bunting was my favorite. Each sighting reminded me of the summer when Nick was six and we rented our first house in the country, intended as a family month of swimming, sunshine, and fresh food. Our plans were shattered when CBS sent Michael off on a last-minute assignment.

Furious, I called my friend Marion Cunningham in the Bay Area, moaning about my misfortune. Marion was an American icon; she'd been James Beard's assistant, she rewrote *The Fannie Farmer Cookbook,* and she acted as den mother to a large group of American food folk.

"Would you like me to come?" She said this as if it was the most natural thing in the world to drop everything and fly across the continent on the spur of the moment. "I could get the next plane out."

She was as good as her word, and she gamely folded her tall body into my battered little car, crammed in with a couple of cats, a mountain of toys, and an entire kitchen's worth of pots and pans. We headed north. I'd rented a farmhouse in the Hudson River Valley, complete with neighboring cows.

It was a wonderful few weeks. Marion and I had been friends for years, but we'd never cooked together. I was enchanted to discover how fearless she could be in the kitchen. She baked cakes and cookies, produced fantastic breakfasts, and when she made a mistake she'd invariably wave her hand declaring, "It won't matter a bit!" Best of all, whenever Nick got bored she'd take him into the kitchen and encourage him to make a mess.

One morning an indigo bunting landed on the lawn. "Look!" she cried. "What a beautiful bird. I think we should celebrate." She and Nick disappeared for a while, and when they rejoined me my son was proudly carrying a pitcher of sour cherry lemonade.

SOUR CHERRY LEMONADE

SHOPPING LIST
1 quart sour cherries
4 lemons

STAPLES
½ cup sugar

Serves 4

The joy of this drink, other than its slightly sneaky flavor, is that you don't have to remove the cherry pits. You do, however, have to remove the stems from a quart (about 2 pounds) of sour cherries. Toss the cherries into a blender, whirring them until they've become a rough mush. Some of the pits will be chopped too; that's fine because you're going to put them in a strainer and press hard, extracting as much puree as you can. Discard the solids.

Place the cherry puree into a pitcher and stir in the juice of the lemons and the sugar. (If you like things really sour, you might want less than ½ cup; if you've got a sweet tooth, you'll want more.)

This will keep for a day or two in the refrigerator. When you're ready to drink the lemonade, pour into glasses and add water (or sparkling water) to taste.

Want to turn this into cocktails? Add a few splashes of vodka or gin, and garnish with a sprig of mint.

Bear pranced past this morning. He probably wanted my sweet salty Vietnamese pork. Who can blame him?

WE'D ALWAYS KNOWN THE BEARS WERE THERE, EVEN THOUGH WE'D NEVER ACTUALLY seen them. They tended to save their visits until after dark, overturning garbage cans while we were sleeping, liberally strewing the contents across the road. But now that I was cooking all day long their visits had become more frequent, and today one of the bears ventured brazenly onto the lawn. I think he was lured by

the tantalizing scent of caramelizing sugar. He ambled around, eyeing the sweet, crisp, salty pork I'd set on the table, surrounded by heaps of fresh mint and basil, wedges of lime, and bowls of crushed peanuts. I hurriedly went inside, closed the windows, locked the doors, and left him to devour our lunch.

EASY VIETNAMESE CARAMELIZED PORK

SHOPPING LIST

2 Armenian
   cucumbers
¾ pound pork
   tenderloin
2 tablespoons
   fish sauce
mint
basil
peanuts
1 lime
Sriracha

STAPLES

2 tablespoons rice
   vinegar
salt
ginger
vegetable or peanut oil
1 small onion
   (sliced thin)
1 clove garlic
   (smashed)
4 teaspoons sugar
pepper
rice

Serves 2

Pour the rice vinegar into a small bowl and add a pinch of salt and 1 teaspoon of sugar. Slice the Armenian cucumbers into thin rounds, along with a small knob of ginger. Put them into the vinegar and allow the flavors to mingle while you make the pork.

Slice the pork tenderloin very thin. (This is easiest if you put the meat in the freezer for half an hour to get it very cold before slicing.) It can be difficult to find small tenderloins; when I end up with more meat than I need, I chop the remainder and save it for another dish.

Get a wok so hot that a drop of water dances on the surface and then disappears. Add a couple of tablespoons of peanut or neutral oil and immediately toss in the onion and the smashed garlic. As soon as it's fragrant, add the pork and 1 tablespoon of sugar and stir-fry, tossing every few minutes, for 10 to 15 minutes, until the pork has crisped into delicious little bits.

Take the wok off the heat and stir in the fish sauce; it should become completely absorbed. Grind in a lot of black pepper.

Remove the ginger from the cucumbers and mix the cucumbers into the pork. (Whether you want to add the marinade is up to you; I like the taste of vinegar, but you might prefer your meat completely dry.)

Serve with rice. Put fresh mint and basil on the table, along with crushed peanuts, lime wedges, and Sriracha, and allow each diner to make a mixture that appeals to them.

This will feed two people very generously. Unless you have a very large wok and a ferocious source of heat, the recipe does not double well; you want the pork to get really crisp.

Gray day, grumpy birds: the bear has made off with their feeder again. Puzzled squirrel glares up at the empty pole.

———

THE BEARS CONSIDER THE BIRD FEEDER THEIR PRIVATE SALAD BAR. THEY RAIDED IT so often that by mid-July we admitted defeat.

It made me sad to see the feeder come down. I'd come to think of it as a kind of living rainbow, the colors changing as one variety of bird flew off to be replaced by another.

Annoyed at the bears, I decided to retaliate by working up a recipe that emitted no olfactory signals. I'd wrap my food up, sealing in every scent until we sat down at the table.

This is a perfect way to cook delicate fillets of fish, because the folded packets protect them from the heat. It also makes serving simple; you put a packet on each plate, offering them to your guests like little presents.

SOLE EN PAPILLOTE

SHOPPING LIST
4 fillets of any variety
  flat fish, 4–6 ounces
  each (gray sole,
  lemon sole,
  or flounder)
2 scallions

STAPLES
vegetable or grapeseed
  oil
soy sauce
rice wine vinegar
ginger
rice

Serves 4

Buy whichever flat fish is most sustainable at the fishmonger's at the moment (gray sole, lemon sole, or the like).

Cut 4 rectangles of parchment paper so that they will make handsome packages for the fish, and lightly brush them with grapeseed or some other neutral oil. Lay a fillet on each piece of parchment, and brush liberally with soy sauce and a bit of rice wine vinegar. Grate a good amount of ginger on top of each one, and scatter some sliced scallions (both green and white parts) across the top. Close the packets, folding up the edges of the paper so that each one is entirely closed, and put them on a baking sheet.

Bake in a hot oven (about 400 degrees) for about 10 minutes, or until just cooked. Serve with rice.

Up early. Vast rose sky, cloud wisps. Wood thrush calling. Cool cucumber soup. Lemon verbena. Threads of mint. Day starts well.

I STOOD OUTSIDE, MY ONE BARE FOOT IN DEW-DAMP GRASS, WATCHING THE SUN come up, contemplating the day's dishes. I love the early morning hours, when nobody else is up and the only sound is the birds, calling to one another from the trees.

I conjured some flavors in my mind: cucumbers—such a refreshingly subtle vegetable—mingled with lemon verbena and mint. Buttermilk, perhaps? Inside, I began concocting this quick little bowlful, which turned out to be light, cool, and bracing. I'm sure it would make a satisfying lunch, but on this late-July morning it was a perfect way to start the day.

The secret here is lemon verbena; the plant has bright green leaves, a gorgeous citric scent, and surprising sweetness. It makes an extremely appealing tea; all you have to do is pour boiling water over the leaves and allow them to steep for a few minutes. Few people can believe that the leaves contain such a wealth of flavors; I'm constantly accused of adding sugar.

CUCUMBER SOUP LACED WITH
LEMON VERBENA, THREADS OF MINT

SHOPPING LIST

4 cucumbers
1 cup buttermilk
1 lime
lemon verbena
mint

STAPLES

red wine vinegar
sugar
garlic
salt
pepper

Makes 3–4 small servings

Peel the cucumbers, seed them, chop them coarsely, and put them in a blender with the buttermilk. (If you don't have buttermilk, yogurt will do, but you may need to thin it with a bit of milk.) Add a splash of red wine vinegar, a sprinkle of sugar, ½ clove of garlic, and a couple of ice cubes. Whirl away until it becomes a beautiful pale puree. Add salt and pepper to taste, squeeze in 1 or 2 teaspoons of lime juice and garnish with some finely julienned lemon verbena and a bit of mint.

Sleepy gray afternoon. Storm blows in: pounding rain. Pasta sizzled in oil. Chile-sparked. Tang of bottarga. Splash of lemon. Awake!

IT WAS ONE OF THOSE DAYS; HAZY AND JUST HOT ENOUGH TO MAKE WORKING DIF-ficult. I sat at my computer, writing recipes, eyelids fluttering over the keyboard as Stella purred beside me. The air began to fill with the electric scent of ozone, and the sky grew dark. I watched the weather moving toward us from far away. Then, with a rush of sound, it was here, rain crashing onto grass and thundering on the roof. Lightning flashed.

I barely breathed, watching the light show. Finally the rain slowed, murmuring gently, a kind of wordless poetry as it moved off, propelled by a curtain of sunlight.

It had taken ten minutes. I was revived. And starving. I went into the kitchen and made a pot of my favorite pasta. Like the storm, it takes all of ten minutes. And like the storm, it's a clash of sound and texture—and utterly delicious.

SPAGHETTI WITH BOTTARGA AND BREAD CRUMBS

SHOPPING LIST

4 ounces bottarga
di mugine (salted,
cured mullet roe)

STAPLES

1 pound spaghetti
(dry, or see pasta
recipe, page 30)
2 cloves garlic
(sliced thin)
red pepper flakes
olive oil
parsley
1 lemon
homemade bread
crumbs (see recipe,
page 17)

Serves 4

Boil a large pot of water for pasta.

While the spaghetti cooks, gently sauté the garlic and a fat pinch of crushed red pepper flakes in about ½ cup of good olive oil just until it becomes fragrant.

Take as much bottarga as you can afford (classic recipes call for 6 ounces for a pound of spaghetti, but bottarga's so expensive, and so powerful, I tend to use about half that much), and shave half of it into thin, delicate curls. Grate the rest.

When the pasta is al dente, drain it and toss it into a bowl with the olive oil mixture and some finely chopped Italian parsley. Toss the bottarga with the pasta, along with the zest of the lemon and a generous handful of bread crumbs, and serve.

Simple pleasure: tiny potatoes, just
out of the earth, roasted until
soft flesh melts inside crackling skins.
The taste of summer.

Like most urban people, I grew up thinking that potatoes aren't really vegetables. They're those brown things that are always available, summer, winter, spring, fall. It took my first visit to a farm to make me understand that potatoes are very much like corn: a few hours out of the earth, before the sugar converts to starch, they taste entirely different than they do later on in life. The flavor is clear, fresh, a little bit sweet. The texture's different, too, melting into something soft and almost creamy.

On this late July morning I found the first new potatoes at the farmers' market, and I filled my basket. There was green garlic too, which is slightly sticky and sprightlier than garlic that's been aged and cured. It's the perfect foil for the innocent taste of new potatoes. This combination is . . . well, perfect.

NEW POTATOES WITH GREEN GARLIC

SHOPPING LIST
6 small newly dug potatoes (up to 18 if they're tiny)
3 cloves green garlic (sliced)
thyme
white wine

STAPLES
olive oil
salt
pepper

Serves 3

Scrub the potatoes well but do not peel them. Toss them with olive oil to coat, along with the garlic, a sprinkling of thyme, and salt and pepper. Toss in a bit of white wine, cover tightly with foil, and roast in a hot oven (about 400 degrees) for about 40 minutes until they're tender. Heaven.

Lightning sizzles. Thunder cracks.
Electric sky at midnight. Rain drums,
hard. Safe inside: huge red wine,
the joy of onion sandwiches.

ONE BY ONE OUR DINNER GUESTS CALLED TO SAY THEY'D BE SAFER STAYING HOME. Michael and I stood at the screen door watching the rain thunder down, sniffing the electric scent the summer storm had spewed into the air. The power was blinking on and off, threatening to desert us for good.

I eyed the hors d'oeuvres, wondering what to do with them. Reading about James Beard, I'd come upon a recipe for what he called "onion rings"; the author said they were one of Beard's favorite party dishes. Intrigued, I'd made them. A *lot* of them.

You might call these little sandwiches elegant in their simplicity. Or you might just call them simple. I eyed the little white circles now, thinking you really have to love onions to appreciate them. I reached for one.

I sipped my wine, looked out at the rain, nibbled an onion ring. "Amazing weather," said Michael, listening to the thrum. He ate a sandwich. We watched. We sipped. At some point I reached for another sandwich and found my fingers scrabbling across an empty plate.

JAMES BEARD'S "ONION RINGS"

SHOPPING LIST
1 loaf sturdy white
   bread (or brioche)
1 bunch parsley

STAPLES
mayonnaise
salt
4 small white onions

Begin with a sliced loaf of sturdy white bread or brioche. Take a 2½-inch round cookie cutter and cut circles out of the bread. Slather them with good commercial mayonnaise and sprinkle that with salt.

Slice onions very thin. Put a slice of onion on a circle of bread and sandwich it with a second piece of bread.

Chop the parsley. Spread mayonnaise on the edge of each sandwich and then roll it in parsley. You are done.

Couldn't sleep. Silver sky.
Fresh morning pulls me outside.
Wandering the woods munching cold
rare duck, a mineral jolt of flavor.

———

AT THE BEGINNING OF AUGUST THE WALKING CAST CAME OFF; SUDDENLY I could go anywhere, do anything. I could drive, I could swim, I could hike. Now I climbed out of bed every morning and went for a walk in the woods. On my way out the door I usually grabbed the first thing I found in the refrigerator: on this morning it was slices of cold duck breast, left over from the night before.

Most Americans think of duck as the gray meat you find in dishes like duck à l'orange or Peking duck. But cooked rare, so the flesh is deep red and the skin crisp, the breast attains a lean, robust character. Cut into thin slices, duck breast can easily stand in for beef. But no steer ever rendered up such delicious fat; it's a bonus, and the basis for fantastic future meals.

I knew I wanted to include some kind of duck breast in the cookbook, but after preparing it a dozen different ways, I returned to a recipe I've been making most of my life. The only trick is allowing enough time to marinate the breast—it really makes a difference.

MAGRET OF DUCK WITH
EASY ORANGE SAUCE

SHOPPING LIST
2 whole boned
  duck breasts
  (4 pieces, each
  about ½ pound)
1 orange

STAPLES
1 large shallot
½ tablespoon salt
parsley
dried thyme
bay leaf
peppercorns
1 large clove garlic
½ cup chicken
  stock (see recipe,
  page 301)
2 tablespoons sugar
2 tablespoons cider
  vinegar
½ tablespoon
  cornstarch

Serves 4

Mince the shallot with ½ tablespoon of coarse salt. Add some minced parsley, a bit of thyme, a crumbled bay leaf, and a dozen crushed peppercorns. Slice the garlic thin and add that. Spread across the duck breasts, sandwich 2 pieces together like hands in prayer, wrap them in plastic, and put the 2 packages in the refrigerator for a few hours or overnight.

Allow the duck breasts to come to room temperature. Wipe off the excess marinade and score the skin by making diagonal slashes with a knife, which will help render the fat.

Get a skillet very hot and put the duck breasts in, skin side down. Turn the heat down to medium and cook slowly, spooning the fat off every few minutes. You'll be stunned by the amount of fat that comes off a single duck breast. Save it; rendered duck fat is a remarkable substance. There's nothing better than potatoes sautéed in duck fat, and its deep flavor transforms a pot of beans into something truly remarkable.

Cook until the skin is very crisp, about 20 minutes, then turn over, turn the heat up to high, and cook for another 4 to 7 minutes until the breast reaches 125 degrees. (The timing will depend on the thickness of your duck breast.) The meat will be rare. Let the duck rest 5 minutes, then slice on the diagonal and serve the beautifully rosy slices as they are—or with this extremely simple orange sauce.

ORANGE SAUCE

Remove the zest from the orange and julienne it into thin shreds. (Don't be too fussy about this, or it will take forever.) Drop the shreds into a small pot of boiling water for about a minute, then drain and set aside.

Juice the orange; you should have about half a cup. Put it in a small saucepan with the chicken stock, sugar, and cider vinegar. Cook until the sugar dissolves. Add the orange zest and a teaspoon of the rendered duck fat. Bring to a boil.

Mix the cornstarch into a tablespoon of water and stir in, just until it thickens a bit. Poured over slices of rare duck breast, this is an entirely modern take on old-fashioned duck à l'orange.

*Bright. Breezy. Hot.
Yellow butterflies dance on the lawn.
Pasta twined into tomatoes. Melting
mozzarella. Basil. Simple. Savory. Fine.*

ONE OF THE GREAT ADVANTAGES OF BEING OUT OF THE CAST WAS THAT I COULD now drive myself around. I began driving into town at all hours, haunting shops and markets, thrilled to be able to navigate on my own.

Most days I found myself at the cheese shop; the world of cheese has been exploding so quickly that there's always something new. Today, however, it was a classic that caught my eye: a shipment of buffalo mozzarella had just arrived from Italy.

Like most New Yorkers, I grew up thinking of mozzarella as the bland rubbery blob sprawled across a slice of Famous Ray's pizza. Then I got an assignment to write about an artisanal mozzarella maker on the Italian coast, halfway between Naples and Rome. Nick was about ten, and I took him along, thinking he'd be enchanted by the water buffalo. But he had eyes only for the cheesemaker, a beautiful old woman who took one look at my son, scooped a ball of cheese from the vat, and held it out, still dripping and warm. Her eyes never left his face as he devoured the entire ball. Wordlessly, she handed him another.

I leaned over to filch a taste. Soft, creamy, subtle, the mozzarella was one of the most delicious substances I'd ever had in my mouth. I became an instant addict, and when I find the real thing—made from the milk of the water buffalo—I never pass it up. With figs or melon, a bit of prosciutto, and a few nuts, mozzarella makes a fantastic

first course. It's wonderful melted onto sandwiches or tossed into salads. It's a great foil for caviar or salmon roe. But to me, mozzarella never tastes better than in this very simple pasta dish, melted into ripe tomatoes and fresh herbs. (If you can't get real mozzarella di bufala, skip this dish. I once attempted to make it with supermarket mozzarella: we ended up eating peanut butter and jelly sandwiches instead.)

PAINLESS PASTA FOR THREE

SHOPPING LIST
fresh basil
5 ripe tomatoes
1 ball mozzarella
  di bufala

STAPLES
3 cloves garlic
olive oil
1 pound spaghetti
  (dry, or see recipe,
  page 30)
salt
pepper

Serves 3 or 4

Slice the garlic and shred a handful of basil leaves into about a half cup of fresh, green-tasting olive oil. This is the time to use the best you've got, since the flavor will inform all the other ingredients. Allow the mixture to macerate for at least an hour.

Cut the tomatoes in half and gently squeeze out the seeds. Chop them coarsely, add them to the mixture, and allow that to sit for another hour or so. Dice the ball of mozzarella into small pieces.

Cook a pound of spaghetti. When it's al dente, turn it into a bowl and top with the mozzarella. Toss it about like crazy until the cheese has become soft and slightly melted. Pour on the tomato and olive oil mixture and toss again. Add salt and pepper to taste.

When you're done you'll probably have olive oil left at the bottom of the bowl. Pour it off and save it for next time.

Perfect summer breakfast.
Lemon-scented peach cobbler,
buttermilk crust, warm from
the oven with splashes of cream.

THERE WERE PEACHES AT THE FARMERS' MARKET THIS MORNING, AND I BOUGHT AS many as I could carry, despite the fact that every one was rock hard. As I put them in my basket I thought how sad it is that an entire generation thinks peaches are supposed to be crunchy. They've never experienced a fragile tree-ripened peach that yields beneath your touch, never known that intense fragrance that can perfume an entire room. A perfect peach is one of life's great pleasures, and it is at its best eaten simply, out of hand.

Less perfect peaches, however, offer other pleasures. Peel back the skin and you discover a secret burst of color, a private sunset, hiding just beneath. Slice these peaches into a pan, top them with a carefree crust, bake them into a cobbler, and they are transformed by the oven's heat so that you instantly understand why "peach" has always been a term of endearment.

FRESH PEACH BREAKFAST COBBLER

SHOPPING LIST

4 large peaches

⅓ cup buttermilk

STAPLES

1 lemon

¼–½ cup sugar

1 tablespoon
cornstarch

1 cup flour

1 teaspoon baking
powder

¼ teaspoon baking
soda

½ teaspoon salt

4 tablespoons
(½ stick) butter

Serves 4 or 5

Peel the peaches by dropping them into a pot of boiling water for about 40 seconds and then putting them under cold running water until they're easy to handle; the skins will slip right off. (If the peaches are not ripe, it might take as much as a minute in boiling water before the skins release their grip.)

Slice the peaches directly into a glass or ceramic pie plate, being sure to capture the juice. Squeeze half the lemon over the fruit. Mix the sugar (I prefer ¼ cup, but you might like it a little sweeter) with the cornstarch and stir it into the peaches.

Mix the flour with the baking powder, baking soda, and salt. Cut in the butter and very gently mix in the buttermilk. Plop the damp dough onto the peaches (it won't entirely cover the fruit, but it will spread as it bakes and give the cobbler a rustic air), and bake in a 400-degree oven for about half an hour.

Serve warm, with a pitcher of cream.

Biting into summer.
Sitting on the lawn, feet bare,
eating hot buttered corn.
Just picked. So good.

_____

ON THIS EARLY AUGUST DAY, WHEN I TOLD THE MAN AT THE FARM STAND TO GIVE me the smallest ears of corn, he shot me a skeptical glance. "You want the puny ones?"

It made me think of my mother, who considered herself the queen of corn. The farmer down the road begged to differ, but he knew exactly what she liked; when she called, he'd go into the field to seek out the smallest, youngest, whitest ears. Mom would hang up the phone, put a pot of water on to boil, and grab her keys. Ten minutes later she'd be back and we'd shuck the ears and cook them just long enough to melt the butter.

"I should write a book telling people how to cook corn," Mom often said. "Most people ruin it." I thought of her as I shucked the ears, pulling back the husk to reveal tiny kernels lined up like pearls. I pulled off the soft silk, wondering as I always do if there's any way to weave with it. Then I dropped the ears into boiling water, counted to sixty, pulled them out, slathered them with butter, sprinkled them with salt, and took them outside to eat.

I ate four ears all by myself, thinking that Mom never permitted herself this solitary indulgence. The thought made me sad.

*Sun-warmed tomatoes sprinkled
with salt. The joy of warm biscuits.
Melting cheese. The scent of basil.
The best old-fashioned recipe.*

WHEN MY FRIENDS LEARNED THAT I WAS WORKING ON A COOKBOOK, IT BECAME A
universally acknowledged truth that I must be in need of tomatoes. Every person
in possession of a garden showered them upon me. I piled them in the kitchen,
and on this morning, when I put the water on for coffee, the sight of those
gorgeous red orbs, fat and shiny as Christmas ornaments, gave me a sudden sharp
taste memory of James Beard's tomato pie.

The first time I met the great man, I told him, breathlessly, that I made his
tomato pie recipe all the time. "Really?" he said, turning a sardonic eye on me. I
immediately wished I'd come up with a more sophisticated dish.

And yet I continue to love this one. There's something so flat-out American
about the flavor of cheese-scented mayonnaise when it curls into the tomatoes on
a biscuit crust. I would not want to write a cookbook that did not include this
classic.

JAMES BEARD'S TOMATO PIE

SHOPPING LIST
¾ cup buttermilk
4–6 ripe tomatoes
  (about 2 pounds)
fresh basil leaves
1 cup grated sharp
  cheddar cheese
1½ cups
  mayonnaise

STAPLES
2 cups flour
2½ teaspoons
  baking powder
salt
½ teaspoon
  baking soda
6 tablespoons butter
parsley
pepper

Makes 6 small servings

Begin by making biscuit dough. Any biscuit recipe will do, and in a pinch you could use the ones you find in the freezer case of your supermarket. But I like the flavor of this buttermilk biscuit, and the way it looks with the little green flecks of parsley dancing through it.

Preheat the oven to 375 degrees. Combine the flour with the baking powder, ½ teaspoon salt, and baking soda. Cut in the butter until it's the size of peas, and add a little flurry of chopped parsley (mostly because it looks pretty). Stir in buttermilk until the dough holds together, then turn out onto a floured surface and knead a few minutes. Pat the dough into the bottom and sides of a buttered 9-inch pie pan.

Cover the biscuit dough with the tomatoes, sliced into nice fat rounds. Sprinkle with salt and pepper. Shower a couple of tablespoons of shredded basil on top.

Mix the grated cheddar cheese with the mayonnaise and spread the mixture on top of the tomatoes.

Bake for about 35 minutes, or until the top is golden brown. On a hot summer night it makes a satisfying little meal.

Fresh morning, no clouds.
Thickly sliced tomatoes, salt sparkling
on top. Freshly buttered bread.
Scent of summer lingers on my fingers.

THE COOKBOOK WASN'T MY ONLY SUMMER PROJECT. I WAS ALSO WORKING ON AN introduction to a new American edition of Elizabeth David recipes. The more I read about England's most important food writer, the better I liked her. Elizabeth David changed the way England ate; she was Julia Child, James Beard, and Chuck Williams (for a while she sold kitchenware products), rolled into one.

American cookbook writers tend to be sensible people. At the very least, we attempt to create the illusion that we are sober counselors handing down sage advice. Ms. David was cut from different cloth. She was, I discovered, a wild woman who sailed off to Europe with a married lover on the eve of World War II. Landing in Sicily on the day Il Duce declared war on England, she spent her war in Greece and Egypt. She lost the lover, married an officer, and apparently ate very well.

Being stranded in strange new lands did not bother Ms. David. Returning to a dreary England was another matter. Food was rationed, the weather was cold, the colors drab. Elizabeth David was depressed. To cheer herself up she wrote about the food she'd eaten in the Mediterranean: lemons, olive oil, tomatoes, sardines . . .

The recipes are as lively as the woman who wrote them. David refuses to take you by the hand and walk you through in measured steps. To her, cooking is a dance; she may be leading, but you need to keep up. She lures you into the kitchen, twirls you around, and then goes waltzing off. To cook with Elizabeth David, I found, is to keep tasting as you reinvent each dish. Even when you follow her directions for a simple dish of tomatoes and cream, you end up making it your own.

TOMATOES AND CREAM

DAVID PEELED TOMATOES, SALTED THEM, AND POURED CREAM OVER THE TOP. I did something even simpler: I sliced ripe tomatoes, showered them with Maldon salt, and covered them with cream. Then I snipped a bit of basil over the top. I like this so much that I sometimes find myself literally licking the plate.

The next day I read her recipe for stuffed tomatoes and went into the kitchen to create my own version. Don't even think about trying this unless you've got really good, perfectly ripe tomatoes.

STUFFED TOMATOES

SHOPPING LIST
4 ripe tomatoes
1 bunch flat leaf
  parsley
fresh basil
black olives

STAPLES
salt
2 cloves garlic
  (minced)
2 anchovy fillets
  (chopped)
vinegar
pepper
bread crumbs
  (see recipe,
  page 17)
Parmesan cheese

Serves 4

Cut the tops off a few plump tomatoes, core them, and cut out the seedy insides. Discard the seeds and reserve the pulp. Sprinkle a bit of salt into the tomatoes and turn them upside down to drain for about an hour.

Chop the parsley very fine, add the minced garlic, chopped fillets of anchovy, a bit of basil, and the tomato pulp. Add a splash of vinegar and salt and pepper to taste. You might also want to add a couple of chopped black olives, a handful of good bread crumbs, and/or a bit of grated Parmesan cheese. This is a forgiving recipe; you can afford to be creative.

When the tomatoes are drained, fill them with the green mixture and allow them to sit for an hour or so, to blend the flavors. Serve as is; these are great with chicken. (They are also great baked in a medium oven for about half an hour.)

Foggy, foggy, foggy. Eating sunshine: tomatoes whirled with cucumbers, onions, peppers. Splash of vinegar. Crunch of crouton. Better weather.

SPENDING TIME WITH ELIZABETH DAVID WAS VERY LIBERATING, AND I FOUND MYSELF walking through the farmers' market looking at the vegetables with new eyes. What would she do with these peppers and onions? When I found a farmer offering slightly overripe tomatoes at a bargain price, I had my answer: gazpacho. The most seasonal dish I know, gazpacho is not worth making with tepid peppers or sad tomatoes.

GAZPACHO

SHOPPING LIST
2 pounds ripe
  tomatoes
  (don't peel them)
watermelon
1 cucumber (peeled
  and chopped)
leafy herbs (optional)

STAPLES
½ onion (coarsely
  chopped)
1 clove garlic
2 tablespoons olive
  oil
2 tablespoons good
  vinegar
salt
pepper
croutons

Serves 4 to 6

Gazpacho is basically a liquid tomato salad. You take a bunch of ripe tomatoes and whirl them in a blender with a few compatible vegetables. I generally add chopped onion, cucumber, and a small amount of garlic, but you could also use bell peppers. Watermelon makes a nice addition. And if you have some leafy herbs, throw them in as well.

When you're filling your blender, put the softest vegetables in first. I began with very ripe tomatoes and a couple of chunks of watermelon. Then I added the onion, the cucumber, and the garlic. I splashed in equal amounts of olive oil and good vinegar and turned on the blender. I like chunky gazpacho, but you can keep blending until it's perfectly smooth if that's your desire. I tasted for seasoning and added salt and pepper and a bit more vinegar. Then I let it rest in the refrigerator for a couple of hours so the flavors could get acquainted.

When it was time to eat, I gave it a stir and poured it into attractive bowls. I diced up a few crunchy vegetables—cucumbers, peppers, or carrots—and scattered them across the top. Sometimes I'll shred a leaf of basil, parsley, or celery onto the soup, and if I have leftover pesto, I'll spoon that on top. A few fat homemade croutons, a couple of drops of olive oil, and the soup is ready to present. Elizabeth David would definitely approve.

Lovely light at 5:30 a.m.
Kitchen in the misty morning. Creamy
corn pudding, sparked with chives.
Back to bed. Delicious dreams.

I'D BEEN DREAMING THAT I WAS BEING CHASED ACROSS A FIELD BY AN ANGRY ARMY of produce. The irate ingredients of all the recipes that hadn't worked, they shook their leaves and rattled their roots as they hurled rotten fruit at my head.

"This is ridiculous," I muttered, getting out of bed. But I knew exactly where the dream had come from: my guilty conscience. It was late August, and the corn I'd bought the day before had been starchy and mealy—what my mother would have derided as "horse corn." Disgusted, I'd shucked two ears and thrown the rest away.

Now, ashamed of the waste, I went into the kitchen to retrieve the shunned ears. I was barely awake, but I grated kernels and broke eggs, watching the sun rise through the trees and paint the sky copper. As the air grew warmer, the birds began their chorus. I chopped some chives and threw them in as well.

The pudding came together quickly, and it was not yet six when I put it in the oven, set the alarm, and went back to sleep for another hour.

This time no angry vegetables invaded my dreams. When the alarm sounded, I went into the kitchen; it smelled like just-picked corn. I made coffee and pulled the puffed golden pudding from the oven.

The scent of caffeine had woken Michael, who came padding into the kitchen. "The cookbook may be giving you nightmares," he said, spooning up some of the soft, sweet pudding, "but as far as I'm concerned it's working out nicely."

"But the cookbook's almost done," I said. Michael gave me a sharp glance; he'd heard the fear behind the words.

"You'll think of something else to do," he said. I wished I had his confidence.

CORN PUDDING

SHOPPING LIST
6 ears fresh corn

STAPLES
1 cup cream
2 tablespoons sugar
¼ cup flour
1 teaspoon salt
5 eggs
6 tablespoons
 (¾ stick)
 unsalted butter

Serves 6

Using a box grater, coarsely grate the kernels off 4 ears of corn. Use a sharp knife to cut the kernels from the other 2 ears.

Put the cobs in a large skillet with the cream and cook over low heat until the cream is reduced to between ½ and ¾ cup and has been infused with the flavor of corn.

Combine all the corn kernels with the sugar, flour, and salt in a large mixing bowl. Stir in the infused cream. Break in the eggs, one by one, stirring to incorporate after each addition.

Put the butter into a cast iron skillet or an 8-inch-square Pyrex pan and set it in a 350-degree oven until it has melted. Pour the butter into the corn mixture and give it a few good stirs. Pour the corn mixture back into the skillet or baking dish and bake for about 1 hour, until it has turned golden and set.

This not only makes a spectacular breakfast, but it's a great side dish with a simple dinner. And the leftovers, reheated, make a very pleasing snack.

Rain-washed, crystalline sky.
Summer ebbing away. Sun-warmed
plums, fragile, fragrant on this bright
morning. Each bite a tiny farewell.

———————

THE SIGHT OF ITALIAN PRUNE PLUMS IN THE MARKET FELT LIKE A BAD OMEN, another sign that the easy season was almost over.

They were everywhere, grinning maliciously at me, and in the end I gave in and bought a quart. Driving home I picked one up and took a bite, forgetting that in their natural state prune plums are squishy and bland. I looked morosely down at the half-eaten plum, thinking it was a sad excuse for fruit.

But in the oven they were transformed, their tender flesh becoming perfumed in the heat. I'd forgotten that, and as I ate the first slice of this extremely satisfying torte I closed my eyes and made a wish: if only fall would turn out to be an equally pleasant surprise.

A SLIGHT VARIATION ON MARIAN BURROS'S FAMOUS PLUM TORTE

SHOPPING LIST
20 small (or 12 large)
  Italian prune plums
¾ cup buttermilk

STAPLES
8 tablespoons
  (1 stick) unsalted
  butter
½ cup sugar
2 eggs
½ teaspoon vanilla
1 lemon
1½ cups flour
1 teaspoon baking
  powder
½ teaspoon salt
½ teaspoon
  baking soda
4 tablespoons
  brown sugar

This is one of America's best-loved cakes. It's incredibly easy and incredibly delicious. I've tinkered with Marian's recipe a bit—made it a bit richer, a bit plummier. I'm sure Marian won't mind.

Butter a 9-inch round springform or cake pan with high sides (if you use a short-sided, inexpensive pan it might overflow), line the bottom with waxed or parchment paper, butter that, then dust lightly with flour.

Cut the plums in half and remove the pits.

Beat the butter with a generous ½ cup of sugar until light. Add the eggs. Beat in the buttermilk (plain yogurt would do, too), the vanilla, and the grated rind of the lemon.

Mix the flour with the baking powder, salt, and baking soda and add to the butter mixture, beating just until combined.

Spoon half of the batter into the cake pan. Cover with half of the plums, cut side down, and sprinkle with 2 tablespoons of brown sugar (white sugar will do if you don't have brown). Spoon in the rest of the batter and cover with the remaining plum halves, this time cut side up. Sprinkle with 2 more tablespoons of brown sugar and bake in a 350-degree oven for 50 minutes to an hour. The cake should be firm, golden, and pulling away from the side of the pan.

Cool on a cake rack for about 15 minutes. then invert onto a plate, peel off the parchment paper, and invert again onto another plate. It's best served warm, with dollops of softly whipped cream, although it's good at any temperature.

Mysterious misty morning.
Crows swoop in, take off wheeling,
cawing. Last tomatoes roasted into soup.
Final flavor. Summer's over.

———

THE TOMATOES IN THE MARKET WERE BARELY RED. THE FIRST FROST LOOMED. THE farmers, no longer willing to gamble on the weather, had snatched them from the vines slightly underripe.

Still, I filled my basket. On a chilly September day, tomato soup is a fine segue from one season to the next. It's the flavor of the last one folded into the temperature of the next—and a good way to make summer last a little longer.

ROASTED TOMATO SOUP

SHOPPING LIST
2 pounds tomatoes

STAPLES
2 onions (quartered)
4–5 cloves garlic
 (peeled)
olive oil
salt

Serves 4

Core the tomatoes, cut them into quarters, and put them on a sheet pan lined with parchment paper. Add the onions and the cloves of garlic. Sprinkle them with olive oil and a few good shakes of salt and roast them in a 375-degree oven for about 45 minutes.

Puree the tomatoes, onions, and garlic in a blender, adding water to get the consistency you like (1 cup will make a fairly thick soup; 2 cups will make a fairly thin one). Taste for seasoning. If you want a completely smooth soup, strain it, but the bits of onion and tomato skin add what I consider a delightful chew. If you're feeling profligate, swirl in a bit of cream just before serving.

Fall's back. Cool silver sky.
Black balsamic-splashed beans. Bright
white rice. Crisp-edged fried egg.
Brilliant habanero salsa: fresh, hot.

WHEN I STEPPED OUTSIDE, THE DEW ON THE GRASS CHILLED MY FEET, MAKING IT VERY clear that the days of outdoor showers and breakfast on the lawn were over until next year. I went inside, laid a fire in the grate, and contemplated breakfast.

I'd made black beans the night before, and I reheated them as I made some rice. On a cool morning there's nothing like a plate of rice and beans to bring the world into focus. I fried an egg and spooned on a dollop of really hot salsa to jolt me into the day.

Beans are easy—if you have a good source. Antique beans are such stale curmudgeons they refuse to get soft. Try to buy your beans from a shop that does a brisk bean business; if you end up with year-old beans, you'll be standing by the stove for hours, cursing.

GREAT BLACK BEANS

SHOPPING LIST
1 cup dried black
  turtle beans
3 tablespoons lard
  or bacon drippings
1 sprig epazote
  (or 1 tablespoon
  dried epazote)
  (optional)
1 chile pepper
  (I prefer habanero)
  (optional)
cream sherry

STAPLES
1 onion (chopped)
garlic (optional)
soy sauce
balsamic vinegar
salt, pepper

You want to soak your beans before you cook them. Wash a cup of them (they're often dusty) and paw through to make sure there are no stones. Cover them with water and soak them overnight. In the morning, drain them and add 3 to 4 cups of water (the water should be a good inch above the beans in the pot), along with the onion and a few tablespoons of lard or bacon drippings.

If you are fortunate enough to have a source for epazote, add that. Epazote is used throughout Mexico and Central America for its herbal flavor—it reminds me a bit of oregano— and because it supposedly reduces the flatulence brought on by beans. Most Latino bodegas sell it dried.

You could add a couple of cloves of garlic if you like, and a chopped chile or two as well. Bring to a boil, cover, turn the heat down, and simmer until the beans are tender; depending on the age of your beans, this could take anywhere from 1 to 3 hours. Remove the epazote and stir in a healthy glug of cream sherry, a few splashes of soy sauce, and a bit of balsamic vinegar. Taste for seasoning. Now add as much salt and pepper as you like.

To make a quick taco, grate some cheddar cheese onto a tortilla, wrap it in a paper towel, and zap it in the microwave for about 30 seconds, until the cheese has melted. Pry the tortilla open, spoon in some warmed black beans and freshly chopped tomatoes, chiles, cilantro, and onions. Roll up and serve with hot sauce.

The lonely sound of rain thrums through this fog-shrouded valley. Need some spice. Yogurt-cloaked chicken scented with curry. So consoled.

———

THE LAST RECIPE TO TEST. I DREW IT OUT, NOT WANTING TO ADMIT THAT THE COOKbook was finished, that it was time to move on to whatever was coming next.

Playing for time, I fiddled with the recipe. It was an old favorite, a dish we developed for *Gourmet's* television show *Diary of a Foodie.* The yogurt marinade turns ordinary chicken legs into something smooth, velvety, and filled with mysterious flavors. The lactic acid tenderizes the meat, allowing the spices to penetrate the flesh until it sings with flavor. The high heat of the oven gives it a few attractive charred spots, which makes the chicken look as delicious as it tastes. But now I began measuring fresh spices and squeezing limes, trying to make a good recipe better.

"TANDOORI" CHICKEN

Pull the skin off the chicken.

Chop up a handful of mint and another of cilantro and stir them into the yogurt, along with the coriander, cumin, turmeric, cayenne, garlic, and a tablespoon of fresh minced ginger. Slice the shallot and add that to the mix. Squeeze in the juice of the lime and add a teaspoon of salt, a lot of freshly ground black pepper, and dashes of cinnamon and paprika.

Slather the chicken all over with this mixture, and allow it to sit in the refrigerator for 4 to 12 hours.

Preheat the oven to 500 degrees. Put the chicken on a foil-lined baking pan and roast for about half an hour. (It's not necessary, but if you have a rack, set the chicken on the rack over the foil-lined pan.) Wonderful finger food—and terrific cold the next day.

Four a.m. Can't sleep. Motorcycle screams up the highway. Strange birds chirp. One lonely siren. Hot fudge on vanilla ice cream. Better!

———

SUMMER OVER, COOKBOOK DONE, I WAS BACK IN A STATE OF ANXIETY. I LAY FRETFULLY in bed at night, knowing what I should be doing and yet reluctant to commit.

I have always wanted to write a novel. I'm an avid reader, and fiction is my first love; the ability to inhabit someone else's space, even for a little while, makes life so much richer. I've dreamed of writing a novel since I was very small, but I'd always put it off, finding all the reasons why I couldn't do it. I had a job, a child, no time. Now my child was grown, my job was over, and my days belonged to me. The time had finally come. Surely it couldn't be that difficult?

But the middle of the night is no time to look for answers. I got out of bed and went into the kitchen. I wanted some hot dark fudge poured over cold white ice cream, and I knew that just stirring up the sauce would improve my mood.

HOT FUDGE TO SOOTHE YOUR SOUL

SHOPPING LIST

⅔ cup heavy cream

¼ cup Dutch
  process cocoa
  powder

½ cup light
  corn syrup

1 teaspoon instant
  espresso powder

STAPLES

⅓ cup brown sugar

salt

6 ounces bittersweet
  chocolate

2 tablespoons unsalted
  butter

1 teaspoon vanilla

Makes about 2 cups

I began foraging for ingredients. Cream, yes, we had it. I poured it into a pot, stirred in brown sugar, a pinch of salt, and Dutch process cocoa. Then I stirred in corn syrup. It's a horrid industrial product, but I keep it around for moments like this; it adds body and shine and prevents sugar crystals from forming. Hot fudge sundaes are not for the guilt-prone.

I chopped the deep, dense chocolate, dropped it into the pot, and watched it slowly give itself to the cream. Stirring constantly, I inhaled the scent: I was already feeling better.

When the sauce began to ripple like satin I stirred in the butter and instant espresso powder. (Coffee, to me at least, makes chocolate taste more chocolatey.) At the very end I added a teaspoon of vanilla.

I poured the warm fudge onto a pint of vanilla ice cream, watched it harden, pulled up a stool, and ate the entire thing. It doesn't happen often, but every once in a while a person needs to utterly indulge herself. Then I went back to bed and fell into an easy sleep.

Clouds coming in. Chilly outside.
In here the generous scent of chicken
stock swirls through the air.
A solace and a promise.

THE LEAVES WERE CHANGING. I SAT AT THE WINDOW THINKING ABOUT A NOVEL, trying to gather my thoughts into a coherent story.

Automatically, I went into the kitchen and began assembling the ingredients for chicken stock. It is the most constant presence in my life; in summer and winter, good times and bad, I make chicken stock.

It is, of course, one of the kitchen's most reliable building blocks. A stock-filled freezer is an insurance policy, a guarantee of future risottos, stews, sauces, and stir-fries. Reduced, stock makes every vegetable taste better. And in a pinch there's nothing better than a bowl of chicken soup with an egg beaten in, a few leaves of spinach, some grated Parmesan cheese.

But mostly I make chicken stock because I enjoy the long, slow ritual. I delight in standing at the stove watching the proteins swirl across the surface like foam on the tide. I like the way the parsley wilts when it hits the hot liquid, and the relentless energy of the onions, rising to the surface no matter how many times you try to push them under.

What I have always loved best is the aroma. As the water turned to broth, filling the kitchen with its cheerful scent, I took a deep breath. It gave me strength and hope. It also gave me an idea. Standing over the pot, I suddenly knew exactly what my novel was going to be about.

CHICKEN STOCK

SHOPPING LIST

1 stewing hen
  (or 6–8 pounds
  of chicken parts)
2 carrots
2 stalks celery

STAPLES

1 or 2 onions
5 sprigs parsley
bay leaf
peppercorns
2 teaspoons salt

Makes about 8 cups

If you can find a stewing hen, buy it; they're the secret to deeply flavored stock. Most commercial chickens are slaughtered at 6 weeks (free-range and organic birds are allowed to live to 14 weeks), but laying hens are spared as long as they're productive. Free-range laying hens generally have 2 years to develop character; at the end of that time they're much too tough to roast, but they make spectacular soup.

If you can't find a stewing hen, buy 6 to 8 pounds of chicken parts (a mixture of legs and wings is good) and put them into a large stockpot. Cover with cold water—about 2 quarts—and bring almost to a boil. Skim off the foam that rises to the top, add the onions (halved), the carrots (washed and cut in half), the celery, the parsley, a bay leaf, and a handful of peppercorns. Add the salt. Partially cover the pot and cook very slowly, so that a bubble rises lazily to the surface every minute or so, for at least 4 hours. Strain the broth, let the liquid come to room temperature, then chill overnight. (The meat will have given its flavor and nutrients to the broth, but you can still shred it for chicken salad if you like.)

Remove the fat from the top of the broth, divide into containers, and store in the refrigerator for up to 5 days, or in the freezer for a few months.

Cool, rainy. Autumn's on its way.
Pasta, perhaps? Cauliflower,
olives, anchovies. Rich red wine.
Ripe pears. So fine.

·————

AS THE DAYS GREW COOLER I TENTATIVELY BEGAN TO WRITE, HEADING OFF TO THE market whenever I ran out of words. My heroine was a young cook with an inspired palate and a passion for food, and I scoured the markets, memorizing sights and sounds and smells, trying to think what she would do with all the foods I found.

The peaches had been replaced by pears, and the leafy greens were making way for the kales and cabbages. Now, strolling between the stalls, I spied a great white cauliflower, as beautiful as a bouquet. I had to buy it.

Cauliflower is the vegetable Michael loves best. I carried it home, wondering what my heroine, with her perfect palate, would make with this lovely vegetable. She'd try bringing out its essential nature by surrounding it with a range of compatible flavors. I conjured up the mellow taste of olives, thinking of how they'd coax out the earthy notes of cauliflower. The bite of capers? The salt of anchovies? And then, just for contrast, she'd probably chop up a few golden raisins to add a subtle note of sweetness.

SAVORY SWEET PASTA FOR MICHAEL

SHOPPING LIST
1 head of cauliflower
¼ cup yellow raisins
  or currants
6 Kalamata olives

STAPLES
olive oil
salt
2 tablespoons unsalted
  butter
6 anchovy fillets
2 cloves garlic
  (minced)
2 teaspoons capers
12 ounces penne
  (dried)
Parmesan cheese

Serves 3

Preheat the oven to 400 degrees.

Separate the cauliflower into florets, gently pulling them apart. Put them on a baking sheet, sprinkle with olive oil and a bit of salt, and roast for 25 minutes, until they just begin to turn golden.

Melt the butter with 2 tablespoons of olive oil in a large skillet and allow the foam to die. Rinse the anchovy fillets and add them to the pan, stirring until they have disintegrated. Add the minced garlic, yellow raisins or currants, and capers, and stir.

Meanwhile, bring a large pot of well-salted water to a boil and cook the penne al dente.

While the pasta cooks, chop up the Kalamata olives and add them to the skillet along with the cauliflower. Cook, stirring, for about 5 minutes. If brown bits are sticking to the bottom of the pan, add a little water to scrape them up.

Drain the pasta, toss with the cauliflower mixture, sprinkle with grated Parmesan cheese, and serve.

The hawks are hunting, hanging motionless in cool air. Sun and fog playing tag. Scent of wood smoke. The season's changed.

EARLY OCTOBER. THE FIRST ANNIVERSARY OF *GOURMET*'S DEMISE. ALL DAY PEOPLE had been calling to commiserate, asking if I'd found a job. "I've been writing," I said, but when they asked exactly what, I tried to keep my answer vague. I had already discovered that when it came to fiction I could either write the book or talk about it. I couldn't do both, and I didn't want to waste a single word.

"Let's go to the movies." Michael sensed that the calls were making me uncomfortable, reminding me of all the *Gourmet* grief.

Rushing around before we left, I put some russet potatoes into a slow oven, washed and shredded a handful of Brussels sprouts, and diced an onion. Just before walking out the door, I set some lamb chops on the counter to come to room temperature.

QUICK, EASY DO-AHEAD DINNER FOR TWO PEOPLE: A TEN-MINUTE MEAL

HOME AGAIN, I CHECKED THE POTATOES; THEY WERE SOFT, FORGIV-ing, perfect. I tossed the onion into a pan with a bit of oil and a smashed clove of garlic and waited for them to grow fragrant. Then I added salt and pepper, some chile pepper flakes, and a generous tablespoon of miso. Finally I threw the shredded sprouts into the pan and stirred them about.

The sprouts began to sizzle and wilt. I salted the chops and put them into a very hot pan, allowing them to get a good crust on the outside while still remaining bright pink within (about 4 minutes a side). While they rested on a platter, I sprinkled a few drops—no more than half a teaspoon each—of maple syrup and soy sauce into the sprouts, for the final layer of flavor.

I lit the candles and poured the wine, and we sat down. The lamb chops were crisp, the potatoes baked almost to melt-ing, the sprouts sweet, salty, and spicy.

The cooking had taken almost no time, but we sat at that table for hours, sharing our thoughts on *The Social Network,* grateful to be together in the quiet calm of the house.

Remembering how miserable I'd been at this time the year before, I smiled. Since then, I'd discovered the many things that I will never need. A year ago, when the movie ended, we probably would have gone out to eat. Someplace fancy, perhaps, where we'd have spent a pile of money to sit surrounded by strangers, minding our manners and lowering our voices each time a waiter appeared. Or we might have chosen one of the chic noisy places and sat shouting at each other over the din. Liv-ing in that fast-paced world, I would not have thought to come home and make a quiet meal.

I looked over at my computer, where the novel was waiting. I poured a glass of wine and sipped it slowly. Then I gathered up the dishes, took them to the kitchen, and plunged my hands into the warm water.

ACKNOWLEDGMENTS

This volume never intended to grow into a book. It was just a little diary I kept for myself, a record of what was happening in my kitchen. But when I showed it to my friends, it suddenly began to blossom.

It started with my agent, Kathy Robbins, who urged me to turn my notes into a book.

My editor, Susan Kamil, liked the manuscript so well she insisted, over my strenuous objections, that it was crying out for photographs.

At that point I turned to the former creative director of *Gourmet,* Richard Ferretti, who said I *had* to call photographer Mikkel Vang.

Richard is never wrong; working with Mikkel was pure joy. "This is not going to look like any other cookbook," he said. "It's going to be just you, me, and a camera. No food stylists, no prop people, no lights, no tricks." For a couple of days each season, he came to my house and I cooked. When each dish was done we went to the cupboard, chose a plate, and Mikkel took the picture. Then we ate. Between dishes we walked in the woods, kicked leaves, and in winter threw snowballs at each other.

It was my good fortune to have my assistant, Sukey Bernard, join us. When I said it wasn't necessary she said, "I'll come anyway; you never know, you might need me." There's no way I could have done it without her. She's kind, smart, unflappable—and she has a wonderful appetite. (On waffle morning, she and Mikkel each ate four.)

Thanks, too, to Robin McKay, who tested all the recipes and gave me great notes. "Sometimes," she wrote about one, "I am glad that I am alone in the kitchen. This was one of those times . . . licked the plate clean!"

Most of the plates I use every day were made by my neighbor, the wonderful ceramic artist Mary Anne Davis. When I told her what I was up to, she threw open the doors to her studio and said, "Take anything you want."

The food folks in Columbia County and the Berkshires are very special people, and I'm grateful to all the farmers, bakers, and artisans who make my cooking possible. Matt Rubiner, at Rubiner's in Great Barrington, is a constant source of inspiration. And on a summer day, a visit to Staron's farm stand in Chatham always lifts my heart.

Special thanks to Susan Turner, who created this gorgeous layout from so many disparate elements. I just wish my father, the book designer, was around to see it. Thank, too, to Evan Sung, for the lovely jacket photo.

My deep gratitude goes to the many people at Random House who nurtured this project: Gina Centrello, Avideh Bashirrad, Theresa Zoro, Sally Marvin, Leigh Marchant, Amelia Zalcman, Molly Turpin, and the indefatigable Christine Mykityshyn.

And finally thanks to all my Twitter friends; you helped me survive a very difficult year. I'm not sure I could have done it without you.

SUBJECT INDEX

Page numbers of photographs appear in italics.

E

Easter, 182, 185
English food, 283, 285
Eriquez, Gina Marie Miraglia, 6

F

Fairway Market, New York City, 150–51,
    164, 164–65
Fannie Farmer Cookbook, The, 259
Farmer, Fannie Merritt, xix, 132
farmers' markets and farm stands, *12, 15, 18,*
    31, *269*, 277
    apple varieties, 35
    end of fall offerings, 31
    first new potatoes, 269
    Italian prune plums in, 291
    last tomatoes of the season, 293
    lobster at, 253
    mid-April, in-season asparagus, 186
    New England, 13–14
    overripe tomatoes and, 286
    peaches, 277
    sour cherries, 254
"Fat Cat" (Reichl), 223
Ferretti, Richard, 5
For You, Mom. Finally (Reichl), 188, 191
Fourth of July picnic, 242–45
    menu, 242

G

Gourmet Cookbook, The (ed. Reichl)
    pancake recipe, 241
Gourmet magazine, xv
    April issue, final year, 95–96
    cessation of publication, xv, 5–6, 163,
        303
    "expanding the brand," xv
    last party, 20
    most requested recipe, 139
    public reaction to magazine closing, 9,
        10, 33, 53, 105, 115
    Reichl and staff, reaction to closing of
        magazine, 5, 6
    Reichl's office, 5
    Reichl's office, cleaning out, 21–22, 27
    rejected custard recipe, 99
    staff reunion, 163–64
    test kitchen, 6, 21

Gourmet Today (ed. Reichl), xv, 27, 59
    "the radio satellite tour," 57
    Reichl on book tour, xv–xvi, 9–10, 19,
        20, 21, 31, 33, 53
Green, Robin, 21, 27–28
Grimes, Paul, 6

H

Henderson, Fergus, 197
Hudson River Valley, 88, 259

I

Île d'Oléron, France, 88
Italy
    Basilicata region, anchovy bread and, 39
    Christmas in Tuscany, 145
    puntarelle in, 163
    Reichl trip, artisanal mozzarella maker
        and, 274

K

King, Carole, 242, 243
Knauer, Ian, 6

L

Lahey, Jim, 130
Le Pigeon restaurant, Portland, Oregon, 191
Lincoln, Mary J., 132, 133
Longchamps restaurant, New York City, 120
Los Angeles, California, 198, 202
Lupa restaurant, New York City, 57–58

M

matzoh, spiced, from Blue Ribbon
    Bakery, 47
McDormand, Fran, 19
Mitsuwa supermarket, Edgewater, New
    Jersey, 25
Mmmmm: A Feastiary (Reichl), xvi
My Bread (Lahey), 130

N

Newhouse, Si, 5
New York City, 142
    artisanal butcher shop, 153
    Asian restaurants, Flushing, 22
    Chinatown, 20, 148
    classic coffee shop and toasted corn muf-
        fins, 115

Fairway market, 150–51, *164*, 164–65
Famous Ray's pizza, mozzarella and, 274
food shopping in, 145, 148, 161, 164–65,
  182
halal cart on the corner of Sixth Avenue
  and Forty-Third Street, 117
Koreatown, 166
Longchamps restaurant, 120
Lupa restaurant, 57–58
old lady begging in subway, 158, 161,
  163
Prune restaurant, 116
Reichl encounter with *Gourmet* reader,
  115
Reichl in, after college graduation, xvi
Reichl rambling in, xvi
Reichl returning home to, 140–41, 145
spring in, *157*, 171, *173*, *179*
Zabar's, *170*
New York state, Reichl/Singer house, 69,
  210
bears and, 260, 262, 264
blue moon in the Berkshires, 76
country fall and, *50*, *69*, 299, 303
country fall and wild turkeys, 43
country spring and, 179, 180, *181*, 185,
  210
country summer and, *227*, 228–29, 236,
  238, 250, *250*, 260, *261*, 262, 264, 265,
  268, 272, 274, 295
country summer thunderstorm, 266
country winter and, 79, 80–81, *82*, 87,
  89, 90, 94, 95, 102, *103*, 107, *109*, 110,
  112, *113*, 119, 123, 129, 136
country winter and moose sighting, 84,
  86
country winter and walking in the
  woods, 75
interior, *239*
kitchen at, xxi, *237*
purslane growing wild at, 247
summer solstice celebration, 240
sunrise, *83*, 265
sunset, *250*
Thanksgiving at, 33–49, 51–52

O

Ochoa, Laurie, 21, 27–28

P

Peconic Bay scallops, 64
Portland, Oregon, 191, 192, 194
  food carts, 194
Prune restaurant, New York City, 116
Puget Sound oysters, 77, *78*

R

recipe writing, xix–xx
  before standardized measurements, 132
Reichl, Ernst, 71
Reichl, Ruth
  **—career, television shows, and
    books**
  Adventures with Ruth launch party, 20
  Adventures with Ruth television show, xv,
    19
  American edition, Elizabeth David reci-
    pes, introduction for, 283, 285
  cookbook idea and development, 164,
    169, 171, 173, 179, 191, 231, 250, 254,
    266, 282, 289, 296
  as food critic and editor, xvi, 41
  For You, Mom. Finally, paperback release
    and book tour, 188, 191, 192, 194, 196,
    197, 198, 202
  as *Gourmet* magazine editor in chief, xv,
    xvi, 27, 95, 96–97, 99
  Gourmet magazine folding and emotional
    consequences, xv, 5–6, 10, 27, 33, 43,
    59, 61, 64, 104–5, 123, 124, 132, 135,
    140, 163, 244, 247, 303, 304
  Gourmet magazine staff, 5–6, 20, 21, 116
  Gourmet magazine staff reunion, 163–64
  Gourmet Today cookbook promotion,
    xv–xvi, 9–10, 19, 20, 21, 31, 33, 53, 57
  interviewed by Anderson Cooper, 140
  job hunt, 141, 142, 146–47, 163
  writing and, xvi, 87, 132, 135, 148, 164,
    221, 266, 298, 299, 301, 302, 303, 304
  Zócalo panel, Los Angeles, 104–5
  —cooking and food
  act of cooking and, xvii
  apples, buying and storing, 35, 90
  apricots, as favorite food, 207
  asparagus in-season and, 186
  best biscuits ever tasted, 231
  best salmon, Copper River, 176

Reichl, Ruth (cont'd):
  breakfast for dinner, 240
  cake baking, 63
  cheese shopping, 274
  childhood food, 230
  chili secrets of, 44
  comfort foods, 141, 142, 145
  cooking as essential to, 225
  cooking as meditation, xvi–xvii
  cooking as therapy, 135, 147
  eggplant and, 151
  favorite morning foods, 240
  first tomatillo, 127
  food shopping, artisanal butcher shop,
    153
  food shopping, as part of the cooking
    process, xvii
  food shopping, Chinatown, 148
  food shopping, country butcher shop, 87,
    188
  food shopping, country winter stocking
    up, 107
  food shopping, Fairway Market, 150–51,
    164, 164–65
  food shopping, Hollywood farmers' mar-
    ket (and what to do with watery, bland
    strawberries), 105 '
  food shopping, inspiration and, 13–14,
    165, 182, 302 (*see also* farmers' markets
    and farm stands)
  food shopping, Mitsuwa Supermarket, 25
  food shopping, new potatoes, 269 (*see
    also* farmers' markets and farm stands)
  food shopping, puntarelle found, 161
  kitchen contents, xx
  old cookbooks used by, 132
  peaches and, 277
  prepared dishes kept on hand, 6
  recipe philosophy, xix–xx
  "Recipes to Try" folder, 102
  scallops, buying and eating raw, 64–65
  sour cherry obsession, 254
  tacos, preference for Yucatecan pork, 198
  turkey recipes and most embarrassing
    example, 41
  yamaimo ("mountain potato") and,
    25–26

—**life, home, and travel**
in Bangkok, 194
in Berkeley, 1970s, 127–28
bird-watching and indigo bunting
    memory, 258–59
a blue moon and, 76
broken foot, surgery, recuperation, 202,
    205, 206, 207, 211, 213, 225, 231, 242,
    272
Carole King and, 244
cats, Halley and Stella, 13, 54, *55*, 61, 63,
    110, 119, 146, 207, *209*, 211, 266, *267*
cats, Halley's death and ode, 222–23
Christmas and, 71–75
Christmas in Tuscany, 145
city spring and, 161, 163–64, 166, 169,
    172, *173*, 173
communal meal with friends, 27–28
country dinner party, with burgers, 237,
    237, *239*
country dinner party rained out, 271
country winter, hoarfrost seen, 75
country winter, moose sighting and, 84,
    86
country winter, storms and power out-
    ages, *89*, 90, 94, 95, 102, *103*, *109*, 110,
    112, *113*, 129, 136, *137*, 137 (*see also*
    New York state, Reichl/Singer house)
dream of angry vegetables, 289
Easter and, 182, 185
eating out with friends, Flushing,
    Queens, 22
Fourth of July at Tanglewood picnic, 242,
    244
grandmother of, 136
homeless woman in subway and, 161,
    163
in Israel, senior year of college, 244
Italy trip, artisanal mozzarella maker story,
    274
lessons learned, xvii
living in France, 88
lobster eating, 253
memories of her father, 71
memories of her mother, and corn, 280,
    289
New Year's Day, 83

New York apartment and city life, 136, 140–41, 142, 145, 148, 153, 163, 169, *170*, 179, *221, 224*

nightmare, recurring, 61

potluck party and, 76

scooter rental, 231

summer solstice celebration, 240

Thanksgiving and, 33–49, 51–52

Twitter and, xvii, xxi, 65, 99, 112, 129

Ripert, Eric, 205, 206

Rochlin, Margy, 21, 25, 27–28

Rodewald, James, 6

Rucker, Gabriel, 191

Ruggiero, Maggie, 6

S

San Francisco, California, 196, 197

Ferry Building, 197

Zuni restaurant, 197

"scientific cooking," xix

Silpat nonstick surface, using, 44, 192

Silverton, Nancy, 21, 25, 27–28

biscuit recipe from, 233

Simmons, Amelia, xix

Singer, Michael, xvi, 10, 13, 54, 59, 61, 123, 258, 303, 304

country summer and, 271

country winter, moose sighting and, 84, 86

country winter and, 94, 95, 110, 119, 136

favorite vegetable, 302

Fourth of July at Tanglewood picnic, 242

grilling top round steak, 250

lobster eating, 253

New Year's, 77

Prune's bacon and marmalade sandwich and, 116

shoulder surgery, 65, 67, 68, 71

waffle-making by, 211

Singer, Nick, xvi, 61, 84, 213, 258, 259

Christmas and, 71, 75

favorite breakfast, 241

and friend Gemma, 213, 217

hummus making by, 219

Italy trip, artisanal mozzarella maker and, 274

Koreatown meal, 166

quiche making by, 216–17

Thanksgiving and, 39

Stanton, Jeremy, 87, 199

Starker's Restaurant, Kansas City, 9

summer solstice celebration, 240

T

Tanglewood music festival, Lenox, Massachusetts, 242, 244

Tapestry (King), 244

Taylor, James, 242, 244

Thanksgiving, 33–49, 51–52

Tranströmer, Tomas, 94

Trillin, Calvin, 47

Twitter (Reichl's tweets)

about fantasy foods, 205

query on bread dough and no oven, 129

recipes in Twitter form, 171

request for banana bread recipes, 112

tweeting about custard making, with no binder, 99

tweeting about raw scallops, 65

tweeting Ruth Reichl, xxi

virtual friendships, xvii

W

Wallace, Tom, xv

Wiest, Dianne, 19

Willoughby, Doc, 5, 116

Wright, Jeffrey, 19

Y

Yangshuo, China, 19

"You've Got a Friend" (King), 244

Yo-Yo Ma, 242, 244

Z

Zabar's, New York, *170*

Zócalo panel, Los Angeles, 104–5

Zuni restaurant, San Francisco, 197

RECIPE INDEX

broccoli rabe
  about, 65–66
  Bruschetta, *66*, 66
Bruschetta, Broccoli Rabe, 66, *66*
Brussels sprouts
  Quick, Easy Do-Ahead Dinner for Two
    People: A Ten-Minute Meal, 304
Buckwheat Blini, 182, *183*
Bulgogi
  about, 166, 168
  Bulgogi at Home, *167*, 168
butter
  brown, how to make, 15
  Buttermilk Potatoes with Brown
    Butter, 15
  Buttery Flaky Fantastic Biscuits, 234
buttermilk
  about, 14
  biscuits, 283
  Buttermilk Potatoes with Brown
    Butter, 15
  Buttery Flaky Fantastic Biscuits, 234
  Fried Oysters, 192, *193*, 194
  Real Fried Chicken, *243*, 245
butternut squash
  Butternut Squash Soup, 32, *32*
Butter-Toasted Apricot Oatmeal, 95
Buttery Flaky Fantastic Biscuits, 234

C

cabbage
  Borscht Salad (À La Fergus Henderson),
    196, 197
  My Grandmother's Cabbage, 136–37
  Spicy Korean Rice Sticks with Shrimp
    and Vegetables, *22*, 23
cakes
  Big New York Cheesecake, *138*, 139
  The Cake That Cures Everything
    (chocolate cake), *62*, 63–64
  Gingered Applesauce Cake Glazed with
    Caramel, *91*, *92*, 93
  January Pudding, 102
  Lemon Pudding Cake, 165
  Mrs. Lincoln's Genuine Sponge Cake,
    133
  Perfect Pound Cake, 38

A Slight Variation on Marian Burros's
    Famous Plum Torte, 292
  Strawberry Shortcake, *232*, 233, *235*
capers
  Savory Sweet Pasta for Michael, 303
  Salsa Verde, *134*, 135
Caramel Glaze, 93
carrot(s)
  Beef, Wine, and Onion Stew, 110
  Butternut Squash Soup, 32, *32*
cashews
  Tart Lemon Tart, 100, *101*
cauliflower
  Savory Sweet Pasta for Michael,
    303
caviar (salmon or trout)
  Buckwheat Blini, 182, *183*
  Sea Urchin Pasta, *204*, 206
cheddar cheese
  The Diva of Grilled Cheese, *85*, 86
  Great Black Beans Taco, 295–96
  James Beard's Tomato Pie, 283
Cheesecake, Big New York, *138*, 139
cherry(ies), sour
  how to pit, 254
  Sour Cherry Crostata, *255*, *256*,
    257–58
  Sour Cherry Lemonade, 260
chicken
  brining, 180
  Chicken Fricassee, 88
  Chicken Liver Pâté, 6, 7, *8*, 9
  Chicken Stock, 301
  Chicken Stock, about, 301
  Chicken Stock, how to reduce, 195
  Food Cart Curry Chicken, 118
  Gluten-Free Egg-Wrapped Dumplings
    from Yangshuo, 20
  Grilled Chicken, 180–81
  Khao Man Gai, 195
  marinade for (curry-based), 118
  marinade for (yogurt-based), 297
  My Version of Pollo Alla Diavola, *56*,
    58, *58*
  Real Fried Chicken, *243*, 245
  Roast Chicken with Potatoes, 76
  "Tandoori" Chicken, 297

D

desserts
  Apple Crisp, *36*, 37
  Apricot Pie, *208*, 209
  Big New York Cheesecake, *138*, 139
  The Cake That Cures Everything
    (chocolate cake), *62*, 63–64
  Cranberry Pecan Crostata, 43–44
  Fresh Peach Breakfast Cobbler, 279, *279*
  Hot Fudge to Soothe Your Soul, 299
  ice cream sandwiches (with Fannie
    Farmer's Classic Yeast-Raised Waffles),
    212
  January Pudding, 102
  Lemon Panna Cotta, 100
  Lemon Pudding Cake, 165
  Linzer Torte, *70*, 71–72
  Mrs. Lincoln's Genuine Sponge Cake,
    133
  Nectarine Galette, 18
  Perfect Pound Cake, 38
  Rhubarb Sundaes, 179
  Roasted Winter Strawberries with Ice
    Cream, 105
  A Slight Variation on Marian Burros's
    Famous Plum Torte, 292
  Sour Cherry Crostata, *255*, *256*, 257–58
  Strawberry Shortcake, *232*, 233, *235*
  Tart Lemon Tart, 100, *101*
  Watermelon Sundae, 206
Deviled Eggs, Pink, *184*, 185–86, *186*
Diva of Grilled Cheese, The, *85*, 86
duck
  about, 272
  curing, 191
  Duck Carpaccio, *190*, 191
  Magret of Duck with Easy Orange
    Sauce, 273
  marinade for, 273
dumplings
  Chinese Dumplings, *48*, 48–49, *49*
  Gluten-Free Egg-Wrapped Dumplings
    from Yangshuo, 20

E

Easy "Bolognese," 28–30, *29*
Easy Vietnamese Caramelized Pork, 262

Easter
  Buckwheat Blini, 182, *183*
  Pink Deviled Eggs, *184*, 185–86
eggplant
  about, 174
  Asian Eggplant Salad, *150*, *151*, *152*,
    152
  charring to remove the skin, 151, 152,
    152
  Eggplant and Arugula Sandwiches, 174,
    175
eggs
  Avgolemono, *96*–97, 97
  Custard in a Crust (quiche), *215*, 216–17,
    217
  French Toast, 171
  Gluten-Free Egg-Wrapped Dumplings
    from Yangshuo, 20
  how to hard-boil, 185
  Longchamps Rice Pudding with Raisins,
    120, *121*
  Matzo Brei, 142, *143*, 144
  Pink Deviled Eggs, *184*, 185–86, *186*
  Shirred Eggs with Potato Puree, 2, *3*, *4*, 4
  Spaghetti Alla Carbonara, 141
  Turkey Hash with Fried Eggs, 51
epazote
  about, 295
  Great Black Beans, 295–96

F

Fabulous Hummus, *218*, 220
  suggested toppings, 220
Fannie Farmer's Classic Yeast-Raised
    Waffles, *211*, *212*, 212
feta cheese
  Purslane Tacos, *248*, *249*, 249
Filet of Beef, 77
fish and seafood
  Creamed Lobster Claws on Toasted
    Brioche, 253
  Fried Oysters, 192, *193*, 194
  raw scallops, with jalapeño shards, 64–65
  Salmon with Rhubarb Glaze, 177
  Sea Urchin Pasta, *204*, 206
  Sole en Papillote, 264
  Spaghetti Allo Scoglio, 149

Hamburgers, 238, *239*
    condiments for, 238
Homemade Bread Crumbs, 17
Homemade Chili Powder, 46
Horseradish Sauce, 77
Hot Fudge to Soothe Your Soul, 299
Hummus, Fabulous, *218*, 220
    suggested toppings, 220

I

ice cream
    Hot Fudge to Soothe Your Soul, 299
    ice cream sandwiches (with Fannie
        Farmer's Classic Yeast-Raised Waffles),
        212
    Rhubarb Sundaes, 179
    Roasted Winter Strawberries with Ice
        Cream, 105
    Watermelon Sundae, 206

J

jalapeño peppers
    Khao Man Gai sauce, 195
    Pork and Tomatillo Stew, *126*, 128
    raw scallops, with jalapeño shards,
        64–65
jam
    Fresh Apricot Jam, 240–41
    Linzer Torte, *70*, 71–72
    My Version of Prune's Bacon and Mar-
        malade Sandwich, 117
    tips for making, 241
James Beard's "Onion Rings," *270*, 271
James Beard's Tomato Pie, 283
January Pudding, 102
Jim Lahey's No-Knead Bread, 130, *131*

K

kale
    Spicy Tuscan Kale, *16*, 17
Khao Man Gai (Thai Chicken Rice),
    195
kimchi
    Bulgogi at Home, *167*, 168
Korean red pepper paste (gochujang)
    Spicy Korean Rice Sticks with Shrimp
        and Vegetables, 22, 23

Korean rice sticks (ddeok)
    about, 22, 23
    Spicy Korean Rice Sticks with Shrimp
        and Vegetables, *22*, 23

L

lamb
    Quick, Easy Do-Ahead Dinner for Two
        People: A Ten-Minute Meal, 304
    Roast Leg of Lamb with Fresh Mint
        Sauce, 154, *154, 155*
leek(s)
    The Diva of Grilled Cheese, *85*, 86
lemon(s)
    Avgolemono, *96–97*, 97
    basic vinaigrette, 181
    Crisp, Lemony Baby Yukons, 251
    Fabulous Hummus, *218*, 220
    Lemon Panna Cotta, 100
    Lemon Pudding Cake, 165
    Sour Cherry Lemonade, 260
    Tart Lemon Tart, 100, *101*
lemon verbena
    about, 265
    Cucumber Soup Laced with Lemon
        Verbena, Threads of Mint, 266
lettuce. *See also* arugula
    Blue Cheese Dressing (with iceberg let-
        tuce), 214
    Bulgogi at Home, *167*, 168
lime(s)
    Asian Eggplant Salad, *150, 151, 152*, 152
    Cucumber Soup Laced with Lemon
        Verbena, Threads of Mint, 266
    garnish, with sour cream, for Pork and
        Tomatillo Stew, 128
    pork marinade, 200
    raw scallops, with jalapeño shards,
        64–65
    Spice-Rubbed Pork Cooked in Banana
        Leaves (Cochinita Pibil), *199*, 200, *201*
    Sriracha Shrimp Over Coconut Rice, 69
    "Tandoori" Chicken, 297
    Thai-American Noodles, 124, *125*
    wedges, served with Easy Vietnamese
        Caramelized Pork, 262, *263*
Linzer Torte, *70*, 71–72

lobster
  Creamed Lobster Claws on Toasted
    Brioche, 253
  how to cook, 253
  just-caught vs. supermarket, 253
London broil
  marinade for, 251
  Michael's Grilled London Broil with
    Red Onions, 251
Longchamps Rice Pudding with Raisins,
  120, *121*

M

Magret of Duck with Easy Orange Sauce,
  273
Ma Po Tofu, 60
marinade
  for beef (Bulgogi), 168
  for chicken (curry-based), 118
  for chicken (yogurt-based), 297
  for cucumbers, 262
  for duck, 273
  for London broil, 251
  for pork, 200
  for shrimp, 69
matzo, 47
  Matzo Brei, 142, *143, 144*
mayonnaise
  James Beard's Tomato Pie, 283
  Pink Deviled Eggs, *184*, 185–86, *186*
Michael's Grilled London Broil with Red
  Onions, 251
mint
  Cucumber Soup Laced with Lemon
    Verbena, Threads of Mint, 266
  Fresh Mint Sauce, 154, *155*
  "Tandoori" Chicken, 297
Moroccan Purslane Salad, 247
mozzarella cheese
  about, 274, 276
  as first course, suggestions, 274, 276
  mozzarella di bufala, 274, 276
  Painless Pasta for Three, *275*, 276, *276*
Mrs. Lincoln's Genuine Sponge Cake,
  133
muffins
  New York Corn Muffins, *114*, 115

mushroom(s)
  Beef, Wine, and Onion Stew, 111
  Chicken Fricassee, 88
  Chinese Dumplings, *48*, 48–49, *49*
mussels
  Spaghetti Allo Scoglio, 149
My Grandmother's Cabbage,
  136–37
My Pancakes, 241–42
My Version of Prune's Bacon and Marma-
  lade Sandwich, 117

N

nectarine(s)
  Nectarine Galette, 18
New Potatoes with Green Garlic,
  269
New York Corn Muffins, *114*, 115
noodles
  My Grandmother's Cabbage, 136–37
  Thai-American Noodles, 124, *125*
nutmeg
  Custard in a Crust (quiche), *215*, 216–17,
    217
  streusel topping, 209

O

oatmeal
  Butter-Toasted Apricot Oatmeal, 95
olive(s)
  Moroccan Purslane Salad, 247
  Savory Sweet Pasta for Michael, 303
  Stuffed Tomatoes, 286
onion(s)
  Beef, Wine, and Onion Stew, 111
  Borscht Salad (À La Fergus Henderson),
    196, 197
  The Diva of Grilled Cheese, *85*, 86
  James Beard's "Onion Rings," *270*,
    271
  Michael's Grilled London Broil with
    Red Onions, 251
  Pickled Red Onions, 201, *201*
  Roast Chicken with Potatoes, 76
orange marmalade
  My Version of Prune's Bacon and Mar-
    malade Sandwich, 117

Roast Leg of Lamb with Fresh Mint
Sauce, 154, *154, 155*

S

Spaghetti Allo Scoglio, 149
Spaghetti with Bottarga and Bread Crumbs,
    267
spareribs
    Venetian Pork, 68
Spice-Rubbed Pork Cooked in Banana
    Leaves (Cochinita Pibil), *199*, 200,
    201
Spicy Korean Rice Sticks with Shrimp and
    Vegetables, *22*, 23
Spicy Tuscan Kale, *16*, 17
spinach
    Sautéed Spinach, 74
    Spinach and Ricotta Gnocchi, *106*, *108*,
    108
Sponge Cake, Mrs. Lincoln's Genuine, 133
squid
    Spaghetti Allo Scoglio, 149
Sriracha sauce
    Bulgogi at Home, *167*, 168
    Sriracha Shrimp Over Coconut Rice, 69
Staples
    freezer, xx
    pantry, xx
    refrigerator, xx
    unusual, xx
    vegetable, xx
Steak Sandwich, 10–11, *11*
stew
    Beef, Wine, and Onion Stew, 111
    Pork and Tomatillo Stew, *126*, 128
stone fruits
    Apricot Pie, *208,* 209
    Duck Carpaccio, *190,* 191
    Fresh Apricot Jam, 240–41
    Fresh Peach Breakfast Cobbler, *279*,
    279
    Nectarine Galette, 18
    A Slight Variation on Marian Burros's
    Famous Plum Torte, 292
strawberry(ies)
    Roasted Winter Strawberries with Ice
    Cream, 105
    Strawberry Shortcake, *232*, 233, *235*
streusel topping, 209
Stuffed Tomatoes, 286
sugar, extra-fine, 133

Szechuan peppercorns, 59
    Ma Po Tofu, 60

T

tacos
    Great Black Beans for, 295–96
    Purslane Tacos, *248*, 249, *249*
tahini
    Fabulous Hummus, *218*, 220
Tart Lemon Tart, 100, *101*
Thai-American Noodles, 124, *125*
Thanksgiving, 33–48, 51–52
    Anchovy Bread, 39–40, *40*
    Apple Crisp, *36*, 37
    Basic Chili Recipe, 45, *46*
    Chinese Dumplings, 48–49, *48–49*
    Cranberry Pecan Crostata, 43–44
    High-Heat Turkey, 41
    Homemade Chili Powder, 46
    Perfect Pound Cake, 38
    Pumpkin Pancakes, 52
    Pumpkin Pie, adaptation for
        back-of-the-can recipe, 44
    Turkey Gravy, 34
    Turkey Hash with Fried Eggs, 51
    Turkey Stock, 34
tofu
    Ma Po Tofu, 60
tomatillos
    green salsa, *249*, 249
    Pork and Tomatillo Stew, *126*, 128
    Purslane Tacos, *248*, 249, *249*
tomato(es)
    Basic Chili Recipe, 45, *46*
    Easy "Bolognese," 28–30, *29*
    Gazpacho, 287
    James Beard's Tomato Pie, 283
    overripe, suggestion for, 286
    Painless Pasta for Three, *275*, 276, *276*
    Pork and Tomatillo Stew, *126*, 128
    Roasted Tomato Soup, 293
    Stuffed Tomatoes, 286
    Tomatoes and Cream, 285
tomato(es), cherry
    Spaghetti Allo Scoglio, 149
truffle salt
    Filet of Beef, 77

turkey
  High-Heat Turkey, 41
  Turkey Gravy, 34–35
  Turkey Hash with Fried Eggs, 51
  Turkey Stock, 34
Tuscan Bean Soup, 146

V

vanilla bean
  Fresh Apricot Jam, 240–41
  tip for removing seeds, 241
Venetian Pork (spareribs), 68
vinaigrette, basic, 181

W

waffles
  Fannie Farmer's Classic Yeast-Raised
    Waffles, *211*, 212, *212*

watermelon
  Gazpacho, 287
  Watermelon Sundae, 206
wine (red)
  Beef, Wine, and Onion Stew, 111
  Three-Day Short Ribs, 214
wine (white)
  Chicken Fricassee, 88
  New Potatoes with Green Garlic, 269
  Spaghetti Allo Scoglio, 149

Y

yamaimo ("mountain potato"), *24*
  about, 25
  preparing, *26*, 26
yogurt
  marinade, for chicken, 297
  "Tandoori" Chicken, 297

ABOUT THE AUTHOR

Ruth Reichl was born and raised in Greenwich Village. She wrote her first cookbook at twenty-one, and went on to be the restaurant critic of both the *Los Angeles Times* and *The New York Times*. She was editor in chief of *Gourmet* magazine for ten years.

She now lives with her husband in upstate New York.

ruthreichl.com
@ruthreichl